Not Hockey

NOT

HOCKEY

CRITICAL ESSAYS ON CANADA'S OTHER SPORT LITERATURE

Edited by

ANGIE ABDOU AND JAMIE DOPP

◊ AU PRESS

Copyright © 2023 Angie Abdou and Jamie Dopp
Published by AU Press, Athabasca University
1 University Drive, Athabasca, AB T9S 3A3

https://doi.org/10.15215/aupress/9781771993777.01

Cover design by Natalie Olsen
Printed and bound in Canada

Library and Archives Canada Cataloguing in Publication

Title: Not hockey : critical essays on Canada's other sport literature / edited by
    Angie Abdou and Jamie Dopp.
Names: Abdou, Angie, 1969– editor. | Dopp, Jamie, 1957– editor.
Description: Includes bibliographical references.
Identifiers: Canadiana (print) 20230223168 | Canadiana (ebook) 20230223184 |
    ISBN 9781771993777 (softcover) | ISBN 9781771993784 (PDF) | ISBN
    9781771993791 (EPUB)
Subjects: LCSH: Canadian literature—History and criticism. | LCSH: Sports in
    literature. | LCSH: Athletes in literature.
Classification: LCC PS8101.S73 N68 2023 | DDC C810.9/3579—dc23

We acknowledge the financial support of the Government of Canada through
the Canada Book Fund (CBF) for our publishing activities and the assistance
provided by the Government of Alberta through the Alberta Media Fund.

Canadä   Albertan
                Government

Contents

Not Hockey

Introduction

A quick survey of Canadian sport fiction, drama, and poetry illustrates that hockey tends to eclipse other sports in our nation's literature. This prevalence should surprise nobody, given the iconic status of hockey in the national imagination. That status led to hockey dominating our earlier collection, *Writing the Body in Motion: A Critical Anthology on Canadian Sport Literature* (2018). Yet Canadians obviously participate in, and care deeply about, plenty of other sports. In this new collection, we deliberately chose to highlight literature about sports in Canada other than hockey. Relatively few of the sports represented involve organized team competition. Some are played by individuals in small groups, while others are largely solitary activities, in which participants compete with their own past achievements more than they compete against each other. Some of the sports are well known and have a long history: mountaineering, rodeo, and curling, for example. Others are relatively new and unconventional, including sports of the sort often labelled "extreme"—high-risk sports whose practitioners deliberately embrace potentially lethal danger.

Not Hockey further develops the goals of its predecessor. We have designed it as a valuable resource for sport literature courses in which students have an opportunity to critique sports culture and analyze the role of athletics in today's society. The essays in this collection will also appeal to scholars and general readers interested in imaginative responses to sport. In our introduction to *Writing the Body in Motion*, we stressed the way that sport literature uses sport to explore larger issues faced by human beings, and we cited Priscilla Uppal's claim that sport literature functions as "metaphor, paradigm, a way to experience some of the harsher realities of the world, a place to escape to, an arena from which endless lessons can be learned, passed on, learned again" (2009, xiv). These broader frameworks of understanding still apply.

The title of this collection suggests a bit of a twist, however. What are the implications of labelling the sports represented in this collection as "not hockey"? At first glance, the label might seem to reproduce the hockey bias we indicated above, as if Canadian sport only falls into two categories: "hockey" and "not hockey." We chose the label, however, as a challenge to the status quo. Canadian sport involves so much more than hockey, just as Canadian identity is so much more diverse than the identity associated with hockey. The sports represented in this collection—and the essays and interviews these sports and their literature have inspired—offer various takes on this diversity.

Each essay takes a critical approach to a work or works of literature in which sport, in one way or another, plays a central role. Interviews with or comments from the authors of these works follow several of the essays, giving readers a chance to see what the authors themselves think of sport and/or their book's relationship to sport. We have grouped the essays and their companion pieces into three sections, which reflect three central themes in the collection.

The essays in the first section, "Niche Sports and Subcultures: Non-commercial Experiences," focus on literary works that feature niche sports, that is, unconventional sports that have a relatively narrow appeal and whose practitioners tend to feel a strong sense of group membership. Such sports often (though not necessarily) attract people who are rebelling against normative values and social expectations, particularly young people who are in the process of asserting their independence and defining themselves as individuals. This element of defiance may include the deliberate embrace of physical danger associated with sports commonly labelled "extreme," three of which—skateboarding, parkour, and ultrarunning—are featured in this part. In the literary works that contributors examine in this section, this defiance manifests itself in the ways certain subcultures associated with niche sports, extreme or not, resist commercialization and commodification, and thereby preserve another, possibly more authentic, experience of sport.

In "'All Lithe Power and Confidence': Skateboarding in Michael Christie's *If I Fall, If I Die*," Heidi Tiedemann Darroch explores skateboarding's potential for fostering reconciliation and allyship, particularly in the way skateboarding offers a less competitive and hierarchical model of sport. Similarly, in "Olympic Athletes Versus Parkour Artists: Sport, Art, and the Critique of Celebrity Culture in Timothy Taylor's *The Blue Light Project*," Angie Abdou posits that Taylor offers parkour-based creative movement as an alternative to the pitfalls of mainstream society, such as consumerism, obsession with celebrity, and fixation on relentless progress. In "Covering Distance, Coming of Age, and Communicating Subculture: David Carroll's Young Adult Sports Novel *Ultra*," ultramarathon runner Fred Mason makes the case that extreme sport can help young people cope with developmental crises and major life obstacles, playing a major role in movement toward adulthood. He explains that Carroll was inspired to write the book through his attempts to explain his sport to his nieces and nephews in a way that truly captured the experience—particularly the sport's transformative spiritual potential. The fourth essay in this group, Jamie Dopp's "Out of the Ordinary: Curling in *The Black Bonspiel of Willie MacCrimmon* and *Men with Brooms*," will seem, at first, an outlier. It begins with curling's peculiar position in Canada, as both an economically marginal and widely popular sport. Then, through an analysis of two comical texts, it develops into a meditation on the blurred line between the ordinary and the extraordinary (or extreme) in sports.

The second part, "Colonialism and Nature," groups together essays on sports that allow their participants to immerse themselves in nature, often in isolation. Such sports provide a temporary escape from the trials of everyday, routine existence, as well as space for reflection and self-grounding that cannot be found in a culture that rewards constant action. However, in Western cultural and literary traditions, this approach to nature often begins from an assumption that the land is "empty" of history, culture, and Indigenous Peoples—that is, that it is a mere vessel for non-Indigenous individuals' self-fulfillment. The chapters in this part, and the literature they discuss, acknowledge and explore this colonial lens in different ways.

In "Sporting Mountain Voices: Alpinism and (Neo)colonial Discourse in Thomas Wharton's *Icefields* and Angie Abdou's *The Canterbury Trail*," Eva-Maria Müller explores two texts that take ecocritical approaches to sports that use nature for human recreation. Each of these texts, Müller argues, offers an important take on the ethical responsibility humans have towards nature, even during such seemingly benign activities as skiing, snowboarding, and mountain climbing. In the next essay, "Getting Away from It All, or Breathing It All In: Decolonizing Wilderness Adventure Stories," Gyllian Phillips encourages readers to reconsider the relationship between humans and land by comparing trekking stories *Into the Wild*, by Jon Krakaur, and *Wild*, by Cheryl Strayed, to Richard Wagamese's *Medicine Walk*. Wagamese's novel, Phillips argues, challenges the settler notion that people become "one with the land" through personal journeys by offering the counter-example of a journey of healing by an Indigenous boy and his dying father. Misao Dean presents a slightly different look at the sportsperson's relationship to nature in her "A 'Most Enthusiastic Sportsman Explorer': Warburton Pike in *The Barren Ground*," an early-twentieth-century memoir of a settler engaged in hunting for sport. Pike's account, according to Dean, offers a remarkable portrait of a sport with many extreme elements. Although the account is dated in some telling ways, it also contains forward-thinking ideas about the relationship of humans to nature and between Indigenous people and settlers in Canada.

Although issues of equity and relative privilege surface throughout this collection, some essays deal more explicitly with social hierarchies and the uneven distribution of power than others. These essays are grouped together in the third section, "Gender, Race, and Class."

In "'Maggie's Own Sphere': Fly Fishing and Ecofeminism in Ethel Wilson's *Swamp Angel*," Cory Willard discusses a novel from the 1950s that takes a unique approach to stories about characters journeying into nature to discover themselves. *Swamp Angel* deals with a strong woman who escapes an abusive husband by her mastery of a conventionally male sport: fly fishing. The novel also explores the kinds of healing, even spiritual, power that nature can retain in the modern world. Veronika Schuchter's "'Don't Expect Rodeo to Be a Sweet Sport': Ambiguity, Spectacle, and Cowgirls in Aritha van Herk's *Stampede and the Westness of West*" focuses attention on the Calgary Stampede and its main sporting event, rodeo. Both the Stampede and rodeo are shaped by histories involving colonialism, sexism, and racism. Van Herk's prose poem collection, Schuchter argues, takes an ambiguous position toward this history, sometimes acknowledging it, other times suggesting that Stampede and rodeo have an openness of definition that mirrors the openness of the West itself. In "Immigration, Masculinity, and Olympic-Style Weightlifting in David Bezmozgis's 'The Second Strongest Man'," Jason Blake considers the immigrant experience of dislocation, the transitory nature of fame, and expressions of masculinity through the lens of a sport long dominated by the Soviet Union. Adrian Markle explores the ramifications of social class in "'It All Gets Beaten Out of You': Poverty, Boxing, and Writing in Steven Heighton's *The Shadow Boxer*." And finally, in "Turn It Upside Down: Race and Representation in Sport, Sport Literature, and Sport Lit Scholarship," Jael Richardson talks about *The Stone Thrower*, her memoir about her father Chuck Ealey, Canada's first Black quarterback to win a Grey Cup, and the impact of racism on his career. Drawing on her experience as the founder and executive director of Canada's Festival of Literary Diversity, she reflects on the lack of racial diversity in sport literature and among those who study it. Recognizing the urgent need for change, she offers suggestions about how writers, scholars, and sport literature associations can draw attention to this problem, work to improve diversity, and include a wider range of voices in the field.

WORKS CITED

Abdou, Angie, and Jamie Dopp, eds. 2018. *Writing the Body in Motion: A Critical Anthology on Canadian Sport Literature*. Edmonton: Athabasca University Press.

Uppal, Priscila, ed. 2009. *The Exile Book of Canadian Sports Stories*. Toronto: Exile Editions.

Part I
Niche Sports and Subcultures
Non-commercial Experiences

1

Heidi Tiedemann Darroch

"All Lithe Power and Confidence"
Skateboarding in Michael
Christie's *If I Fall, If I Die*

Skateboarding debuted as an Olympic sport in the 2021 Tokyo Summer Games, signalling the legitimacy achieved by an activity first viewed as a children's pastime and later as an emblem of urban youth counterculture (Willing, Green, and Pavlidis 2020, 832). From its inception, skateboarding has enabled the creative repurposing of city streets. One of Canada's earliest portrayals of skateboarding, a 1966 National Film Board documentary entitled *The Devil's Toy*, directed by Claude Jutra, juxtaposes the alarm that street skateboarding aroused in Montréal police and bureaucrats with the innocent exhilaration of young riders claiming space in the city. In keeping with the long association of youth and skateboarding, young adult fiction has featured the sport frequently, including in Nick Hornby's first young adult novel *Slam* (2007), Blake Nelson's *Paranoid Park* (2006; adapted to film by Gus Van Sant in 2007), and the Canadian novel *Torn Skirt* (2001) by Rebecca Godfrey, alongside multiple high-interest books for developing readers.

More unusually, Canadian novelist and short story writer Michael Christie explores skateboarding as a source of freedom and adventure in *If I Fall, If I Die* (2015), an adult novel that draws on Christie's family history and his experiences as a professional skateboarder (Creagan 2020). Christie provides an accessible introduction to a notoriously jargon-ridden sport by minimizing his use of technical terms and emphasizing grace and fluidity through motion, portraying skateboarding as an act of joyful (albeit bruising) autonomy and an accessible means of intercultural understanding and solidarity, specifically between Indigenous and non-Indigenous youth. Christie does not idealize skateboarding's potential for fostering reconciliation of settlers and Indigenous people, but he does point to the possibilities for allyship between young people who share values of community and personal excellence in sport. The novel presents skateboarding as an activity that is more collaborative than competitive, and that builds relationships of mentoring and care in which skaters celebrate one another's growing prowess and develop their budding senses of self and autonomy. In Christie's portrayal, skateboarding also sets its youthful practitioners at odds with the racially segregated and socio-economically fractured culture of Thunder Bay. By the end of the novel, the central characters have become part of a diverse and inclusive community that counters their city's cultural and racial divides.

* * *

If I Fall, If I Die centers on the lives of eleven-year-old Will and his mother Diane Cardiel—a last name Christie borrows from one of his own skating idols, John Cardiel, who fought his way back into professional skateboarding after a devastating accident (Creagan 2020). They live in a residential neighbourhood in Thunder Bay, Ontario, in the 1980s. Diane is a former experimental filmmaker who has agoraphobia, an overwhelming fear of the outdoors that prevents her from leaving the house. Her disorder was sparked by a series of family tragedies, including her older brother Charlie's death in an industrial accident for which Diane feels partly responsible. After the dissolution of her brief marriage to an architect and a frightening experience on a subway platform in Toronto, Diane flees with Will, then a toddler, to Thunder Bay where she grew up, hoping to regain a sense of safety. Instead, her world grows increasingly constricted. Panic attacks began to plague her in the car, at the grocery store, even in her front yard, and she retreats indoors.

When the novel opens, it has been several years since Diane stopped going outside. Will, now eleven, has not ventured outside either, to assuage his mother's hypervigilance about his safety. Even within their home, Diane has adopted elaborate safety measures. She requires that Will don a helmet and wetsuit to change a lightbulb, limits their meals to foods that are not choking hazards, and insists on baths rather than showers to prevent fatal falls. Diane's precautions are intended to protect Will, but in practice they impede him from developing an age-appropriate level of independence, including sleeping in his own bed and forming peer relationships.

As Will's need for autonomy grows, the story begins to shift, soon becoming a fast-paced boys' adventure story complete with dangerous bootleggers, an encounter with a vicious wolf, a tussle over a *Treasure Island*–like map, and a search for a missing friend. As David Berry's 2015 review in the *National Post* points out, "one of the book's background ironies is that the world Will steps out into proves . . . to be just as terrifying as Diane's faltering mind has conjured it up to be." When Diane finally, and belatedly, allows Will to attend school after years of largely unstructured homeschooling, he struggles with the sudden expansion of his world. To overcome the loneliness he experiences in his new environment, where he struggles to understand expectations, Will turns to sport, setting his sights on becoming "the most electrifying practitioner in the short but storied schoolyard pantheon of ice sliding" (*If I Fall*, 96). He sands down the treads on his winter boots so that he can skid even more rapidly down a treacherously icy hill, inventing a range of moves that he executes with fluid and controlled motions. "Helmetless and unafraid, Will could dance, spin, slide backwards, and do 360s on one foot" (95), his classmates looking on in admiration. Will's skill attracts particular attention from Jonah, a classmate who is both a gifted artist and an adept skateboarder. When Marcus, another classmate, disappears, and authorities appear indifferent, Will and Jonah decide to embark on a search for him. Jonah teaches Will to skateboard so that they will be able to cover more ground more quickly, and this enhanced mobility becomes central to Will's burgeoning sense of confidence.

* * *

If I Fall, If I Die introduces skateboarding as a practical means of transportation for boys too young to drive, but the sport represents more than pragmatism. It appeals to the novel's socially marginalized characters as a broader part of their identity development as boys growing into young men without male parental role models. As sports historian Emily Chivers Yochim (2010) notes, skateboarding has predominantly been an adolescent and male activity from its inception, evolving over the course of the twentieth century from a children's pastime created by attaching roller-skate wheels to boards, to the preserve of countercultural adolescents who dominated the burgeoning field of professional skateboarding from the mid-1970s on. The popularity of skateboarding waxed and waned from the late 1950s, when the first professional skateboards were produced, to the 1980s, when Canadian actor Michael J. Fox's character Marty McFly famously skateboarded throughout the film *Back to the Future*. Skateboarding's history is rife with concerns about safety and the purported anti-social behaviour of skateboarders, whose appropriation of public and privately owned urban spaces often involves trespassing or skirmishes with vehicle traffic. Given its limited emphasis on competition, and like surfing, its parallel recreational form, skateboarding was not initially recognized as a "sport" but rather as a leisure activity. As a solo form that relies on dexterity, speed, and grace, skateboarding is perhaps more akin to performance, much like figure skating.

The subsequent professionalization of skateboarding, and its heightened public profile, are closely linked to ESPN's creation of the X Games in 1995, a competition for "extreme" sports. The categorization of sports such as snowboarding, street luge racing, and wakeboarding as "extreme" marks them as physically risky, and they showcase displays of hyper-masculinity (Wheaton 2004, 16). Though they shared appreciation for these elements, the amateur skateboarding community critiqued the mainstreaming, commercialization, and commodification of their sport through ESPN's televised coverage of the X Games, viewing it as "a perversion of the core ethos that has driven skateboarding subculture since its inception" (D'Orazio 2020, 2).

By 2015, when *If I Fall, If I Die* was published, skateboarding was no longer the preserve of a subculture but was firmly entrenched in the mainstream, in substantial part thanks to ESPN. The book is set, however, in the 1980s, a pre-mainstreaming decade that saw some of the earliest efforts to create teams of skaters. The Bones Brigade, which included Tony Hawk alongside fellow future stars Ray Rodrigues, Steve Caballero, and Rodney Mullen, was perhaps the best known of these teams, finding renown within a then-tight-knit skateboarding community thanks to impresario Stacy Peralta's films of their urban exploits (Willing, Green, and Pavlidis 2020, 836). Only later would Hawk—who became the first person to execute a "900," two and a half aerial rotations, on a skateboard at the X Games—be derided within the skateboarding community for representing "the corporate face of the new skateboarding industry . . . a symbol of what skating is *not*"

(Clark 2016). It is the subculture of dedicated, hard-core practitioners in a time before the X Games that appeals to Christie's characters and from which they draw inspiration in constructing their own community of oddball outsiders.

In electing to skateboard, Will and his friends run counter to Canadian sports ideals, particularly in northern cities where hockey is central to the community. Unlike hockey, lacrosse (Canada's official summer sport), or basketball, which have lengthy national histories, skateboarding has had a limited Canadian presence, substantially hampered by the climate. As Christie explains in an interview, his hometown of Thunder Bay, in the northwestern part of Ontario, experiences seven months of snow, limiting the sport's appeal (Creagan 2020). Despite the climactic disadvantages, Christie, like his fictional protagonist, became passionate about skateboarding at the age of eleven, drawn to it because it had "no coaches, no teams, no registration fees. It took place *out there*, in the world" and offered a sense of freedom from his mother's intense anxiety (in Rice 2015). Christie's early start is characteristic of how most skaters begin skateboarding, without formal lessons or coaching. As a lifestyle sport characterized by its "nonconformist, free-spirited, self-directed, and creative elements" (Beal et al. 2017, 11), skateboarding is open to a range of participants for whom organized competitive sports have less appeal or accessibility. The downside is the activity's intense physicality and high risk of injury. Videos of Christie filmed during his professional skating career show him "launching himself into the air, landing tricks that defy gravity—grinding on handrails and kick-flipping over park benches" (Medley 2015), but these feats came at a cost. Christie broke "wrists, fingers, a tibia, a fibula, chipped a handful of teeth, cracked a vertebra . . . snapped a collarbone," and sustained multiple concussions (Christie 2015a).

While his novel documents skateboarding's bruising toll, Christie wanted to steer away from depicting the sport as the exclusive domain of the "adrenaline junkie" (Creagan 2020). Instead, he focuses on two critical elements that reflect his own experience as a former skater: skateboarding as a form of community that bolsters physical courage and transcends racism and cultural differences; and skateboarding as graceful performance, akin to dance, where style and creative use of space are valued.

* * *

Christie examines Thunder Bay's division between its white and Indigenous populations by portraying systemic racism's impact on stereotypes, institutions, and personal relationships. Will's mother Diane, who grew up in Thunder Bay, recalls how her own father spoke slightingly of the capacity of Indigenous people for hard work, how white children would recoil at the accidental touch of a racialized classmate, and how her beloved brother, desperate to get out of Thunder Bay, exploited Indigenous people by severely underpaying them to work illicit overnight shifts at a grain mill. Twenty years later, in the novel's present, relatively little has changed in Thunder Bay—but Will, having grown up in isolation from this world, is innocent of prejudice.

Will ventures out of his home for the first time in the novel after hearing a small explosion. In the yard, he encounters Marcus, who is trying to steal their garden hose. While the boys' conversation is brief, Will, who is familiar with peer relationships only from books and films, is left with the impression that by concealing Marcus's attempted theft, he has sealed a bond of friendship. Marcus disappears shortly after his encounter with Will, having gone into hiding to evade a local gang of bootleggers (who believe that Marcus has stolen their map to the liquor they've stashed all over town). Marcus's foster mother assumes he has returned to his extended family, and no one in a position of authority is keen to mount a search. Jonah, like Marcus, is Indigenous, and as Jonah points out to Will, who is concerned about Marcus, "Indian kids go missing all the time. Especially orphans. Nobody in Thunder Bay even blinks" (132).

Christie's attention to the nonchalant way Marcus's disappearance is treated is central to the novel's exploration of systemic racism in policing, education, and child welfare. Thunder Bay has a long history of marginalizing Indigenous people (Fiddler 2019). Racist attacks are so frequent that, as historian Travis Hay bluntly puts it, "Thunder Bay, Ontario, is not a safe place for Indigenous youth" (2018, 1). In *If I Fall*, Christie focuses on how the city's prosperous period as a shipping centre was followed by a long economic decline through the 1970s and 1980s, accompanied by increased racial tensions. As the largest city in northwest Ontario, Thunder Bay is also the only secondary schooling option for Indigenous youth in northern, fly-in communities. Students must leave homes to continue their education after grade 8, living in boarding homes where they may receive scant supervision. Tanya Talaga's award-winning book *Seven Fallen Feathers* (2017) explores the deaths of seven such young people, assessing the complex circumstances of their families' lives, which have been disrupted by colonialism, including residential schooling, over multiple generations. Like other observers, Talaga indicts the cursory investigations into these young people's deaths; the police, relying on stereotypes, attribute the multiple drownings and other fatal incidents to alcohol misuse. Anti-Indigenous racism was also evident in the Thunder Bay death of Barbara Kentner, struck in the abdomen by a trailer hitch thrown from a truck by Brayden Busby, who was ultimately found guilty of manslaughter (Walters 2020). A litany of similar abuses has been documented in this city, the source of about 37 percent of Indigenous murder victims in Ontario even though it has only about 5 percent of the province's Indigenous population (Jago 2017). In January 2019, after two detailed inquiries into systemic racism on the force, Thunder Bay police services issued a formal apology to the community and committed to improving practices (Fiddler 2019). This broader context is crucial to understanding the vulnerability of Indigenous youth depicted in Christie's novel.

The dismissive attitude of the police toward Marcus's disappearance is only one of the ways in which Indigenous children and young people in the novel experience systemic discrimination. Will notices that his Indigenous classmates are ignored by teachers. During his search for Marcus, he learns that the social welfare system removes Indigenous children from their families and places them in overcrowded, white foster homes. As *If I Fall* makes clear, every sector of Thunder Bay life is inflected by racism. For instance, when Jonah's older brothers start a roofing business that does not attract customers despite intensive marketing efforts, they are chided by a government bureaucrat at the employment office who spouts racist stereotypes, claiming, as Jonah's older brother repeats to him with heavy sarcasm, that "homeowners in Thunder Bay knew we haven't lived under them for long enough" to know "the first thing about roofs" (160). Casual racism and racist epithets in the novel are voiced by a range of characters of varying social statures, suggesting the prevalence of anti-Indigenous sentiment in the city.

Even sport is segregated in Thunder Bay, with both ethnicity and social class playing a role. Will learns that the city's sport culture is centered on hockey, but "none of the Indian kids at his school played because the Kevlar pads cost a small fortune" (77). Skateboarding is more financially accessible to young Indigenous people, but it lacks the community support and infrastructure available for hockey. In response, Will and Jonah initiate their own, alternate community. They ignore popular hockey players' taunts and insults and spurn their classmates' clothing styles in favour of "flannel button-ups and work pants" from thrift stores, which are better suited to the hazards of skateboarding (164). To bolster their knowledge of the sport, Jonah collects US-based magazines *Thrasher* and *Transworld* alongside a small cache of treasured skateboarding videos—a genre popularized in the early 1980s as home VCRs were becoming more affordable. Poring over their videos and magazines, the boys gain both a point of entry into skateboarding culture and role models for their own developing styles. They dream of escaping Thunder Bay after high school and moving to California to become professional skateboarders, just as Will's mother and her brother once dreamed of escaping to Toronto for higher education.

While Will and Jonah are partly drawn to skateboarding's connections to a broader world, they also appreciate it as an art form. Mirroring Christie's own vision of skateboarding as "a kind of structured dance that's enacted out there, situationally, in the world" (in Isaacs 2015), Will is awestruck by the "regal grace and fluidity" that Jonah exhibits while performing a common skateboard trick, an ollie: "[H]e crouched, frozen like a cat stalking a robin, before cracking the rear of the board down, rocketing himself upward with the apparatus clinging impossibly to his feet like a burr. After this, the silence of flight but for the sibilance of wheels spinning, then a growling return to the asphalt and his lackadaisical ride-away" (*If I Fall*, 120). Christie's use of alliterative and figurative language in this passage conveys the activity's poetic and graceful character through Will's admiring eyes. Similar bird and animal comparisons are used several times in the novel to characterize Jonah's skating, like when Christie describes how Jonah "was ever more elegant, languid, full of feline poise, all lithe power and confidence" (319). While Will's initial attempts are faltering, he becomes more confident when he realizes that skateboarding is fundamentally "about mastery—a *seizure* of control, not a loss," and experiences startling joy as the skateboard "danced or flipped or spun successfully" beneath him (166). Even Diane, who at first cannot bear to watch Will on a skateboard for fear of him hurting himself, increasingly appreciates the aesthetic element, finding the activity "as beautiful as any dance, with its arcing turns and graceful little leaps" (152).

Christie's portrayal of skateboarding's beauty and grace aligns it with what philosopher Jason Holt, drawing on the foundational work of David

Best (1974), describes as the "aesthetic sports, in which aesthetic judgment figures into determining the outcomes" (2019, 19). In sports such as figure skating, diving, and gymnastics, "it is of the first importance that there should be no wasted effort and no superfluous motion" (19) and "form" is accorded credit when evaluating performance (22). Conversely, in the majority of both team and individual sports such as running, tennis, or hockey—sports that David Best terms "purposive" (1974, 201)—aesthetic appeal does not determine the activities' outcomes, although grace may be appreciated as a subordinate element. For instance, as Holt observes, in hockey or soccer, "two garbage goals always beat one beautiful goal, although we still enjoy beautiful goals" (20).

Skateboarding is physically strenuous and requires a high tolerance for injury. Will's early efforts send him crashing to the ground, "the board toma-hawking off in the opposite direction, his knees and elbows quickly bashed and gored by the tyrannical pavement" (*If I Fall*, 137). Even with Jonah's careful coaching, Will suffers countless accidents, "flaying the tender skin of his lower back, knees, and hips like an invisible monster was dismant-ling him cell by cell" and waking up in the mornings with "a symphony of aches" (137). The richly metaphorical language allows Christie to convey the physical experience of the skater as an alternative to the daunting, tech-nical vocabulary of skateboarding's dozens of basic moves. In an interview with *Thrasher* magazine, Christie explains his longstanding concern that "skateboarding couldn't be represented . . . in a way that both remained true to the act itself while at the same time making it interesting for the non-skateboarder public" (Creagan 2020). Jonathan Russell Clark (2016) makes a similar claim in his discussion of fictional portrayals of skateboard-ing, including Tom Perrotta's *Little Children* and Hornby's *Slam*, which he argues fail to convey skateboarding culture and skaters with any degree of verisimilitude. Even skateboarding memoirs that provide detailed descrip-tions of technique do not, he suggests, capture skateboarding's essential features. Clark wonders if "something about skating . . . resisted narrative description," arguing that portraying skateboarding tricks "by explaining their literal movements strips skating of its unconscious wonder, its strange, dance-like beauty." Christie demonstrates this in an interview, offering a parodic and jargon-ridden example of how an adept skateboarder might describe the sport to informed peers: "'Will and Jonah waxed a ledge by the old gas station and Will learned switchstance frontside tailslides and had almost learned to shove-it out when his kingpin broke.' How's that grab you, general reader?" (in Rice 2015). By electing to emphasize skateboarding as physical experience and aesthetic performance while minimizing technical language, Christie alternates between the perspective of the skater and the spectator, ensuring the book is accessible and engaging for readers who don't have specialized knowledge of the sport.

* * *

Will's skateboarding places him on the opposite trajectory to his mother's insularity. He explores forests and rivers, the waterfront, and abandoned urban areas, moving further away from home while achieving greater confidence and even joy in his efforts: "That the board did their bidding—danced or flipped or spun successfully beneath them—afforded the most sublime pleasures of their short lives" (166). In contrast to the fear that constrains Diane's life, Will experiences a sense of freedom through expansive movement out into the world, relishing the "emotional and experiential dimensions that are an important part of the attraction of the culture [of skateboarding]" (Willing, Green, and Pavlidis 2020, 835).

Christie creates a vivid portrayal of Thunder Bay's depressing, post-industrial decline and its paradoxical allure to skateboarders as a site of resistance to capitalism's values. Architectural theorists have pointed out that skateboarding sets itself in opposition to the notion that urban space exists to create wealth: "[S]kateboarding shows that pre-existing uses of buildings and city spaces are not the only possibilities, that architecture can instead be consumed by activities which are not explicitly commodified" (Borden 2019, 225). When the novel opens, Thunder Bay, once heralded (as Will's mother ruefully notes) as Canada's own Chicago, is two decades into the economic decline prompted by the end of shipping that has reshaped the city. The downtown storefronts are "now mostly shuttered and vacant"; only the "strip clubs, strip malls, taverns, and hockey rinks" survive (22). On the deserted waterfront, with its decaying grain elevators, Will and Jonah seek out the forbidden spaces that skateboarders find most inviting, recuperating unused public or abandoned private property for their own purposes. Christie suggests that "skateboarding is at its very essence a creative adaptation to the bleak urban spaces of the world" (in Rice 2015). As Will and Jonah explore the industrial environment, they locate "the crannies of the city that no upright citizen had reason to frequent," imbuing these "discarded nooks and leftovers" and "the abandoned, unused architecture that people preferred to ignore" with purpose and excitement (*If I Fall*, 164, 166).

Skateboarders also need to negotiate shared access to neglected urban spaces occupied by other marginalized users, including people who are insecurely housed. In Christie's novel, the boys' search for Marcus leads them to a disheveled hermit, Titus, whom they first meet in the woods. Later in the novel, Will and Jonah care for Titus in his new-found home in a grain elevator while he recovers from an attack by the bootleggers. To pass the time, they create an ersatz skateboard park in the grain elevator, a boon in the icy winter, "a time of despair and unimaginable yearning" for skateboarders. They borrow a design from a skateboarding magazine and scavenge wood to construct ramps on which to practice, "threading their way between pillars and hoppers and conveyance vents, back and forth at breakneck speeds." Instead of suffering through the monotony of school, they suffer through "unplanned splits, shinners, debilitating knee whacks, wrist tweaks, bent fingers, hippers, elbow bashings, back scrapes, rolled ankles, and chin abrasions" (251). Christie's vivid language conveys both the intense physicality of skateboarding and the boys' contagious enthusiasm for hurling themselves around in space.

The boys' friendship with Titus brings them to the attention of the Butler, the leader of the bootleggers, who believes that they either know the location of the grid map he's seeking or can provide information about Marcus's whereabouts. To ferret out the truth, the Butler imprisons the boys along with Titus and then pays Will's mother Diane an unnerving visit. Diane quells her panic enough to seek assistance from Jonah's older brothers, who rescue the boys. In a Dickensian twist, Titus is revealed to be Diane's older brother, Charlie, who was believed to have died many years earlier. Will's family is almost magically reconstituted: Charlie/Titus moves in with Will and Diane, who in turn establish a less suffocatingly interdependent relationship. Christie does not minimize the severe mental illness that both Diane, still suffering from agoraphobia, and her brother, traumatized by losses and grief, continue to experience, but things do begin to change for them. With Will's support, Diane embraces photography and inches back into the world by observing it through her camera. While Charlie's symptoms still emerge periodically, "most of the time he was all right" (316).

Christie again turns to skateboarding's aesthetic qualities in the book's final pages, in which Will shows Diane a film he's made, also titled *If I Fall, If I Die*. In the film, Will juxtaposes skateboarding tricks with contrasting images of his friends, family, and the city of Thunder Bay. When Diane asks him why he has included falls in the final version of his film, wondering if this might harm his chance of using to film to attract potential sponsors, he tells her, "We don't want to lie and make it look like we don't fall. Because we do. All the time" (321). In producing his film, Will matches Christie's own artistic achievement, celebrating skateboarding's wild inventiveness and exhilaration while highlighting the impossibility of achieving perfection in either art or life.

If I Fall, If I Die is the story of a young boy on the brink of adolescence who negotiates a path to growth and self-discovery through the creativity and physical courage embodied in skateboarding. Will's constricted life indoors is supplanted by his exploration of the outside world, a place that is terrifyingly unpredictable but where friendship prompted by shared love of the sport creates tight bonds. By the end of the novel, although they have not succeeded in locating Marcus, Will and Jonah have formed a thriving community with other young skateboarders, including "a Chinese kid who bruised easily and had to hide both his bruises and his skateboard from a strict father who taught chemistry at the college; an only-child girl whose father was the city's best hockey coach"; and "a motor-mouthed Irish kid who used to be a soccer prodigy but quit when his mother died" (319). While this passage betrays some stereotyping, it also reflects Christie's recollection of the diverse community of "wild, strange boys" he skated with as a budding professional—young people who turned to skateboarding as a refuge (Christie 2015a). The novel celebrates the athleticism, the beauty and grace, and the friendships that can be forged through the sport.

WORKS CITED

Beal, Becky, Matthew Atencio, E. Missy Wright, and ZaNean McClain. 2017. "Skateboarding, Community and Urban Politics: Shifting Practices and Challenges." *International Journal of Sport Policy and Politics* 11 (1): 11–23. https://doi.org/10.1080/19406940.2016.1220406.

Berry, David. 2015. "Michael Christie's Ever-Expanding *If I Fall, If I Die*." *National Post*, February 2, 2015. https://nationalpost.com/entertainment/books/michael-christie-interview-if-i-fall.

Best, David. 1974. "The Aesthetic in Sport." *The British Journal of Aesthetics* 14 (3): 197–213.

Borden, Iain. 2019. *Skateboarding and the City: A Complete History*. London: Bloomsbury.

Christie, Michael. 2015a. "All Parents Are Cowards." *New York Times*, February 12, 2015. https://opinionator.blogs.nytimes.com/2015/02/12/all -parents-are-cowards/.

Christie, Michael. 2015b. *If I Fall, If I Die*. Toronto: Emblem/Penguin Random House Canada.

Clark, Jonathan Russell. 2016. "Skateboarding in Fiction: A Brief History of Failure; On Accuracy and Authenticity in Art." *Literary Hub*, March 24, 2016. https://lithub.com/skateboarding-in-fiction-a-brief-history-of-failure/.

Creagan, Adam. "Michael Christie: The Novelist Who Rips." *Thrasher Magazine*, May 18, 2020. https://www.thrashermagazine.com/articles/michael-christie-the-novelist-who-rips/.

D'Orazio, Dax. 2020. "Skateboarding's Olympic Moment." *Journal of Sport and Social Issues* 45 (5): 1–31. https://doi.org/10.1177/0193723520928595.

Fiddler, Willow. 2019. "Thunder Bay Police Board Apologizes for Systemic Racism." *APTN National News*, January 14, 2019. https://www.aptnnews .ca/national-news/thunder-bay-police-apology/.

Hay, Travis Andrew. 2018. "Foreclosing Accountability: The Limited Scope of the Seven Youth Inquest in Thunder Bay, Ontario." *Canadian Review of Social Policy* 78: 1–24. https://crsp.journals.yorku.ca/index.php/crsp/article/view/40328/36472.

Holt, Jason. 2019. *Kinetic Beauty: The Philosophical Aesthetics of Sport*. London: Routledge.

Isaacs, Julienne. 2015. "Michael Christie." *Full Stop*, February 24, 2015. https://www.full-stop.net/2015/02/24/interviews/julienneisaacs/michael-christie/.

Jago, Robert. 2017. "The Deadly Racism of Thunder Bay." *The Walrus*, December 11, 2017. https://thewalrus.ca/the-deadly-racism-of-thunder -bay/.

Medley, Mark. 2015. "Michael Christie's Second Book Examines Living Life to the Fullest." *Globe and Mail*, January 30, 2015. https://www .theglobeandmail.com/arts/books-and-media/michael-christies-second-book -examines-living-life-to-the-fullest/article22722183/.

Rice, Joel. 2015. "Theories of Literature: An Interview with Mike Christie, Author of *If I Fall, If I Die.*" Flip: A Column about Skateboarding. *McSweeney's*, March 25, 2015. https://www.mcsweeneys.net/articles/column-26-theories-of-literature-an-interview-with-mike-christie-author-of-if-i-fall-if-i-die.

Talaga, Tanya. 2017. *Seven Fallen Feathers*. Toronto: House of Anansi.

Walters, Jeff. 2020. "Kentner Family Pleased with Brayden Busby Manslaughter Conviction." *CBC News*, December 15, 2020. https://www.cbc.ca/news/canada/thunder-bay/thunder-bay-bushby-trial-reaction-1.5841559.

Wheaton, Belinda. 2004. *Understanding Lifestyle Sport: Consumption, Identity and Difference*. London: Routledge.

Willing, Indigo, Ben Green, and Adele Pavlidis. 2020. "The 'Boy Scouts' and 'Bad Boys' of Skateboarding: A Thematic Analysis of the Bones Brigade." *Sport in Society* 23 (5): 832–46. https://doi.org/10.1080/17430437.2019.1580265.

Yochim, Emily Chivers. 2010. *Skate Life: Re-imagining White Masculinity*. Ann Arbor: University of Michigan Press.

Burn the Scoreboards

Michael Christie on Skateboarding and Olympic Sport

I have something to confess: I detest the fact that skateboarding is now an official Olympic event. And though I know a few of the skaters who represented their nations in Tokyo in 2021, and I've spent decades of my life standing on a board that rolls on four little wheels, I can guarantee that I'm not going to watch a single second of it.

Let me tell you why. I grew up in Thunder Bay, a place that has reportedly spawned more NHL players per capita than anywhere in Canada. It was a pretty working-class town, and most boys my age harboured NHL dreams, including me. I had a friend on my hockey team whose father had once tried out for the Toronto Maple Leafs. During our games, he would bark angry instructions from the stands whenever my friend was on the ice. And I remember my friend once confessing that if he didn't get a point in our game, he wouldn't get dinner that evening. As a result, he'd often go to bed hungry, and at school I'd often split my bagged lunch with him.

Though I loved the physical sensation of gliding across the ice, I distinctly remember skating around during those hockey games and glancing up at the scoreboard and just *hating* the sight of it. It had nothing to do with whether my team was winning or losing, I instead hated the fact that one number was higher than the other, and that everyone (most particularly the adults and coaches) cared so much about the difference between them. I loathed the scoreboard's very *existence*, the way it watched over us and determined who would be angry and who would be happy, and, in some tragic cases, who would be eating dinner that night.

And so, when I was around eleven years old, I quit. The hockey players in my class were horrified. A teacher took me aside and told me that I was ruining my life and I would have no friends and no girl would ever be interested in me. But that summer I was lucky enough to discover something that no adult could possibly understand: an activity with no rules, no rankings, no competition, no rep teams, no national organizations, no 6:00 a.m. practices, no body-checking, and definitely no scoreboard.

Skateboarding was all I thought about for the next twenty years, and I moved away from Thunder Bay at age eighteen so I could skate year-round in California and BC. I went on to garner a few sponsors, and eventually skateboarding led me to writing and film and photography. I wouldn't be the writer or the person I am today without it. (It chills me to consider how things could have gone differently, and it could be me up in those stands today, yelling at my poor child as they struggled to whack a little disc of black rubber into a net.)

There remains much debate in skateboarding circles about whether skateboarding is a sport or not. And though the argument is mostly boring and semantic, I contest that skateboarding is instead a kind of improvisational dance, one that takes place not on a stage but out in the street. Its tricks are a kinetic language that skaters use to express themselves upon the architectural spaces of the world. Because you definitely don't do a difficult skateboard trick to score points and win a competition. You do it for the pleasure it brings you. You do it simply to do it.

Which brings us back to the Olympics, and the fact that skateboarding will now be getting its very own scoreboard, albeit one determined by the absurdly subjective whims of judges. This "event" will take place in an arena, upon contrived, purpose-built obstacles, with corporate sponsors adorning every surface. The competition will be fierce. The skateboarding that was a salvation for me and countless others will be nowhere in sight.

So please, instead of watching Olympic skateboarding, Google some great, innovative skateboarders like Leo Baker, Mark Gonzales, Cher Strauberry, Tyshawn Jones, Breana Geering, or Rick McCrank. Watch how freely their bodies vault and turn and whirl through space. Watch how they make a playground of their bleak urban environments. Watch their resilience and their focus and their determination to cut their own path, the exuberant, rolling joy they take in being alive.

And let's just leave the scoreboards out of it.

2

Angie Abdou

Olympic Athletes Versus Parkour Artists

Sport, Art, and the Critique of Celebrity Culture in Timothy Taylor's *The Blue Light Project*

An intense and compelling exploration of contemporary existence, Timothy Taylor's *The Blue Light Project* (2011) is a novel fueled by the energy of urban life: hostage-takings, reality TV gone wrong, parkour, drug addiction, street art, downtown explosions, corrupt journalists, disillusioned Olympians, resilient children, and a creative brother who appears to have dropped out of it all. With profound insight, Taylor explores our society's obsession with celebrity and follows the desire for fame along its potentially catastrophic trajectories. The connections between contemporary sport and celebrity culture are clear, but Taylor also examines the role art plays in today's fame-driven world. Of most interest within the context of this essay collection, Taylor includes creative, athletic movement within the sphere of art he explores, thereby expanding the definitions of both sport and art.

As Eve, the protagonist of Taylor's novel, explains, this creative, athletic movement is "a sport . . . [T]hey jump off very high things. Run creatively." Readers might be tempted to use the term *parkour* to describe this movement. After all, Eve's description aligns with definitions of parkour: "an art whose main themes are escape and spatial appropriation" (Guss 2011, 75) and an activity that "involves moving rapidly through the urban environment, reflexively interpreting the objects encountered not as obstacles but as opportunities for movement" (Bavinton 2007, 392). Though these definitions match the activities in the novel, the characters of *The Blue Light Project* make a deliberate decision *not* to use the term *parkour*—or *freerunning*, as some practitioners refer to it (Saville 2008, 892)—to describe their version of creative movement: "These were Parkour moves, although Rabbit didn't use that term. Freesteal was what people around Rabbit called what they did: a combination of running, climbing, exploring places off limits to the public, and leaving public art on the walls wherever they went" (*Blue Light*, 63). The combination of movement with art is an extension of how real-life parkour practitioners perceive their sport. In an extensive study of website material, media articles, and interview data, Bavinton sees three intersecting definitions and representations of parkour: "as 'sport', as 'discipline', and as 'art'" (2007, 401). By tying the physical movement to the practice of public art, Taylor intensifies the third aspect. His characters' rejection of the word *parkour* stems not only from the added element of public art but also partly from the disdain for "anything vaguely commercial" (*Blue Light*, 94). Freestealers—a fictional term invented by Timothy Taylor and that, for simplicity's sake, I use synonymously with *parkour* in this chapter—do not like the term *graffiti artists* either. Unlike graffiti artists, freestealers do not tag their art; they leave it "as a gift to the cityscape so the free eye might freely find it" (42). The anonymity of their freesteal movement, like the anonymity of the art, aligns with this goal. Both the creative movement and the art objects exist as gifts to whomever happens to see them. Rabbit stands as the novel's main freestealer, claiming that the activity of freestealing defines how he wants to fit in the world: "making his quiet way without confrontation, leaving his marks for those who would see" (42). The novel offers this crossover between art and sport—freestealing—as a redemptive space in a world much in need of redemption.

Freesteal is a decidedly non-commercial activity. On the other side of the non-commercial–commercial sporting spectrum, we find the novel's protagonist, Eve Latour, an Olympic biathlete who has attained fame for her heroic gold-medal completion of a race under circumstances so harsh that nobody could reasonably have expected her to complete it. Early in *The Blue Light Project*, Eve, not at all comfortable with her own celebrity, claims: "Finishing is just what you do. I imagine it takes more courage to quit" (41). This message applies to a variety of "races" in our current culture (the technological race, the consumerism race, the resource-extraction race, the fame/celebrity race), and Taylor asks readers to pause and consider our society's current trajectories: Might we be able to quit courageously rather than blindly staying the course? Parkour, with its focus on movement artists "creatively choosing their own trajectories" (Guss 2011, 74), serves as a fitting metaphor for avoiding the predictable, predetermined course and forging a new path.

The Blue Light Project, then, sets up a juxtaposition between Olympic sports and the parkour-style movement of freesteal, a comparison that works to expose—and condemn—our society's obsession with both fame and relentless, linear forward movement. Drawing explicitly on Werner Herzog, Taylor laments our culture's dearth of adequate images to deal with a culture in crisis, a lack caused, in part, by our obsession with clichéd sport heroes as celebrities (Taylor 2014). Social scientists often exclude parkour and other extreme sports from this notion of sport as clichéd and fame-ruined. They tend to link the same hopefulness to the growth of parkour that Taylor links to freesteal. Of parkour, Nathan Guss claims that this "new global art," in its free use of space and its collaborative process, is "a sign and potentially a harbinger of the emergence of new forms of human relations and political power" (2011, 83). Such scholars position parkour as a form of rebellion "through which participants reinterpret material spatial restrictions upon public behavior to facilitate unscripted leisure practice and creative play . . . empowering the individual to wrest (admittedly partial and momentary) control of the power relations embedded within public urban spaces" (Bavinton 2007, 391). Of course, since parkour's emergence, it has become quite popular—and therefore mainstream to the extent that marketers have used it to sell everything from soda pop to automobiles, robbing the "new global art" of some of its purity and counterculture political power. Perhaps that shift accounts for Taylor choosing the term *freesteal* over *parkour* in his fiction.

Does counterculture sport, represented in *The Blue Light Project* by freesteal, offer an escape from the limitations and pitfalls of mainstream sport? Is such creative movement thereby a more "authentic" endeavor? Can creative movement (similar to parkour but without its consumer implications) act as a bridge between the artistic world and the athletic one? If so, what does that kind of artistic-athletic endeavor offer the troubled world? *The Blue Light Project* explores these kinds of questions to show

how counterculture sport can offer contemporary society a space of social resistance and the gift of hope.

In *The Blue Light Project*, Eve Latour is desperate to escape mainstream society's scripts and expectations. Eve's society defines her solely as the Olympic Gold Medalist—an identity within which she feels very uncomfortable. People continually want to tell Eve where they were when she crossed the Olympic finish line: "Ah, let me tell you!" they say. "We were all cheering!" they say. "My gosh, that was something," they say (*Blue Light*, 139). Eve remains mystified by the attention. She competed in biathlon (a combination of shooting and cross-country skiing) in an Olympics in Geneva and quickly became the media darling. She entered the race as an underdog, pitted against Austrian Giselle Von Kemper, a "slab-muscled woman from Innsbruck" (27). In the years since the Olympics, Eve has learned to tolerate and survive the "retellings" of her event, "the visuals and audio ramped up" (27), but these retellings make her distinctly anxious. Her discomfort arises because she knows the truths of the moment, visceral truths that those dramatic retellings miss, less heroic truths such as the "the paralyzing nerves [that] had threatened to overcome her" (27). The readers learn about the media version of the intense race: Eve's fall, the commentator's assumption that she could not possibly complete the race, her heroic finish against all odds (as the saying goes), her staggering across the end line in first place, and the final reveal that Eve's fall had been more than a fall.

"Eve hadn't stumbled," we read, "because she was clumsy. She'd stumbled because something had hit her, just above the ankle of her left boot. Something small, hard and traveling at extremely high speed. Like a bullet, exactly" (30). We learn that Eve had been shot by "a crazed Belgian" wielding a slingshot "who decided a good way to get Eve's attention would be to take her opponent out of the race. He'd been aiming for Von Kemper, he told police" (30). Eve skied her way to victory on what everyone would later discover was a broken ankle. These "heroics" (air quotes are Eve's) grab the attention of media and audiences everywhere. Eve goes down in history as a "come-from-behind underdog with suffering and justice" (24). She does not thrive on this attention. The text's first description of her reads: "People who spend their lives in the public eye develop a kind of radar. They feel the eyes, the longing, the volatile desire. Some love it, thrive on it. Others are smartly wary. Eve Latour was wary" (4). Despite her wariness, Eve's fame takes on a life beyond her control. The journalist narrator tells us:

> Forget about all those interviews and profiles after her gold-medal win in Geneva eight years before. The tide of curiosity as her athletic fame so quickly morphed into something bigger. The celebrity engagement to the French film director. The paparazzi outside her Paris hotel after he left her for the tennis player. Her high profile term as UNICEF Global Ambassador. She'd faced them all squarely, the photographers and the networks. She'd accommodated the local press on her return home from Europe, their loved daughter. Always gracious, never minding that they called her Evey like she wasn't thirty-two years old but still a kid. It was true, that she had lived in the media, lived in our gaze. (5–6)

Living in the gaze is an existence Eve fights (in her internal monologues if not in her polite outward actions), but cannot ultimately escape. The disconnect between her reality as a thirty-two-year-old adult and the childish nickname the media uses for her points to a larger disconnect between Eve's representation and her reality, highlighting the stultifying effect celebrity can have on personal growth. Eve becomes an image frozen in time rather than an evolving human being and autonomous adult with personal agency. Like the biblical Eve, the world defines this Eve-athlete by her fall. Where the biblical Eve falls out of grace, our biathlon Eve falls *into* the public's grace. However, with the name parallel, Taylor emphasizes that in her move to celebrity, Eve Latour falls *out of* a purer, more desirable state. Through the story of Eve's struggle (and failure) to escape the media's diminishing gaze, Taylor depicts Eve's athletic celebrity as a claustrophobic cell, not a glorifying or energizing state to be envied and sought after.

In her post-Olympic life, Eve redirects the intense physical energy that she once dedicated to training. She runs the street at night. We might read these running passages as a typical image of the ex-Olympian turned recreational runner, but Eve is not running recreationally. In fact, we can interpret these late-night outings as *less* recreational than her Olympic training. Eve dons her running shoes in the dark to look for her brother, the street artist / parkour practitioner / drug addict / freestealer who has vanished. Here, Eve has given her athleticism a real-world purpose, one with unambiguous meaning and import. Significantly, she undertakes this activity at night, does it unknown, stays where she can be anonymous. These vigorous late-night outings stand as the antithesis of her Olympic athletic career. Where she cannot quite attach meaning to her Olympic race—cannot find the sense in it, cannot identify with the media's image of her—the dark runs hold great meaning for her. The Olympic Gold Medalist runs at night both to escape the unwanted limelight and to find her lost street-artist brother. "She had never had a single hero," the text tells us, "other than [her brother] Ali. Ali, the smart, the brave, the fast. Ali of no fear" (139). In the protagonist's mind, the hero of this story is Ali, the missing freestealer who lives completely outside the fame-cage she knows so well. Ali who has managed to escape from mainstream society's scripts, expectations, and imposed identities. Ali and his sister function as opposites through most of the narrative: the brother who has disappeared and the overly visible sister who *cannot* disappear.

Early in the novel, a company called Double Vision presents Eve with an opportunity to cash in on her celebrity. This company specializes in packaging and selling the lives of former athletes. They want her story. "We've worked with many top former athletes," the representative of Double Vision explains to her, "and I can tell you there is always an appetite for the right sort of former athlete. It's recession proof. It really is. It's like a hunger that doesn't go away. And your story . . . Eve, let me tell you, it's one in a million. It gives us tremendous material to work with" (22). In an interview marking the novel's release, Timothy Taylor explained that he sees a certain class of celebrity who evokes our admiration but not our envy. "These are people who have done something so singular and so unimpeachably good that we cannot either imagine ourselves doing the same or resent them for their accomplishment. . . . Eve is that kind of celebrity. People do not measure themselves against her" (quoted in Sherlock 2011). This undiluted form of fame accounts for Taylor choosing an athlete for his celebrity protagonist, and it is the exact kind of fame that creates a consumer "hunger that does not go away," drawing a company like Double Vision to pursue Eve the Olympic Gold Medalist.

Taylor illustrates the catastrophic downside of fame in a story that most reviewers see as the novel's main plot. There, the cast of a reality TV show called *KiddieFame* has been taken hostage and a man (whose actions have made him instantly famous) holds several fame-seeking children at gunpoint. A *Canadian Literature* review that calls this storyline "the major plot arch" describes *KiddieFame* as "an insidious reality show where the audience votes celebrity-craving preteens off the program"; the review argues that the novel offers "an abstract interrogation of contemporary culture" and a portrayal of an artistic revolution "that overthrows greed, chaos, and corruption" (McFarlane 2012, 185–86). The main difference between the "art" of *KiddieFame* and the "art" of freesteal is that *KiddieFame* exists solely as a manifestation of the human obsession with celebrity, whereas freestealers define themselves predominantly by their eschewing of that celebrity. The dire conclusion of *KiddieFame* makes clear the novel's unambiguous position on fame. The novel's children-in-peril situation is the fault of "the machinery of yearning and dissatisfaction that delivered to people fame on the one hand and ruination on the other" (*Blue Light*, 233), the exact same machinery that shapes Eve's life. The most direct critique of celebrity culture comes from freestealer Ali's response to the hostage emergency: "How alive are those kids outside of their competitive desire to be famous? How alive are we letting them be? Telling them fame is everything?" (293). The novel repeatedly shows Eve to be right to fight against the pull of fame and applauds her desire to follow the alterative pull of artistic revolution represented by freesteal. In fact, *The Blue Light Project* aligns that artistic revolution with an essential life energy, one lacking in the novel's representation of mainstream pursuits.

Despite Eve's "one in a million story," she resists Double Vision's pitch that she feed her own life to the insatiably hungry beast. Her live-in partner Nick, however, does not. Nick is a kind of celebrity himself, a former Gerber baby, his "face on a million bottles of pureed peas, tomatoes and rice, chicken and pasta" (25). Fame is intrinsically woven into his earliest sense of himself and his own worth. Nick embraces an unquestioning, uncritical desire for celebrity; he wants Eve to cash in on her own fame, and he does everything he can to persuade her to do so. Eve, however, remains unconvinced: "I guess I'm having a mixed reaction. Licensing. Buying the rights to part of my life story, to copy and reproduce. To sell. Is it just me or is that weird?" (33). The athletic life as commodity is, unfortunately, more commonplace than weird. A simple Google search produces a wealth of sports articles with headings like "Stop Treating Athletes Like Commodities," "Athletes Are Just Commodities These Days," "When People Become Commodities," "Inside the Game You Are Still a Commodity," "The

Commodification of Sport" "Student Athlete or Commodity?" and "How Do Athletes Commodify their Personal Brand." The best way to eke out a post-competitive living is for the sports heroes to sell their image—and the physical excellence they represent—while their story and prowess are still fresh in the public's mind.

Taylor foregrounds this notion of athlete-as-brand (and Eve's resistance to it) when, in the novel's first section, journalist Thom Pegg expresses surprise at Eve shaking his hand: "Strange thing, that. They don't really touch in my experience. I mean the really big stars. The name brands. The people of iconic wealth and wellness. The people who could surely envy only God. It's less a germ issue than it is a matter of observing the sacred separation between you and them" (4–5). In the face of Eve's refusal to be packed and sold as a brand, Nick continues to encourage her to cooperate with Double Vision to do exactly that, saying "work is work" (38). She rejects the idea of "peddling [her] former self" (38) and cringes at the Stalinist ring of the Double Vision phrase "personal story management" (39). Through the character of Eve—her lack of contentment, her discomfort with the media's image of her, her unwillingness to exchange her personal story for monetary profit, her sense of disconnect between Eve the person and Eve the media darling, and her continued search for authenticity and meaning—Taylor strips Olympic celebrity of allure. Readers are left to look to the other end of the sport spectrum—to the novel's freestealers—for representation of a more authentic, hopeful existence.

FLOW AND EDGEWORK

When scholars discuss the relationship between sport and authenticity, they almost always draw on Victor Turner's concept of flow. According to Turner, flow "denotes the holistic sensation present when we act with total involvement" (1982, 55), a sensation in which we have no sense of time or place and no self-consciousness, but are instead completely immersed in the task at hand. In other words, we experience this state "as a unified flowing from one moment to the next in which we feel in control of our actions, and in which there is little distinction between self and environment; between stimulus and response; or between past, present, and future" (56). The athlete in flow state is completely unaware of an audience, or of the performance such an audience requires. Eve Latour's athletic career is not operating within this ideal flow state or allowing her to access a more authentic existence and unselfconscious self. Run as she might, she cannot escape society's attempts to impose a script upon her. In fact, the script—the intensified and dramatized version of her Olympic story, the clichéd and worn notions of courage and heroism—has become more real to society and to the media than Eve herself, a now thirty-two-year-old woman who would like to move on from her moment of Olympic glory. Eve's celebrity has eclipsed any flow she might have achieved in those far-off moments of her physical acts as a biathlete, "loping down the groomed tracks. Popping off the targets. She had a resting heart rate of forty-nine. She loved the feel of rifle in her hands" (*Blue Light*, 107). In *The Blue Light Project*, Taylor captures her immersion in flow state in only this one small moment in her narrative, and it is not the aspect of sport that interests those determined to monetize her existence. Whatever flow Eve may have achieved has now been eclipsed by her celebrity.

Within the novel, freestealing would be a logical place to search for a more successful, sustained achievement of flow since scholars of extreme activities link the idea of authenticity in high-risk sport to Victor Turner's flow state. Because the extreme athlete participates in an activity that takes maximum focus and attention, the rest of the world fades away and the athlete becomes fully in the moment, not aware of time, space, or audience. In this state, the athlete achieves an immediate sense of self rather than a performing self—because how can a person or person's actions be performative if there is no awareness of audience and no distinction between self and environment? The selfhood an athlete achieves in that moment is more authentic for its lack of performativity. Edgework theorists draw a similar connection between extreme sports and authenticity. The term *edgework*, coined by Stephen Lyng, describes activities that push the safety-danger boundary and offer a temporary escape from "social conditions that produce stunted identities and offer few opportunities for personal transformation and character development" (2005, 6). From this perspective, extreme sports offer a space of social resistance and allow athletes to have an experience antithetical to fame-driven performance. Edgework theorists argue that extreme sports thereby offer a space of social resistance, allowing athletes to escape, momentarily at least, from scripted existence and have an experience antithetical to fame-driven performance. Elizabeth Creyer, William Ross, and Deborah Evers, in an article called "Risky Recreation," posit three reasons for undertaking high-risk activity: normative (response to peer pressure), self-efficacy (need to feel competent), and hedonic (quest for a pleasurable or even spiritual experience) (2003, 242). Those who achieve the flow state fit within the third category marked by spirituality or transcendence. Rabbit lives exactly this way, performing his physical acts not for an audience but for the way they make him feel: "*If* I am to be truly alive, *then* this is what I must do whether you see it or not" (*Blue Light*, 64). This vitality through art and creative movement is what "sped his heartbeat and fired his imagination" (64). In connecting with Rabbit and searching for her brother Ali, Eve attempts to access the same vitality that they locate in freestealing. Eve's literal search for her brother functions as a metaphor for her attempt to find the life energy, agency, and autonomy that sport celebrity has taken from her.

Jackie Kiewa highlights the subversive and authentic potential of extreme sports in her study of one small group of climbers in Queensland, Australia. "[C]limbing is depicted as a 'free area' in which climbers attempt to achieve relative freedom from this society," she argues. In such areas "our identity, our true self, can best be discovered" by positioning ourselves outside of society, and participating in dangerous activities is one way to achieve this position (2002, 145–46). Lyng agrees, arguing that "playing with boundaries in acts of transgression and transcendence, exploiting limits, and crowding edges may be one of the few possibilities for human agency that can be found in the disciplinary society" (2005, 47). These dynamics are evident in Taylor's novel in the act of freestealing. Rabbit undertakes death-defying jumps, playing along the inside edge of the in-control/out-of-control boundary, and his risky movement thus requires his full attention. In this activity, he not only finds the human agency emphasized by Lyng, but also experiences a pure pleasure that corresponds to Turner's flow state. He thus achieves a kind of freedom and authenticity denied Eve. Ameel and Tani identify such freedom as the chief draw of parkour, connecting parkour with the idea of the ludic city and the playful use of space: "This idea of a playful attitude, ready to explore the possibilities of any given space on the basis of structure rather than for what it is intended, is central to the ludic character of parkour, but also to other loosening, playful and confrontational behavior in urban space" (2012, 26). Tellingly, the activity that allows Rabbit to achieve this freedom and playfulness also requires a kind of anonymity that is the antithesis of fame. Authenticity exists far outside the realm of celebrity. Throughout the novel, we read variations on the idea that "[c]elebrity is a con" with the sports fan as its mark (*Blue Light*, 2). But as Eve's life makes clear, the fan is not the only one to suffer from the machinery of fame; the celebrity suffers, too.

In comparison to Eve, readers cannot help but envy Rabbit and Ali their vitality, freedom, authenticity, and "willingness to act," to celebrate the moment of their passions (108). Eve envies them, too. More than this, she desires them: Rabbit as the love interest and Ali as the brother she wants to find. Jungians argue that when we long for another person, we have most often projected onto them something we miss in ourselves, some aspect of our life that needs developing. Both Ali and Rabbit have achieved the freedom and life energy that eludes Eve.

THE OLYMPIAN VERSUS THE FREESTEALER

Eventually Nick and Eve's argument about selling her story to Double Vision winds down (as much as marital arguments ever wind down). To change the subject, Eve introduces Nick (and the reader) to the idea of parkour. "I saw the most incredible thing today," she says (41). She refers to a parkour move she happened to see Rabbit execute, the first of the novel, a seemingly superhuman flight. In the world beyond the novel, athletes also tend to appeal to the superpower aspect of parkour when attempting to explain its allure: "Imagine having superhero abilities," one anonymous athlete says, "able to leap from rooftop to rooftop as if nothing not even buildings could stop you. This is parkour, the *anarchic* new sport of free-runing" (quoted in Saville 2008, 892). Eve spots the novel's superhero while she ignores the Double Vision pitch. She stares out the boardroom window and sees the stranger who reminds of her of Ali balanced on a roof's edge.

> He filled the empty space, his arms spread for balance, his legs tucked. And then, impossibly, he rolled at the top of his arc. He flipped in midair, which brought about a millisecond of complete silence and stillness in her. The whole movement was completely dangerous and completely harmonious. And it pinned her to the spot. (37–38)

The danger of the act is matched, for Eve, by the fact that he performs it without an audience: "Without a sound. Without a reason. No motive, nobody chasing him. No audience that he could have known of, since he hadn't looked down to see that she was there" (38). Her reaction is unambiguous: "It was breathtaking. The most beautiful thing she'd seen in years" (38). Nowhere in the novel does Taylor undermine this sense of awe and reverence that Eve attributes to freestealing. Its freedom, anonymity, and originality work to make freesteal an ideal form of recreation (and re-creation) throughout *The Blue Light Project*.

Twenty pages later, readers revisit the same scene—the roof-leaping trick—from Rabbit's perspective. It occurs in the first section that gives readers access to Rabbit's point of view. The inspiration for the stunt begins in a moment of frustration:

> After he broke the unit he'd been trying to install on top of the Peavey Block and banged up his hand in the process, Rabbit paced and swore and stared at the sky briefly as if it might offer an explanation for his own stupidity. And it was this irritation more than anything that inspired him to jump across the alley and onto the roof of the adjacent building. With a front flip, no less, which was insane on every level. Insane to risk being seen in the middle of the day. Insane . . . well, insane to risk dying. (59)

Frustration with the challenges of the everyday—with the aggravating consequences of working a regular job—provoke him to attempt the impossible, to push the limits of what humans can do, and thus achieve momentary escape, even at the risk of dying. He moves in "controlled strides with much reserved energy, like a jungle cat" (59), the animal imagery highlighting the way his action exists in contradistinction to the constraints of regular human society. Theorists emphasize that parkour does not get rid of constraints but finds freedom and originality within constraints. In the words of Bavinton, "the spatial practices of appropriation and creative reinterpretation central to Parkour identify it as a practice of resistance. Yet, the creative play characteristic of Parkour is not achieved by abolition of constraints, but by the reinterpretation and negotiated utilization of constraints" (2007, 400). Bavinton describes the athletes he studies as "non-conformist relationship to objects" and finds ways of "transforming obstacles into opportunities" (405)—descriptions that could just as easily describe Taylor's Rabbit.

The transformation of fear into play is another way Rabbit achieves a kind of freedom currently unavailable to Eve. He is not immune to the fear felt by Eve—her visceral reaction as she watches him preparing for the jump—but unlike her, he acts despite the fear. John Saville refers to this as a "mobility of action" that parkour practitioners can access through their sport: "fear can become a familiar link to space, a riddle to solve. In parkour the answer is not to dispense with fear but is found in process, trying, testing, working out and becoming fluid" (2008, 910). Saville argues that the sport allows athletes to break from iterative performances of negative emotions through playfulness: "specifically, certain types of unpleasant fear can be supplanted, experimented with and reflected on, through practices like parkour that attempt to cultivate more 'enjoyable' kinds of fear" (910). Throughout the novel, Eve appears attracted to this playfulness—and seeming fearlessness—as it manifests in both Rabbit and Ali, especially in their practice of freesteal.

After Eve explains Rabbit's fear-defying feat to Nick, he responds: "You're not saying that was courage, I hope. That's just dare deviling" (41). Readers have already seen the way "courage" has attached itself to the narrative of Eve's Olympic success. With the introduction of courage in this discussion of parkour-style movement, Taylor invites readers to compare the two athletic endeavors and think about which is courageous, which is heroic, and what these notions of heroism and courage even mean in contemporary society. The privacy and anonymity of Rabbit's act put him in direct opposition to Eve who must constantly exist in the public and cannot escape the public versions of herself. This opposition between public and private comes up repeatedly in the novel with preference always given to private acts—ones that are not undertaken to achieve public recognition or celebrity. Rabbit's existence is the opposite of Eve's, whose history, having been caught up in fame, has been robbed of its life energy, of her true and visceral feelings and ambivalence in the moment, and then packaged and sold. But Rabbit understands his life outside of the framework of fame. Rabbit's desire to live creatively (and for creation's sake) is linked to DNA and presented as an unavoidable way of being. His mentor says: "We have archaic creative threads in our DNA, you and I. We're the guys who would have been cave-painting, laying out rocks in lines, making circles in wheat fields. We're creators, not destroyers, we reveal and don't hide. We're the people bringing the world those images it needs for survival" (124). From Werner Herzog, Rabbit takes the idea that if art does not innovate, art dies, and with it human civilization (95): "If we don't find adequate images, we'll go the way of the dinosaurs" (69). The novel makes it clear that Rabbit also applies Herzog's concept about the necessity of innovation to movement.

The art Rabbit erects is unsigned and only exists as long as the installation lasts. In explaining why he does not use the word *parkour* to refer to his own athletic/artistic performance in the streets, he says as soon as parkour has a name it is not a rebellion any more—it is subsumed into the mainstream. Mainstream recognition is not the goal. The goal is to exist outside the named, outside the mainstream, outside fame-driven, celebrity-driven culture. Instead of fame, Rabbit's aim is to achieve the kind of innovation encouraged by Herzog, to create adequate images, and thereby keep art alive—to work against humans going the way of the dinosaurs.

INNOVATION AND HOPE IN ART AND SPORTS

The Blue Light Project asks: Can we be saved from our superficial celebrity culture? Celebrity has, in Taylor's vision, ruined much of what is good about sport and reduced athletic lives to commodities. Will art save us? Will the combination of art with creative movement save us? Will freesteal save us? According to Taylor's imaginative offering, the individual choice to behave authentically is still available—though choosing it is an act of resistance, one that must be continually re-invented as the original resistance is exploited and drained of vital energy by marketers. Eve, the novel's protagonist searching for an alternative to the deadening effect she feels from her own athletic fame, is drawn to the freedom of freesteal. She particularly admires the way Rabbit does not engage in freesteal for media attention or public accolades, the way it is "enough just to do it and keep on doing it" (201).

Conversely, Taylor highlights the way mainstream athletics can have a ruinous effect through the names he chooses for the novel's two central freestealers, Rabbit and Ali. Anyone familiar with sport literature or with the contemporary novel will read Rabbit as a reference to the central character in John Updike's novel *Rabbit, Run*. Updike's Rabbit was a high school basketball player, so defined by his youthful prowess and early success that the rest of his life reeked of anticlimax. Taylor nods to this parallel late in the novel when Eve asks Rabbit if his name is an "Updike tribute" (204). Ali, as Eve explains, is named after Muhammad Ali because their father was a big fan (208). Despite being a boxing world-champion, Ali also experienced the (fatally) detrimental effects of sport, eventually getting brain damage from the long-term effects of too many blows to the head and arguably dying as a result (Eig 2017). Taylor reinvents Rabbit and Ali, attaching the iconic names to a new kind of athlete-artist who can find vitality through their sport well into middle age. The novel thus offers a more appealing alternative to mainstream athletic existence.

In 2014, Taylor gave a live interview at the Fernie Heritage Library about *The Blue Light Project*. When the host introduced him to the library audience, she announced, "Art will save us! Books will save us!" and said that Taylor's book proved as much. Taylor's response indicated a more moderate view: "I don't *know* if art will save us. But. . . ." Readers can be grateful for that *but*, on which the rest of his talk hinged. On the balance between hope and despair in relation to the creative process, Taylor claimed: "Without hope, why bother with anything, let alone novels? But there is hope, sure there is. My friend, the photographer Lincoln Clarkes, once said to me: 'You know, the only way to explain street art is to think of it as a gift. It only makes sense as a response to some other value, outside ourselves, on some higher perch.' Art still might not save us. But that higher value might, that capacity to give." Parkour-style movement can, in the novel and in wider society, function as that same kind of gift.

The novel's climax comes as just this kind of gift—a moment of anonymous art firing into existence, "a shimmering blue-light dance of hope" (*Blue Light*, 345). *The Blue Light Project* unites Rabbit and Eve, links creative moment and creative object, and provides an offering that is real and original and free, in contrast to the synthetic and commercial non-art offered by both Double Vision and *KiddieFame*. Two ideas are explicitly repeated throughout the novel. One is Herzog's concept that if art does not innovate and find adequate images, humanity dies. The other is the command: "*Keep up the good work, you beautiful, beautiful young artists*" (218). *The Blue Light Project* asserts the life-saving value of art, when it can stay fresh and alive. For sport to remain vital and worthwhile, Taylor suggests, it too must innovate. It too must offer hope. Similarly, John Stephen Saville links innovation and hope to parkour: "The extended and serious practice of parkour is always a questing, a search for new and more elaborate imaginings, it is an opening out of possible, but necessarily attainable motilities" (Saville 2008, 892). Rabbit—and through him Eve—embraces this questing for new and more elaborate imaginings, including the way such creation can be manifested through movement. The novel does not, then, reject sport as a potential vehicle for self-discovery, creation, and vitality, but it does reject sport clichés. It rejects sport that commodifies athletes. It rejects sport that encourages obsession with fame. It rejects sport that robs athletes of agency. To stay alive, sport must innovate.

To those ensuring that it does, we can also say: Keep up the good work you beautiful, beautiful young athletes.

WORKS CITED

Ameel, Lieven, and Sirpa Tani. 2012. "Parkour: Creating Loose Spaces?" *Geografiska Annaler: Series B, Human Geography* 94 (1): 17–30. https://doi.org/10.1111/j.1468-0467.2012.00393.x.

Bavinton, Nathaniel. 2007. "From Obstacle to Opportunity: Parkour, Leisure, and the Reinterpretation of Constraints." *Annals of Leisure Research* 10 (3–4): 391–412.

Creyer, Elizabeth, William Ross, and Deborah Evers. 2003. "Risky Recreation: An Exploration of Factors Influencing the Likelihood of Participation and the Effects of Experience." *Leisure Studies* 22 (3): 239–53. https://doi.org/10.1080/026143603200068000.

Eig, Jonathan. 2017. *Ali: A Life*. New York: Houghton Mifflin Harcourt.

Guss, Nathan. 2011. "Parkour and the Multitude: Politics of a Dangerous Art." *French Cultural Studies* 22 (1): 73–85.

Kiewa, Jackie. 2002. "Traditional Climbing: Metaphor of Resistance or Metanarrative of Oppression?" *Leisure Studies* 21 (2): 145–61. https://doi.org/10.1080/0261436021015 8605.

Lyng, Stephen, ed. 2005. *Edgework: The Sociology of Risk Taking*. New York: Routledge.

McFarlane, Brandon. 2012. "Literary Thrills." *Canadian Literature* 214 (Autumn): 185–86.

Saville, John Stephen. 2008. "Playing with Fear: Parkour and the Mobility of Emotion." *Social and Cultural Geography* 9 (8): 891–914.

Sherlock, Tracy. 2011. "Timothy Taylor Shines Light on Inspiration for *The Blue Light Project*." *Vancouver Sun*, May 5, 2011. https://vancouversun.com/news/staff-blogs/timothy-taylor-shines-light-on-inspiration-for-the-blue-light-project.

Taylor, Timothy. 2011. *The Blue Light Project*. Toronto: Alfred A. Knopf Canada.

Taylor, Timothy. 2014. Interview at the Fernie Heritage Library Literary Reading Series, February 21, 2014.

Turner, Victor. 1982. *From Ritual to Theatre: The Human Seriousness of Play*. New York: PAJ Publications.

Updike, John. 1960. *Rabbit, Run*. New York: Alfred A. Knopf.

On *The Blue Light Project*

An Interview with Timothy Taylor

This interview took place via email between Angie Abdou at her home in Fernie, British Columbia, and Timothy Taylor at his home in Vancouver in March 2021.

ANGIE ABDOU: Why did you choose an athlete—as opposed to another kind of star—as the novel's celebrity protagonist?

TIMOTHY TAYLOR: A word about celebrity in the arts, first. A positive public verdict on your work, whatever it might be, is one of the headiest possible highs. A great review. A bestsellers list. Media requests. Someone stopping you in the street or recognizing you in a restaurant. I don't know many people who aren't thrilled by that kind of attention. But there is a bitter flipside. If you accept the public verdict, that the approval and interest is a true indication of value, then the work itself is rendered provisional. If acclaim signals value, after all, then being ignored must be a true sign of irrelevance. The writer Mavis Gallant once said to me that she didn't read reviews of her work because, were she to revel in the positive ones, she'd by extension have to treat negative reviews as a legitimate repudiation. So she resisted.

Athletics run parallel to the arts in at least this one respect. If the athlete accepts that value is determined externally—by fame, by celebrity—then the athlete fails in its absence regardless of what internal objectives may have originally motivated the effort. But much more than artists, the prowess of even successful athletes is expected to fade. If you buy celebrity's verdict under those circumstances—ignoring Gallant's warning, as it were—you are virtually guaranteed to suffer a crisis of withdrawal in later years. And it seems to me that being recognized in the street with nostalgic gestures years later—old jerseys and programs to autograph, recounts of pinnacle moments from decades prior—will not compensate. Indeed, that phenomenon might only serve like looking through a telescope in reverse, miniaturizing what was once all-consuming, distancing it, making it smaller than it should be.

Eve handles this all without much anxiety in the book. But it was my intent to show her living in the shadow of what came before, to show her vulnerable to provisionality, even if she does not in the end succumb to it.

AA: You made up the term *freesteal*, right? Why did you need an original, fictious term rather than using already existing terms that describe the activities (i.e., parkour and graffiti)?

TT: There is a term for the free movement of people around built objects not really designed to be traversed. That's *parkour*. And then there are terms for unsanctioned public art, like *graffiti*, *street art*, and so on. But there wasn't a single word for what happened when a practitioner combines these things. *Freesteal* combines these two qualities in the work as I observed it, mostly in Vancouver, and mostly around the years 2007 and 2008. First, that the art itself is free to the viewer. Second, that the work does involve borrowing, even theft, as not-strictly-public locations must be accessed. Parts of the city must be borrowed and used in ways that the city might not otherwise agree. There are fire escapes to climb, rooves to traverse, catwalks and highway overpasses to cross, tunnels to enter strictly against the rules. And the more the moves of parkour are integrated with this artistic practice—as they are in my novel—the more this becomes a flowing interchange of what is given and what is taken. That was the idea.

AA: It's noted in the novel that Rabbit has the same name as Updike's famous ex-basketball-player and Ali of course calls to mind iconic boxer Muhammad Ali. Neither fared well in their post-sport existence. What do those sport allusions add to our understanding of the characters of your Rabbit and Ali or our understanding of the novel's commentary around sport?

TT: Well, this is interesting. Neither Ali nor Rabbit were named with that post-sports tailing off in mind. Eve owned that dynamic more or less on her own, in my mind. The naming of those two characters was more the product of a changing method. In every novel I've written, names have come about in ways that live towards one or the other end of a spectrum from careful and planned, to intuitive and spontaneous. *Blue Light* falls to the latter end of the spectrum. In these cases, the names are often first chosen as place holders. So you name a character thinking it's just for compositional purposes. A hundred thousand words later and the name has bedded down by usage to be inextricable. That happened to Jeremy Papier in *Stanley Park*, whose name was first chosen just to get a French surname on the page, to get a name literally on "paper." *Blue Light* was maybe a degree less impulsive in that I looked for names that, to my ear, sounded right for the character's mood. But I got them down quickly and in every case they stuck. Ali was supposed to sound situationally ambiguous. Eve slips through the air, to my ear. And Rabbit. Well Rabbit is elusive and free.

3

Fred Mason

Covering Distance, Coming of Age, and Communicating Subculture
David Carroll's Young Adult Sports Novel *Ultra*

David Carroll's novel *Ultra* (2014) incorporates many of the usual features of the young adult coming-of-age novel. The main character, thirteen-year-old Quinn Scheurmann, uses his sports participation to overcome developmental crises and grief. Supporting characters include an unsure but supportive mother, an absent father who casts a shadow over everything, a female best friend / potential love interest, and a joke-cracking younger brother, all of whom figuratively, and quite literally, help guide Quinn to the finish line. However, Carroll's novel is not your usual coming-of-age sports story. This is because he centres his novel around the unusual sport of ultrarunning, whose participants run races that begin at fifty kilometres and spiral upwards in distance from there. Quinn's coming-of-age occurs not on the ice rink or soccer pitch, but over a twenty-four-hour period as he runs a tough, hundred-mile trail race. *Ultra* is unique in the genre of sports fiction in that it gives *young* readers a glimpse inside the lesser-known sport of ultrarunning. What's more, Carroll, who has first-hand experience in ultrarunning including finishing hundred-milers, is able to give readers a realistic, insider's perspective on the sport and the people who do it, and on the spiritual journey that many ultrarunners understand their runs to be. He portrays the toughness of races, the willingness of ultrarunners to experience pain and altered states of consciousness, and some of the unusual aspects of the subculture such as the older average age of the athletes and the competitiveness of elite women with men. He also shows aspects of the sport that create a deep sense of community, such as high levels of social support amongst the runners.

Ultrarunning refers to any running event over the marathon distance of 26.2 miles (42.2 kilometres). Races take place over set distances or times, with some events spanning multiple days. Typical race distances in ultrarunning are 50 kilometres, 50 miles, 100 kilometres, and 100 miles, with 200 miles a rare but increasingly popular distance. Some ultrarunning events are based on time instead of distance, with participants running on loop courses over a set period of time—usually twelve or twenty-four hours—aiming for the highest accumulated distance. Multi-day events see participants cover set distances each day, often in extreme environments such as deserts or mountain ranges.

The sport has been around since the early 1970s. Until the 1990s, it was considered quite fringe. Although it still seems extreme to many, the sport has seen real growth since the first decade of the 2000s. *Ultrarunning* magazine reported that there were only about 339 races in Canada and the United States in 2005 (Quicke 2017); by 2016, this had mushroomed to 1,473. A global study published in 2020 and sponsored by the International Association of Ultrarunners found that the number of yearly participations in ultramarathons increased 345 percent since 2010, with 611,098 people recording a finish at an ultrarunning event over that ten-year period (Ronto 2020). This data does not capture smaller, local or informal "Fat Ass" style events—less organized events in which the athletes are self-supported—that do not publish results to the web.

Magazines such as *Ultrarunning* (published monthly since 1981) and *Marathon & Beyond* (published between 1997 and 2015) began printing race results, reporting on current events and personalities in the sport, and publishing stories from ultrarunners themselves mainly because the sport did not receive much coverage in the mainstream press, or even other running-specific media. In my research, I have only been able to find thirteen book-length works about the sport published between 1979 and 2001. This included a guide to the sport (Osler and Dodd 1979), David Horton's diary of record-setting runs on the Appalachian Trail and across the United States (Horton and Trittipoe 1997), stories of runners trekking or racing across Death Valley (Benyo 1991; Johnson 2001), and a musing on running and evolution from anthropologist and champion ultrarunner Bernd Heinrich (2001). The growth in ultrarunning's popularity since the early 2000s runs parallel to a growth in popular literature related to the sport over the same period. Dean Karnazes, an elite ultrarunner with a self-promotional streak (leading him, for example, to run on a treadmill suspended over Times Square) wrote his first book, *Ultramarathon Man*, in 2005; it became a bestseller. After this, there was a surge in autobiographies and memoirs written by ultrarunners, from the elite to the back-of-the-pack (e.g., Ayres 2012; Reed 2006; Zahab 2007). Journalist Christopher McDougall's 2009 book *Born to Run* told the story of a trip to Copper Canyon in Mexico, where elite American runners raced with the Tarahumara, an Indigenous group who incorporate ultrarunning-length feats into their religious rituals and who travel by foot (although not necessarily in the ways described by or with the frequency claimed in popular media about them; see Plymire 2006). McDougall's book stayed at the top of the New York Times hardcover nonfiction bestseller lists for fifteen weeks, greatly increasing popular attention to the sport of ultrarunning and serving as a catalyst for the rise of the minimalist running shoe industry. The publishing surge continued: in 2012 alone, as many books on ultrarunning were published as there were in the entire period between 1979 and 2001.

While there are many ultrarunner memoirs, few books target young adults or children. There are four English-language, nonfiction titles aimed at grade school readers, all of which attempt to introduce the sport in different ways. Nate Aaseng's book *Ultramarathons: The World's Most Punishing Races* (1987) provides an overview of eight different races and their inherent challenges, including the Rarahipa, the traditional Tarahumara race featured in McDougall's *Born to Run*. Chris Hayhurst's simply titled book *Ultra Marathon Running* (2002) serves mostly as a guide to training and participation. Jim Whiting's *Ultra Running with Scott Jurek* (2007) explores the sport through the career of Jurek, the elite runner who would later become the star of McDougall's *Born to Run* and go on to pen his own memoirs (Jurek 2012, 2018). *Running to Extremes: Ray Zahab's Amazing Ultramarathon Journey* (Pitt and Zahab 2011)—also a Canadian grade school nonfiction book, though it is more substantial than the others—explores the early years of Zahab's transition into ultramarathon running, including racing in the Amazon and across multiple deserts. This book was released to coincide with the launch of youth educational expeditions led by Zahab through his organization Impossible2Possible.

Ultrarunning-related fiction, particularly fiction geared toward young readers, is rarer than nonfiction. The only ultrarunning-related fiction aimed at adults are a survival novel where the ultrarunner uses his abilities to attempt to find help for his family after a plane crash in northern Québec (Essinger 2017) and a postapocalyptic novel in which a group runs from Edinburgh to southern England after a meteorite shower destroys much of the country (Walker 2016). In 2011, Puffin Canada—the publisher that released Pitt and Zahab's *Running to Extremes* in the same year—published *Just Deserts*, a novel by prolific young-adult-fiction writer Eric Walters, written in collaboration with Ray Zahab. The novel features a teen protagonist forced into a desert-crossing trek that becomes a life-changing experience. Walters based the story on his experience of getting lost while on a desert expedition with Zahab. Although Puffin Canada marketed *Just Deserts* as being connected to *Running to Extremes*, the latter book specifically focuses on Zahab's ultramarathon career while the former focuses on an expedition, not on ultrarunning as such. As a piece of fiction that focuses on ultrarunning and that is aimed at young adults, Carroll's novel *Ultra* is unique.

YOUNG ADULT SPORTS NOVELS, THE COMING-OF-AGE STORY, AND *ULTRA*

Historically, and even today, proponents of youth sport argue that sport teaches young people things like fair play and sportsmanship, and that it contributes to overall character development (Mangan 2000, Messner 2009). Young adult sports novels began to appear in the late 1800s, and for decades they generally mirrored these positive assumptions and depictions of sport (Sherrill 1984). Into the 1950s, young adult sports novels focused on the action on the field rather than the characters' lives off the field (Crowe 2011), and they typically featured a young, male hero whose unwavering strength of character helped him achieve success in his sport and overcome any challenges from people who wanted to ruin the sanctity of that sport (Oriard 1982). Chip Hilton, the main character of an eponymous book series by Clair Bee from the 1940s and 1950s, is an example of such a hero. He listens to coaches and rises above politics and the influence of gamblers to achieve glory on the field, which readers vicariously experience (Gildea 2013; Sherill 1984). Broader social issues such as race and social class crept into young adult sports novels in the 1950s and 1960s, but the way authors portrayed the hero was much the same (Blair 2009; Sherill 1984). The terrain shifted in the 1970s. Writing specifically about baseball novels for young adults (but with insights applicable to young adult sports novels more broadly), Cheré Blair notes that books of this period are "marked by concerns we associate with adolescence itself," which include "constructions of identity and the search for self, awakenings and discovery . . . questions of authority and individual autonomy, preoccupations with the body, and unique and even symbiotic relationships to pop culture and the larger cultural landscape" (2009, 191). In other words, rather than focusing on sports action, many young adult novels began to make sport the backdrop to broader issues (Schneider 2011), with most sports novels mapping onto themes already popular in young adult literature more generally, specifically the tropes of the coming-of-age story (Crowe 2011). Indeed, Pamela Carroll and Steven Chandler (2001) suggest that coming of age has been the prevailing theme in young adult sports novels ever since. *Ultra* certainly falls into this category.

The coming of age for *Ultra*'s main character Quinn Scheurmann occurs over twenty-four hours during which he runs, and ultimately wins, the fictional Shin-Kicker 100 race. The novel is structured as an interview between Quinn and television host Sydney Watson Walters. This interview format allows for a first-person narrative around the experience of the race while also dipping into other aspects of Quinn's life in flashbacks. Mileage is signposted in most chapter titles so that readers can keep track of distance gone and remaining in the race narrative. Major events during the race constitute the chapters, including challenges faced at different times, conversations with other racers, interactions with family and volunteers at aid stations, and Quinn's hallucinations, which help him work through the relationship troubles, developmental crises, and grief at the centre of this coming-of-age story. Quinn's support crew plays an important role in helping Quinn through both the race and his personal troubles. Thanks to a cellphone he got from his best friend Kneecap (whose real name is never mentioned), Quinn can talk to her, his brother Ollie, and his mother throughout the race.

Early on, Kneecap joins Quinn on the racecourse and walks up a mountain with him. They discuss how he's been depressed, a "fun vampire," for the last few months (59–66). Over the phone, Quinn tells his brother that since he does not have a pacer—someone who accompanies ultrarunners to offer encouragement and ensure they stay on course—Ollie must tell him jokes and keep up his spirits. At the end, after a storm blows away most of the trail markers, Quinn's cellphone connection is what allows him to complete the race, with his family and friend coaching him to use the phone's GPS to navigate to the finish line.

The major life crisis that Quinn needs to deal with in his coming of age is the absence of his father, Tom Scheurmann. Tom is a soldier who has been serving in Afghanistan on his third tour. Through most of the book, this absence and the "long shadow" (a chapter title late in the novel) that it casts over Quinn's life explain Quinn's withdrawal from friends and his strained relationship with his mother. Tom had a strong influence on Quinn's decision to take up running, and he is extremely well-loved by the ultrarunning community. He is described as a big guy, muscular, two hundred pounds, and five-foot-eleven—someone who "didn't look like your typical runner" (13). He is also known as a legendary pacer, not least because he is such a good storyteller. Some of Quinn's flashbacks show us as much, with Tom describing psychological "trail demons" and telling far-fetched stories as they run and hike together. As race director Bruce puts it, "we always had a good time when he was around" (47).

Quinn and his father had both registered for the race and were supposed to run it together, but when race day arrives, Tom is not there. Late in the race, however, at a remote aid station eighty-three miles and twenty hours into the race, Quinn has a conversation with his father, apparently in person. Tom says he took a late flight home from Afghanistan to be at the race. The conversation is surreal, and Quinn thinks, "You really can't be here . . . It's not possible" (137). Quinn's father offers him advice, but nothing more. It is a volunteer, not Tom, who fixes Quinn's feet and feeds him. While it's foreshadowed throughout the novel, it's only at mile ninety-seven, when Quinn is visiting a trail-side shrine, that we learn Tom was killed in Afghanistan.

In a call with Ollie, Quinn says he cannot finish the race because it hurts too much, and Ollie asks if it hurts "as much as we hurt when Daddy died" (166). At the end of the race, Quinn and his mother have a cathartic argument and collective cry, both about her letting Quinn run the race and about her letting his father go back to Afghanistan. Quinn regrets not having said goodbye to his father, but his mother comforts him, saying, "That's alright . . . you're doing it now" (189). Thus, the coming of age in the novel centers around dealing with grief and loss, and the use of sport to process and overcome them. Quinn honours his father's memory in running the race and unintentionally shares in the local ultrarunning community's collective grief.

Dead fathers are frequent plot devices in young adult sports novels. In her study of young adult baseball novels, Blair argues that "'[g]ood' dads die in the baseball novels of YA lit, and their sons are left with memories of catch" (2009, 207), or in Quinn's case, memories of running with his father. Common plot device or not, there are certainly ultrarunners who use the sport as a means of coping with all sorts of issues in their lives, including grief (Johnson 2001), addictions (Corbett and England 2018; Engle 2016), and mental health issues (Reese 2021), or as a means to "reset" or manage an otherwise busy life (Whalley 2012). The idea of a race as a journey—an experience that changes the runner—is often voiced in ultrarunning, even by runners repeating a race they have finished before. This idea lines up with research and writing around ultrarunning that discusses spiritual experiences and feelings of being connected to some divine unity through the effortful trek through natural environments (Atkinson 2012; Jones 2005).

Carroll alludes to this kind of experience early in the book when Bruce, the race director, gives the runners instructions at the starting line: "Two minutes from now, you'll cross this line. And in roughly twenty-four hours, if you're lucky, you'll cross it again, only by then you'll be a totally different person" (5). At another point, another runner, Kara, refers to running in nature as her church, a form of worship (26). Quinn experiences something similar. His race serves as a journey, almost a pilgrimage, that helps him work through his loss and pain by supplanting it with a strenuous physical challenge. As his father tells him in their hallucinated conversation at mile eighty-three, Quinn is journeying down a dark hallway, at the end of which new doors will open (142). He will finish his race, but he will also be able to move on in life.

REPRESENTING THE SPORT OF ULTRARUNNING

In discussing what makes a good sports novel, *Horn Book Magazine* editor Dean Schneider suggest that "[f]ew sports novels are only about sports;

if they are any good, they're about lots of things in life—family, friends, the street, jock culture, and the like." He goes on to assert that books that miss the boat have "too much mental drama, not enough play-by-play; nonstop action but weak characterization; or sports lingo misused, revealing a writer who doesn't really know the game" (2011, 68). Schneider makes the case that the writer of young adult sports fiction needs to find a balance between storytelling and characterization on the one hand and including sports-related action in an accurate way on the other. This appears to be exactly Carroll's goal in writing *Ultra*. In his author's note, Carroll describes how the novel was inspired by his nieces and nephews asking him what ultrarunning was like. Initially, he felt he did not give them very good answers, so he made a point of becoming a better storyteller of his experiences. At the same time, he devoted himself to providing a realistic portrayal of the sport, including the human experience of it and the many unusual aspects of the sport and its subculture. As the stories grew, they became the novel.

Carroll does not shy away from portraying the physical challenge of ultrarunning events and the punishment inflicted on runners' bodies and minds. As Kara, an elite athlete in the novel who runs much of the race with Quinn, says, "[W]e're running a hundred miles. Something always hurts" (127). At mile sixty-seven, Quinn describes the pain in his feet as feeling "like I was running on thumbtacks—thumbtacks dipped in acid. It felt like the soles of my feet had been shaved off with a rusty chisel" (128). At the mile eighty-three aid station, a volunteer pops his blisters and seals them with Krazy Glue. Earlier at mile twenty-nine, low on water due to a leaky hydration bladder, Quinn "bonks." He experiences a loss of time: miles go by in a blip, without his awareness. He has hallucinations quite frequently during the race, and they often serve as a means of advancing the coming-of-age crisis. At one point, Quinn has a conversation with the wind in which it asks him to find his shadow. The wind deposits a pair of camouflage combat pants (his father's) in front of him, and he later hallucinates that a bear is wearing them. Late in the night, Quinn thinks he has walked out on a broken railway trellis, and from there takes a ride on a singing whale (something associated with one of his father's stories). He wakes up to find himself on the abandoned railway track at the trail's edge. And of course, Quinn hallucinates the conversation with his father at the mile eighty-three aid station. Hallucinations are quite common for ultrarunners, especially in the night (Johnson 2001; McDougall 2009), to the point of being something anticipated in races of one hundred miles or more, and later discussed with humour. Carroll attempts to explain the frequency of hallucinations and the somewhat nonchalant attitude to them in a flashback sequence with Quinn's father. Tom suggests that hallucinations amount to "trail demons" constructed by your mind to get your body to stop when it can, in fact, still keep going (40–41).

Given the pain and suffering described, it may seem ridiculous to have a thirteen-year-old running a hundred-mile race. One competitor in the novel does question whether someone as young as Quinn should run the Shin-Kicker 100, but race director Bruce brushes this concern aside, pointing out who Quinn's father is and implying that Tom's experience and respected status is enough to vouch for Quinn's ability. Robert Lipsyte (2014), some of whose work is considered classic young adult sport literature, offers the criticism that modern sports novels need to deal with player health and moral and ethical questions around sport. Carroll sidesteps this criticism somewhat by giving Quinn what he calls "his superpowers" throughout the novel. In a flashback, we learn that after running a surprisingly long distance with his father at the age of eight, Quinn was tested in a physiology lab. They found that he had a larger-than-average heart and that his body produced very little lactic acid, so he could run almost to exhaustion with-out feeling any "burn." This may seem unrealistic, but it has a basis in the literature. Ray Zahab, for example, wrote about having almost no lactate threshold in his 2007 book and media reports on him frequently talk about this surprising aspect of his physiology. So even Quinn's "superpowers" are physiological possibilities known within the sport, which Carroll borrows for his own purposes.

In addition to capturing the prevalent sense of the "journey" experi-ence in ultrarunning, and the willing acceptance of pain and distress by its participants, Carroll's novel displays some of the unique demographic aspects of ultrarunning related to age and gender. For example, a fair number of the supporting and side characters competing in the race are older than some might expect for those participating in extreme athletic endeavors. At the beginning of the race, Quinn runs with a group of grey-haired men who discuss their bowel movements (which is a frequent topic of conversation in the ultrarunning community). At mile thirty-eight, Quinn meets a runner named Kern Gregory, whom he perceives to be the age of a grandpa. Kern confirms his age when the pair discuss Kara, who looks to be in her forties; Kern says she's young enough to be a girl to him. A recurring character who Quinn calls "the Dirt Eater" because the back of his shirt reads "Eat my dirt" is also described as an older man with gray, wispy hair. Elite ultrarunners often tend to be in their thirties or forties. Demographic analysis shows that the average ultrarunner, elite or not, is in their forties, and that they tend not to lose much in pace as they age (Ronto 2020). There is a well-worn mythos in the sport that the younger runners are not yet tough enough to be successful. Only in recent years, as the sport has become more popular and commercialized, have elite runners in their twenties risen to prominence in the sport (David and Leheka 2013).

Carroll's choice to place Kara among the elite runners also accurately reflects a gender-related trend in the sport. In conversation with Quinn, Kara reveals she was the outright winner of the race the previous year. In Quinn's race, Kara ultimately places second despite getting lost and running extra miles at different times. While only making up a small number of the overall participants in ultrarunning, women tend to perform well relative to the overall field, and it is common for women to win major hundred-mile races outright (Harris 2012; McDougall 2009; Reed 2006). At distances of two hundred kilometers and above (admittedly, a small number of races), women consistently and collectively outperform men (Ronto 2020). Having a woman character contending to win the race might seem odd to the uninitiated, but it is an accepted part of the sport. In my own experience, male ultrarunners are much less worried about "getting beaten by a woman" than men running shorter distances, likely because it happens so often.

Carroll also includes many scenes and sections of dialogue that depict the deep levels of social support among ultrarunners, showing the sense of community that exists in the sport across typical social boundaries of age and gender, and how it enables runners to get through the physical challenges of the race. Quinn describes the scene at one large aid station to Sydney Watson Walters, the television host, and emphasizes the amazing volunteers. The aid station features pounding music, dozens of people cheering for the runners, all kinds of food, and volunteers checking on the runners to see if they are okay and if they need anything. Quinn later talks about all the gross things volunteers cheerfully put up with from sometimes cranky runners, including sweat, vomit, blood, blisters, and all kinds of other body fluids. Many times in the novel, characters help each other, even when they are among the leaders. For instance, Kara runs with Quinn frequently during the race, engaging in friendly conversation and offering advice that helps Quinn overcome problems. Near the end, Quinn finds Kara disoriented, and they walk-run together to the finish. Kern Gregory also offers crucial assistance to Quinn during the race. When Quinn runs out of water at mile twenty-nine and bonks, Kern offers him his water and helps him refill his supply using the water purifier in his pack. Kern then runs with Quinn for an hour and a half, until they get to the next aid station, so that he can keep an eye on him. Qualitative and ethnographic research studies point to this sense of community as something that continues to draw runners back to these races again and again, despite the pain and suffering (David and Leheka 2013; Harris 2012; Quicke 2017). As someone who participates in the sport myself, I have personally seen injured runners show up to volunteer or crew for people when they would rather be running; pacers run over the marathon distance to keep their runners going, with no individual reward for themselves; and runners sacrifice personal goals to stick with and help someone else finish. I have even seen runners sacrifice their race, for which they had likely trained for months, to assist others or ensure that someone in trouble gets safely out of a wilderness environment. Carroll gives an accurate depiction of how ultrarunners see themselves as a community.

While Carroll follows the genre conventions of young adult sports novels in providing a standard coming-of-age story, including the trope of the dead father, his focus on the sport of ultrarunning is something new for the genre. While ultrarunning is growing in terms of the number of races and participants, there is little media about it, and it is still generally seen as a fringe sport. By writing an engaging young adult novel, Carroll likely does more to promote interest in the sport among young readers than earlier writers of overviews or how-to guides. The novel's strength lies in Carroll's insider perspective from running many such races himself, which he uses to render for young people a realistic picture of the sport and its subculture, including the acceptance of pain, the journey and its spiritual elements, the social support, and the community, all of which combine to bring people back to the sport on an ongoing basis, despite its extremes. Although it is a somewhat generic coming-of-age story, *Ultra* gives readers a realistic picture of what goes into this lesser-known sport of ultrarunning, and what the athletes get out of it.

WORKS CITED

Aaseng, Nate. 1987. *Ultramarathons: The World's Most Punishing Races*. Minneapolis: Lerner Publications.

Atkinson, Michael. 2010. "Entering Scapeland: Yoga, Fell and Post-sport Physical Cultures." *Sport in Society* 13 (7–8): 1249–67.

Ayres, Ed. 2012. *The Longest Race*. New York: The Experiment.

Benyo, Richard. 1991. *The Death Valley 300*. Forestville, CA: Specific Publications.

Blair, Cheré. 2009. "'I Would Have Been Happy Just to Catch While the Father Pitched': The Father-Son Game of Catch in Young Adult Literature." *Aethlon: The Journal of Sport Literature* 36 (1): 189–214.

Carroll, David. 2014. *Ultra*. Toronto: Scholastic Canada.

Carroll, Pamela S., and Steven B. Chandler. 2001. "Sports-Related Young Adult Literature." *Strategies: A Journal for Physical and Sport Educators* 14 (5): 35–37.

Corbett, Catra, with Dan England. 2018. *Reborn on the Run: My Journey from Addiction to Ultramarathons*. New York: Skyhorse Publishing.

Crowe, Chris. 2001. "Young Adult Literature: Sports Literature for Young Adults." *The English Journal* 60 (6): 129–33.

David, Gary C., and Nick Lehecka. 2013. "The Sprit of the Trail: Culture, Popularity and Prize Money in Ultramarathoning." *Fast Capitalism* 10 (1): 55–70. https://doi.org/10.32855/fcapital.201301.006.

Engle, Charlie. 2016. *Running Man: A Memoir*. New York: Simon & Schuster.

Essinger, Dave. 2017. *Running Out*. Charlotte, NC: Mint Hill Books.

Gildea, Dennis. 2013. *Hoop Crazy: The Lives of Clair Bee and Chip Hilton*. Fayetteville, AK: University of Arkansas Press.

Harris, Amy. 2012. "Beyond Limits: Exploring Motivation and the Lack of Women in Ultramarathoning." *Journal of Undergraduate Research at Minnesota State University, Mankato* 12 (1): article 3. https://cornerstone.lib.mnsu.edu/jur/vol12/iss1/3.

Hayhurst, Chris. 2002. *Ultra Marathon Running*. New York: Rosen Publishing.

Heinrich, Bernd. 2001. *Why We Run: A Natural History*. New York: HarperCollins.

Horton, David, and Rebekah Trittipoe. 1997. *A Quest for Adventure: David Horton's Conquest of the Appalachian Trail and the Trans-America Footrace.* Lynchburg, VA: Warwick House.

Johnson, Kirk. 2001. *To the Edge: A Man, Death Valley and the Mystery of Endurance.* New York: Warner Books.

Jones, Peter N. 2002. "Ultrarunners and Chance Encounters with 'Absolute Unitary Being.'" *Anthropology of Consciousness* 15 (2): 39–50.

Jurek, Scott, with Steve Friedman. 2012. *Eat & Run: My Unlikely Journey to Ultramarathon Greatness.* Boston: Mariner Books.

Jurek, Scott, with Jenny Jurek. 2018. *North: Finding My Way While Running the Appalachian Trail.* New York: Little, Brown.

Karnazes, Dean. 2005. *Ultramarathon Man: Confessions of an All-Night Runner.* New York: Tarcher/Penguin.

Lipsyte, Robert. 2014. "Speaking My Mind: Sports Books—The Four Questions." *The English Journal* 104 (1): 94–95.

Mangan, J. A. 2000. *Athleticism in the Victorian and Edwardian Public School: The Emergence and Consolidation of an Educational Ideology.* Abingdon, UK: Routledge.

McDougall, Christopher. 2009. *Born to Run.* New York: Alfred & Knopf.

Messner, Michael. 2009. *It's All for the Kids: Gender, Families, and Youth Sports.* Berkeley: University of California Press.

Oriard, Michael V. 1982. *Dreaming of Heroes: American Sports Fiction, 1868–1980.* Chicago: Nelson-Hall.

Osler, Todd, and Ed Dodd. 1979. *Ultra-Marathoning: The Next Challenge.* Mountain View, CA: World Publishing.

Pitt, Steve, with Ray Zahab. 2011. *Running to Extremes: Ray Zahab's Amazing Ultramarathon Journey.* Toronto: Puffin Canada.

Plymire, Darcy C. 2006. "The Legend of the Tarahumara: Tourism, Overcivilization and the White Man's Indian." *International Journal of the History of Sport* 23 (2): 154–66.

Quicke, Jenna. 2017. *The Phenomenon of Community: A Qualitative Study of the Ultrarunning Community.* Master's thesis, Prescott College. ProQuest (no. 10276702).

Reed, Pam. 2006. *The Extra Mile.* Emmaus, PN: Rodale.

Reese, Corey. 2021. *Stronger Than the Dark: Exploring the Intimate Relationship Between Running and Depression.* Self-published.

Ronto, Paul. 2020. "The State of Ultra Running 2020." *RunRepeat,* September 21, 2020. https://runrepeat.com/state-of-ultra-running.

Schneider, Dean. 2011. "What Makes a Good Sports Novel?" *The Horn Book Magazine* 87 (1): 68–72.

Sherrill, Anne. 1984. "The Male Athlete in Young Adult Sports Fiction." *Arete: The Journal of Sport Literature* 2 (1): 111–30.

Walker, Adrian J. 2016. *The End of the World Running Club*. New York: Del Rey.

Walters, Eric, with Ray Zahab. *Just Deserts*. Toronto: Puffin Canada.

Whalley, Buff. 2012. *Run Wild*. London: Simon & Schuster.

Whiting, Jim. 2007. *Ultra Running with Scott Jurek*. Pembroke Park, FL: Mitchell Lane Publishers.

Zahab, Ray. 2007. *Running for My Life*. Toronto: Insomniac Press.

4

Jamie Dopp

Out of the Ordinary

Curling in *The Black Bonspiel of Willie MacCrimmon* and *Men with Brooms*

> *For many people, curling conjures up images of corn brooms, tams, paunchy middle-aged participants, and lots of tippling.*
>
> Nancy Lee, CBC Radio broadcast in 1987

> *There are no secrets—you play hard and go to the bar.*
>
> Ed Werenich in 2004

Curling was reintroduced into the Winter Olympics in 1988 after an absence of over sixty years. In order to select a Canadian team, the Canadian Curling Association (CCA) organized a qualifying tournament for April 1987. One of the favourites to win this tournament was a rink skipped by Ed Werenich, the winner of the 1983 Canadian and World Championships. Werenich, however, almost didn't get to participate. Worried about the image that might be created if Canadian curlers showed up at the Olympics looking less than athletic, the CCA organized a "training" camp in the fall of 1986 to help prospective Olympians get into shape. Werenich appeared at camp as his usual paunchy self and the CCA gave him an ultimatum: lose weight or be disqualified.

Werenich lost eighteen pounds before the Olympic trials, which were held April 19 to 25, 1987. His rink finished third, two behind the rink skipped by Ed Lukovich, who went on to win a bronze medal at the 1988 Winter Olympics in Calgary. Though he never complained about his third-place finish in the 1987 trials, the embarrassment of the CCA's weight-related ultimatum stayed with Werenich. It also divided the curling community. For many traditionalists, the incident made Werenich a folk hero who embodied (literally!) a version of the game with which they identified.

Though there is some controversy about the origins of curling, what can be said with confidence is that the activity of playing with stones on ice originated in Europe in the Middle Ages. In *Curling: The History, The Players, The Game*, Warren Hansen reports the first hard evidence of curling comes from Paisley Abbot in Scotland, with the earliest stone dated from 1511 (1999, 20–21). Hansen stresses that, although there is evidence of similar games elsewhere in Europe, it was the Scots who "nurtured the game [curling], improved it, established rules, turned it into a national pastime, and exported it to other countries" (20).

Curling arrived in Canada with Scottish immigrants. According to one story, soldiers of the 78th Fraser Highland Regiment melted cannonballs to make iron curling "stones" to play with during the long winter of 1759–60 in Québec, after the Battle of the Plains of Abraham. W. O. Mitchell repeats this likely apocryphal story at the beginning of *The Black Bonspiel of Willie MacCrimmon*. What is more certain is that curling clubs sprang up in various locations in Canada during the first quarter of the nineteenth century. Curling clubs were established in Montréal (1807), Kingston (1820), Québec City (1821), and Halifax (1824) during this period (Hansen 1999, 25–6). The late eighteenth and early nineteenth centuries saw significant immigration from Scotland to Canada, and of Scottish Loyalists to Canada from the United States, with high concentrations in the places where curling took hold. By 1850, curling was well established in eastern Canada, and, around the same time, began to spread across the Prairies. In *The Stone Age: A Social History of Curling on the Prairies*, Vera Pezer suggests that curling became popular on the prairies because of the railway and the Scots who rode it. The Prairie settlers also saw something of their own character reflected in the game: "Its requirement of self-discipline, persistence, patience, and co-operation parallel the qualities of the early settlers" (2003, 1–2).

An important part of curling's popularity has had to do with the game's "democratic traditions," which include a welcoming of all classes, ages, and physical abilities (Redmond 1988, 556). The curling clubs established across Canada in the nineteenth century were open to a wider membership than most other athletic associations, which were often restricted to "gentlemen." (For example, amateur hockey clubs, which began appearing in the 1880s, tended to be restricted in this way.) The training controversy around the 1987 Olympic trials gave Ed Werenich a platform to defend this democratic tradition. The beauty of curling, he stressed in a 1987 interview, is that it doesn't matter if you are "seven or eight years old or eighty," since "anybody can play"—including someone, like Werenich himself, a little on the paunchy side. Curling is not a "physical fitness sport," Werenich said, but "a finesse sport . . . like a chess game on ice" (3:00–3:20).

The availability of curling to all types of players strengthens the claim that curling is the game of choice for "ordinary" Canadians. In the afterword to *The Black Bonspiel*, W. O. Mitchell impersonates the sportswriter Bill Frayne to emphasize this point. "These days," the fictionalized Frayne writes, "curling is the great Canadian game. Forget lacrosse (most people have). Take away hockey, which is only for those who are young and healthy, with a good dental plan. . . . No, pound for pound, curling is the great participatory sport in Canada" (133). The belief in curling's popularity with ordinary Canadians—and the rivalry this popularity implies with hockey—is well-articulated in "The Curling Song," Bowser and Blue's 2003 anthem that is to curling what Stompin' Tom Connors's "The Hockey Song" is to hockey. The second verse makes the comparison with hockey explicit:

> When it comes to winter sports
> It is generally thought
> that hockey is the game
> to which we flock
> But if you actually play,
> then curling wins the day
> In Canada more people curl
> than hock. (47)

The corniness of the rhyme of "flock" with "hock" reinforces the message that curling is the game of ordinary people (who, apparently, have a taste for simple wordplay)—though, ironically, "The Curling Song," which Bowser and Blue deliver with their characteristic stellar harmonies, is more musically sophisticated than "The Hockey Song."

Curling's reputation as an "ordinary" sport is exploited for comic purposes in two of the most well-known imaginative responses to the game in Canada: W. O. Mitchell's novella *The Black Bonspiel of Willie MacCrimmon* (1993), which I've already introduced, and Paul Gross's film *Men with Brooms* (2002). Each of these texts takes the "ordinariness" of curling as an ironic backdrop for extraordinary events. *The Black Bonspiel* tells the story of a small-town cobbler, Willie MacCrimmon, who is so fanatical about curling that he makes a deal with the Devil for a chance to win the Brier. *Men with Brooms* centers on four flawed, small-town men, once members of a legendary curling rink, who are called back together in bizarre fashion to compete in a bonspiel called the Golden Broom. Each text has an ending that is wildly out of the ordinary, with events that strain credulity, the laws of nature, and, perhaps, good taste. In this way, *Men with Brooms* and *The Black Bonspiel* complicate the question of what is ordinary and what is extraordinary in sport and life, while satirizing what is perhaps the most extreme promise of sport: that one great triumph on the field of play can magically transform a life.

THE DEVIL AND WILLIE MACCRIMMON

The Black Bonspiel of Willie MacCrimmon is a novelization of W. O. Mitchell's play *The Black Bonspiel of Wullie MacCrimmon*, which premiered, in its full-length form, in 1977. According to Ormond Mitchell and Barbara Mitchell, *The Black Bonspiel* began as a short story written (but not published) around 1947, then was adapted over the years into "almost every other medium—radio, television, [and] stage" before the full-length play and subsequent novelization (2009, 1). When the novella came out in 1993, Mitchell was a beloved figure in Canada and near the end of a long and successful literary career, with his best known work, the 1947 novel *Who Has Seen the Wind*, a Canadian classic.

   The Black Bonspiel is a comic retelling of the Faust legend, perhaps inspired by Mitchell's familiarity with Stephen Vincent Benét's 1936 story (and later play) "The Devil and Daniel Webster" (Mitchell and Mitchell 2009, 3). Benét's story, like Mitchell's, is about someone who makes a deal with the Devil but manages to escape, in contrast to tragic and cautionary versions of the legend, like Washington Irving's 1824 story "The Devil and Tom Walker" and Christopher Marlowe's classic sixteenth-century play *Doctor Faustus*. A related text would be George Abbott and Stanley Donen's 1958 film *Damn Yankees*—another sport-themed version of the Faust legend. *Damn Yankees* centres on a frustrated Washington Senators superfan, Joe Boyd, who says he would give anything to beat the Yankees, which leads the Devil—in the form of a smooth-talking man named Mr. Applegate—to appear with an offer.

Willie MacCrimmon, the eponymous main character of *The Black Bonspiel*, is a resident of Shelby, Alberta, "a community of five thousand, many of them devout curlers" (3). Willie is the "most dedicated" curler in town. He began playing at the age of ten during his Scottish childhood, coached by his father. Now, after the death of his wife and the closing of his beloved Presbyterian church, curling remains "his only active religion" (6). One day Willie indulges in an extended daydream of curling glory and swears that he would "gi'e anything . . . utterly anything . . . for to skip the winning rink in the Brier!" (44). The Devil, in the guise of a travelling salesman named Mr. Cloutie, duly appears, proclaiming, "That's a bargain, Willie MacCrimmon" (44). The Devil's proposal contains a twist on the standard "soul-for-fair-recompense" arrangement: he wants Willie's soul not just to have it, but so that Willie can curl third for him in Hell.[1] It turns out that, as badly as Willie wants to win the Canadian Brier, the Devil wants to win the Celestial Brier (49–51). Rather than dismiss the Devil's temptation as his Presbyterian faith would counsel, Willie makes a double-or-nothing counter-proposal. He offers to play a one game challenge: Willie's current rink against the Devil's. If Willie wins, he gets to not only skip the winning rink in the Brier, but also save his soul. If the Devil wins, Willie's soul goes to Hell to curl third for the Devil, and Willie doesn't skip at the Brier (51–52).

Willie's agreement with Mr. Cloutie sets up a number of jokes in *The Black Bonspiel* about Hell and the Devil. Many of these jokes are simple wordplays in which the words *Hell* and *the Devil* become ironic because of the literal presence of the Devil in the story. A few jokes work by inverting what is typically assumed to be ordinary or extraordinary. For example,

---

1 The four members of a curling rink are known as the *lead*, *second*, *third*, and *skip*, based on the order in which they throw their stones. The lead and the second are collectively known as the *front end*. That the Devil wants Willie to play third is significant, because the third most directly sets up the skip to score points. Thirds in high level competition are often skips at other times.

when Willie reveals that the Devil recently brought him a pair of curling boots to be repaired, Mr. Pringle, the local United Church minister, exclaims, "A Devil bringing in a pair of curling boots?" and Willie replies: "Aye. It's a wee bit unusual. Most curlers just use overshoes" (31). The Devil himself is made comic in the novella by his obsession with curling, which seems a trivial concern for someone dedicated to the cosmic struggle between Evil and Good. The Devil is also plagued by ordinary concerns. Hell, it turns out, has a single-resource economy much like Alberta's, and, like Alberta, Hell has not been able to diversify. As a result, the Devil is worried that "when the brimstone runs out . . . I don't know what—in Hell—we can do" (48). He also explains the apparently extraordinary fact that there is ice in Hell in the most ordinary of ways: Hell's curling rink uses "artificial" ice (47).

Various details in *The Black Bonspiel* stress the ordinariness of curling, of the places in which it is played, and of the players who play it. The novel's small-town setting—Shelby, Alberta—taps into a long tradition of using small-towns to represent "ordinary" Canadian identity. Like other such locations in Mitchell's fiction, Shelby is populated with small-town types. The most explicit indicators of ordinariness are the other players on Willie's rink. Each of them is named Charlie Brown. Each Charlie Brown is distinguished by a nickname based on his blue-collar occupation: "Malleable" (blacksmith), "Cross-cut" (carpenter), and "Pipe-fitting" (plumber). Nobody on this team is an athlete in the conventional sense. Willie is sixty-nine years old; Pipe-fitting and Malleable are both fifty-two and have Ed Werenich–like physiques, being "built for comfort, with comfortable front porches" (134).

There is also something ordinary about Willie's desire to skip the winning rink in the Brier. To win the Canadian Curling Championship brings only limited fame (despite curling's popularity in Canada) and very little fortune. Even in 2020, after significant increases in prize money over the years, the winning rink at the Brier only received $105,000 to split four ways (Bamford 2020). For comparison, the 2021 prize for first place in the Masters golf tournament is $2,070,000 split no ways at all (Luciani 2021). Willie's fantasy includes meeting the Prime Minister and the Governor General, with the Prime Minister inviting him to dinner at the Senate restaurant and the Governor General saying, "Let me pick up the check" (42). That Willie bets his soul to satisfy such humble desires seems so ordinary as to be comical.

The contrast between the ordinariness of curling and the extraordinariness of the Faustian bargain runs through *The Black Bonspiel of Willie MacCrimmon.* The comedy inspired by this contrast echoes the high culture / low culture coupling often found in sports comedy. Such couplings play on the assumption that sport is, by definition, a low-culture activity, so any high-culture references in relation to it will be comic. A famous example is Paul Quarrington's *King Leary* (1987), which uses a jokey mix of references from Shakespeare's *King Lear* and the life of King Clancy to underpin a tragic-comic tale about an early hockey star. In *The Black Bonspiel*, the Devil's front end is made up of Guy Fawkes and Judas Iscariot, and his third—the player whom Willie is slated to replace if he loses his bargain—is Macbeth. Macbeth's speeches in the novel are quotations from Shakespeare with curling references inserted. When Willie's rink first encounters the Devil's rink, Cross-cut Brown overhears the Devil's third muttering to himself a parody of lines from *Macbeth*:

> Tomorrow, and tomorrow, and tomorrow,
> Curls on this pretty pace from end to end,
> Till the last-thrown rock of recorded time;
> And all our yesterdays have lighted fools
> The way to icy death. (93)

Compare Shakespeare's original:

> Tomorrow, and tomorrow, and tomorrow,
> Creeps in this petty pace from day to day
> To the last syllable of recorded time,
> And all our yesterdays have lighted fools
> The way to dusty death. (*Macbeth* V.v.19–24)

Note how the comedy here combines high and low: the seriousness of Shakespeare creates an ironic contrast with the triviality of curling.

But is curling really trivial compared to Shakespeare? A fascinating thing about jokes based on high-low combinations is that they invite us to think not only of contrasts but of similarities. One of the earliest and most celebrated works of sport literature, Bernard Malamud's 1952 novel *The Natural*, works this way. As Michael Oriard has pointed out, *The Natural* treats baseball "in a consciously mythic way" (1982, 212). It does this both by incorporating into the life of its protagonist, Roy Hobbs, many events from baseball history that have been elevated to the status of myth, and by associating Hobbs with the heroes of classical literature. Hobbs, for example, has a magical weapon like King Arthur's sword Excalibur in the form of a hand-carved bat named Wonderboy that he keeps in a bassoon case. The mythic echoes can be understood to satirize America's obsession with baseball; they seem to make fun of the impulse to elevate such trivial events to the status of myth. Yet the echoes also work in reverse. Who gets to decide what is important enough to be elevated to mythic status?

Myths, as Karen Armstrong has noted, are rooted in the human need for meaning. From early in our history, we have invented stories to connect ourselves to "a larger setting" or "an underlying pattern" in order to reassure ourselves, against a lot of evidence to the contrary, that life has "meaning and value" (2006, 2). Literature is one way we have done this, religion another, and sport yet another. All of these activities have an underlying mythic component, which means that comparisons between them will capture not only differences but similarities. Take another common high-low combination: religion and sport. This combination is often invoked ironically. To say that someone's favourite sport is their "religion" can seem like a statement of disapproval, as if to have a religious attachment to a sport means the person must be shallow. Yet the seemingly exaggerated responses people have to sports are not fully explained by the competitiveness of players or the tribalism of fans. Sports are also symbolic activities in which humans act out desires that are fundamentally religious in nature. Michael Novak makes a strong argument for this in his 1967 classic *The Joy of Sports*. "[T]he underlying metaphysics of sports," he writes, "entails overcoming the fear of death. . . . A game tests considerably more than talent. A game tests, somehow, one's entire life. It tests one's standing with fortune and the gods. . . . To win an athletic contest is to feel as though the gods are on one's side, as though one is Fate's darling" (47). What better way to test whether or not you are "Fate's darling" than by engaging in an athletic contest with the Devil?

Though *The Black Bonspiel* carries the theological implications of Willie's contest with Old Cloutie lightly, the Faustian environment hints at life-and-death issues beneath the ordinary surface of a curling match. One explanation for why curling is Willie's "only active religion" is that he is a widower: his wife, Mary, died of breast cancer ten years before (6). The match, then, has a subtle aura of Willie challenging death, perhaps even expressing his defiance of it—Satan, after all, is the one who tempted Adam and Eve to sin, and thus made death part of being human. More immediately, Willie uses the match to cope with his loss of faith in non-curling religious consolations caused by Mary's death.

Faustian narratives tend to highlight two critical questions for humans. The first has to do with how much a person is willing to—or must—give up to achieve success. The second has to do with how to define success itself. The implications of these questions are well set out in Marlowe's original *Doctor Faustus*. At the beginning of the play, Faustus is a gifted but restless man who cannot settle on the kind of career he wants. He considers a series of traditionally esteemed professions—doctor, professor, minister—but rejects them all. The problem, he feels, is that even if he achieved the greatest success at one of these professions, he would still remain "Faustus and a man." What he truly craves—and why he makes his deal with the Devil—is set out in these lines:

> Couldst thou make men to live eternally,
> Or, being dead, raise them to life again,
> Then this profession were to be esteem'd. (I 23–25)

Faustus, then, is attracted to magic—and, ultimately, makes his bargain with Mephistophilis—with the hope of acquiring a god-like power over life and death. If there is a reason to bargain your soul, this might, perhaps, be the one. Sadly for Faustus, the power he acquires, like many magical wishes granted in fairy tales, turns out to be ephemeral: he can trick other humans with his illusions, but ultimately the illusions are no more than that. A key moment in the play is in Scene XIII when Faustus has Mephistophilis raise the spirit of Helen of Troy and orders her to "make me immortal with a kiss" (XIII 114). With the kiss, however, Helen's lips "suck forth [his] soul"—suggesting that the "spirit" of Helen is in fact a demon in disguise (XIII 115).

There is something especially poignant about Faustian bargains when it comes to sport, since athletes often make enormous sacrifices, and pay significance costs, for possible success. The rewards of sport are also highly variable. Some sports promise mythic-level wealth and fame; others—like curling—offer little. That Willie is willing to bet everything on a sport as non-commercial as curling suggests the imaginative power that sport has. No sport can make a person truly immortal, even if it feels like you are "Fate's darling" at the moment of victory. Yet athletes and fans are often seduced by the promise that sporting success can bring a mythical—or magical—transformation: from zero to hero with one great victory. The extreme ending of *The Black Bonspiel* satirizes this magical promise and hints at other ideas for what sporting success might bring. Before I examine the ending in detail, however, let me turn to another text that satirizes the ordinary Canadian sport of curling.

FORTY-TWO POUNDS OF EXPLODING GRANITE

Men with Brooms, the 2002 film by Paul Gross, signals its intention to play with tropes of Canadian identity from before the opening credits. The theme music on the DVD index is "O Canada," first on an organ, as if at a hockey game, then on a wailing electric guitar, reminiscent of Jimmy Hendrix's version of "The Star Spangled Banner." As the film itself begins, credits flash against a dark screen with forest sounds in the background—a loon, a moose—until the title appears to the sound of a bagpipe drone. Fade in to a shot of a rushing northern stream, then the bagpiper himself, kilted and astride an outcropping of granite. As shots of the stream and the piper alternate, the piper's song resolves itself into "Land of the Silverbirch." After a verse through on the bagpipes, the ersatz-Indigenous chanting of the song begins. Then a manly group of men begin to sing:

> Land of the silver birch
> Home of the beaver
> Where still the mighty moose
> Wanders at will
> Blue lake and rocky shore
> I will return once more
> Boom, chitty, boom, boom,
> Boom, chitty, boom, boom, boom.

As if to complete the montage of Canadian tropes, the scene shifts during the singing of the song to a group of beavers industriously chewing through the trunks of trees. A large beaver completes its work and rises on hind legs, seemingly to call "timber!" Its gnawed tree tilts and ultimately falls down a slope towards a lake, upon which is revealed a white motorboat—the location of the film's first scene.

This first scene involves an old man, Donald Foley, and his daughter Amy. Amy surfaces from the lake in diving gear and gives the thumbs up to Donald, who begins to haul something up on a winch. A shape appears in the water, at first blurry and mud-streaked, then revealing itself to be a curling rock. To readers of Margaret Atwood, this rock-hauling sequence will bring to mind the climactic scene of *Surfacing* (1972) in which the protagonist dives into a northern lake to discover the submerged traumas of her life. The curling rock, indeed, turns out to represent submerged trauma: it is part of a set thrown into the lake ten years before by the story's protagonist, Chris Cutter, when he renounced curling after a series of personal and on-ice failures. The excitement of discovering the lost rocks is too much for Donald. He has a heart attack and dies on the boat in Amy's arms. Then a voice-over begins, as if Donald is narrating from the afterworld. To a montage that introduces the setting of Long Bay, Northern Ontario, and that introduces the main characters, Donald speaks of his love of curling and family. His voice is eventually revealed to be coming from a video played at the reading of his will. The video contains a last request: that the rink he used to coach, skipped by Chris, reconstitute itself and seek to finally win the Golden Broom curling tournament, using the lost-and-found rocks seeded with his ashes.

After the set-up, *Men with Brooms* proceeds like a typical sports redemption story. Each member of the Cutter rink has a flawed life in need of fixing. Neil Bucyk, the lead, is a reluctant undertaker trapped in a loveless marriage. Eddie Strombach, the second, is in a very loving marriage, but his low sperm count prevents him and his wife from having children. James Lennox, the third, left Long Bay years ago only to become a drug dealer. He returns with a rent-a-girlfriend named Angela, whose name he keeps forgetting, pursued by a four-hundred-pound giant of a gangster named Stuckmore, to whom he owes money. Cutter himself has multiple issues to deal with. The immediate cause of his renouncing curling was that he failed to call a burned rock during his rink's last tournament.[2] The shame he feels about this, the film implies,

---

2 If a rock is touched by a member of the rink during sweeping it is considered *burned* and removed from play. There is no referee in curling, so calling or not calling a burned rock is up to the players—and is considered a point of honour.

drove him away from Long Bay and the game. But this dishonourable act is only one demon he has to exorcise. Related to it, in an unspecified way, is the fact that he abandoned his fiancée, Julie Foley—daughter of Donald and sister of Amy—at the altar. He is also estranged from his father, Gordon Cutter, whose own fanaticism about curling caused him to neglect Chris's mother when she was dying.

The plot then continues on two tracks, one having to do with the Cutter rink's preparation for the tournament, the other having to do with their personal lives. The scenes of preparation combine jokes about Canadianness with jokes about curling. Early on, for example, the members of the rink attempt to re-establish their bond by jumping naked from a cliff into a lake. The image of them leaping parodies the idea, epitomized by Molson Canadian's 2010 "Made from Canada" beer commercial, that Canadians are a hardy people who have turned their wild northern homeland into a playground. The water is so cold, however, that the naked curlers scream in shock and their manly parts retreat into their bodies (23:45). The first warm-up game the newly reconstituted rink plays is against a team of elderly men. On the way to the game, Cutter reminds his teammates to play with "honour and dignity" and not to mention "incontinence." At the beginning of the game, however, Lennox trash talks the other rink by vowing to "sweep those diapers right off your arses" (27:00). The elderly team, inevitably, trounces the Cutter rink—an instructive illustration of the "democratic" tradition of the game.

Alongside jokes about Canadianness, *Men with Brooms* plays with the small-town and populist roots of curling. When the Golden Broom tournament begins, an announcer describes the curling rink in Long Bay in religious terms: "In the Mecca of Long Bay, there may be a dozen churches, but make no mistake, this is where everybody comes to worship" (53:30). The people shown are working class in appearance and the arena itself is the size you would expect in a small town.

The Cutter rink loses the first game of the tournament. Afterwards, Chris's father Gordon—played by Canadian acting icon Leslie Nielsen—gathers the rink in an outdoor sauna and lectures them on the history and spirit of the game:

> In the town of Stirling, in the country of Scotland, a man took a
> granite block, cut it, rounded it, and carved a date in it. 1511. The

first known curling rock. Since that day curling has been a game of the people. It has forgone trappings of commerce, embraced all comers, and cherished the truth that all who play the game on any rink, on any given day, can be victorious. (1:08:00)

Gordon Cutter's sermon stresses not only that curling is a "game of the people," in which anyone can be victorious on "any given day," but that the game's populist roots impose an ethic: to forgo the "trappings of commerce."

The rink to beat at the Golden Broom, skipped by Alexander "The Juggernaut" Yount, embodies "the trappings of commerce." The team members make their entrance in silver, spacesuit-like uniforms, backed by a soundtrack of hip-hop music, a fireworks display, and an entourage of Dallas Cowboy-style cheerleaders, which leads Gordon Cutter to call them the "Empire of Evil" (55:00). To top it off, when Chris Cutter offers Yount the traditional expression of pregame sportsmanship—"Good curling"—Yount responds with trash talk: "Whatever" (55:30). Yount represents a hypermodern, celebrity-culture version of curling divorced from the traditions of the game, yet in the preliminary match, it is ironically Cutter who violates curling's traditions by failing (again) to call a burned rock. This appalls his father, who sees what has happened from the stands, and leads to the sauna sermon. Afterwards, Cutter and his mates renew their commitment to the true "honour and dignity" of the game by, among other things, switching to traditional corn brooms. Then they run the table in the rest of the preliminary round to earn a chance at redemption in the championship match against Yount.

EXTREME ENDINGS

The Black Bonspiel of Willie MacCrimmon and *Men with Brooms* both have endings that are, in various ways, extreme. In the case of *The Black Bonspiel*, Willie and his rink, after falling behind, come back to defeat the Devil's rink. They do this with two tactics. First, Pipe-fitting Brown reminds Macbeth that if the Devil's rink wins, he will be replaced as third by Willie. This throws Macbeth off his game. Second, Willie repairs the Devil's curling boot with a silver tack. At the crucial moment of the game, the tack bites the Devil's foot, which responds with excruciating pain (since the Devil is allergic), and the Devil hogs his shot (129).[3] Shortly thereafter, the Devil disappears—a sore loser in more ways than one.

Defeating the Devil (and, by association, death) is an extreme feat, but in a comic text Willie's victory is less an adrenaline rush than a cause for laughter. A more extreme feat, in the context of the story, is the transformation of Cross-cut Brown's wife, Annie. Annie Brown is a caricature of a small-town puritan, a later version of Mrs. Abercrombie, the bullying antagonist in *Who Has Seen the Wind*. Annie wants to ban Shakespeare and Chaucer from the schools (10–11); she reports on the local doctor for visiting a brothel (despite the fact that he visits to assist a woman with appendicitis) (13); and she is trying to reinstate prohibition (21). Most importantly for the story, her puritanism extends to her championing an ordinance that bans curling on the Sabbath. When she gets news of Willie's match against the Devil, she bullies Reverend Pringle, the local United Church minister, into going with her to shut it down.

Annie Brown is a difficult character to accept from a gender point of view. She is so obviously the stereotype of a small-minded, small-town woman. Ormond Mitchell and Barbara Mitchell explain that her creation was "influenced by the spate of censorship incidents across Canada" in the 1980s, which included the attempted banning of *Who Has Seen the Wind* by Pentecostal Christian groups (2009, 4). W. O. Mitchell, in *The Black Bonspiel*, gets a measure of revenge about this by making Annie so odious. Her presence in the story also adds a sly twist to the Faustian narrative because, from her point of view, any game played on the Sabbath is by definition a deal with the Devil.

Annie's transformation at the end of *The Black Bonspiel* is as magical as possible without the actual casting of a spell. Once she gets to the rink, she gets caught up in the action. After the Devil's rink injures her husband with a dirty play, she flips from the scolding Puritan she has been throughout to a diehard fan. More than this, despite trying to get Shakespeare and Chaucer banned for their profanity, she calls out profane encouragement to

3 In curling, players throw their stones from a *hack* (an indentation in the ice that allows them to push off) but must release their stone before a line on the ice called a *hog line*. Stones must cross a second hog line near the top of the house in order to be considered in play. A player may *hog* his or her stone by failing to release it in time or failing to throw it hard enough to get over the second line. Hogged stones—like burned stones—are removed from play.

Willie: "I want you to give [the Devil's rink] the shit-kicking of their curling career—'specially their skip!" (115).

The extreme nature of Annie's transformation suggests something shallow, even hypocritical, about her narrow-minded puritanism. In his writing, Mitchell consistently contrasts characters who, like Willie, affirm life in all its earthly wonder against those who, for whatever reason, do not. Annie lacks the spirit of fun necessary to enjoy life (no pregame dram for her!). She also fails to appreciate the value of imagination (enough to want to ban Shakespeare and Chaucer!). Willie, on the other hand, lacks neither quality, which helps to explain what might seem like a contradiction in the text: Willie is said to be not very religious, yet he argues in favour of a literal Devil and Hell, which, he claims, are the only basis for a true religion (27). Why would he make this argument? In a nutshell, because belief in a literal Devil makes a better story (imagine *Hamlet* without the ghost of Hamlet's father, or *Macbeth* without the witches).

The ending of *The Black Bonspiel*, then, plays with ordinary and extraordinary in revealing ways. It demonstrates how a game that is the embodiment of ordinariness can create extraordinary effects. Sports always do this: they take ordinary human activities (running, climbing, throwing a rock) and turn them into something greater—something with mythic possibilities. At the same time, the ending of the story, by its very extremity, is a reminder that sports always involve an element of sheer fun—and that we should be careful about taking it (or ourselves, if we are the players) too seriously.

Though the ending of *Men with Brooms* doesn't involve any obvious supernatural forces, it is even more extreme than the ending of *The Black Bonspiel*. The climax, as is conventional in sport literature, has to do with a championship game. Chris Cutter and his mates face the Yount rink again, this time in the championship of the Golden Broom. Predictably, they fall behind early but claw their way back into contention. The climactic sequence occurs in the tenth end.[4] Cutter is down one and has the hammer, but the Yount rink builds up a seemingly impenetrable wall of stones to

---

4 An *end* of curling consists of sixteen stones, two thrown by each player, alternating between one team and the other. Games traditionally consist of ten ends. If a game is tied after ten ends, it carries on into extra ends, which are sudden death (first point scored wins).

prevent him from scoring.[5] Scoring two to win is out of the question; as Cutter prepares to throw his last rock, he has no other rocks in the house.[6] The best he can hope for is to make a miraculous shot to score one and fight on in extra ends (with the disadvantage that Yount will now have the hammer). Cutter makes the one-in-a-million shot, but, during the sweeping, his front end burns the rock (again!). This time, Cutter, having made peace with the spirit of the game, calls the foul. Under normal circumstances, this would mean his defeat, but Yount, in a surprising act of sportsmanship, allows Cutter a do-over. Cutter, realizing he is unlikely to make a one-in-a-million shot twice, tries another approach. He throws the rock (which is still loaded with the ashes of Donald Foley) hard down the middle of the sheet. It hits the wall of Yount rocks and explodes, sending fragments into the air. Two fragments land near the button, which gives the Cutter rink two points and the victory.[7] One extreme aspect of this ending is its violation of the official rules of curling. Section 4.5 of the Canadian Curling Association's *Rules of Curling for General Play*, published in 2022, states: "If a stone is broken in play, a replacement stone shall be placed where the largest fragment comes to rest"—which means that Cutter, despite the amazing good fortune of the exploding stone, should only have scored one. That the film plays fast and loose with the rules, however, is consistent with the extremity of its ending. The exploding stone, which scatters Donald Foley's ashes in a way that must please his eternal curler's spirit, not only gives a miraculous victory to the Cutter rink but causes a series of other miraculous fixes. Cutter, of course, redeems the various faults of his life and finds true love in the arms of Amy Foley. Neil Bucyk escapes a loveless marriage and finds true love with Angela. Eddie Strombach and his wife conceive a child. Julie Foley, Amy's sister and Chris's ex-fiancée, heals her broken heart and gets a chance to fly into space. RCMP Officer Frances Dart finds true

---

5 The *hammer* is the last rock thrown during an end of curling. If a team scores a point, the other team gets last rock for the next end. There is a great advantage to having the hammer. Rinks who lead during a game will often seek to blank ends (to have no points scored) so that they can hold onto it. To have the hammer going into extra ends is also a significant advantage, though it doesn't always lead to victory.

6 The house is the set of concentric rings painted on the ice into which teams try to curl their stones to score points.

7 The button is the dot at the centre of the rings: the bull's-eye.

love with a waitress at a local diner. In addition to all this, the beavers from the opening sequence show up to parade through town!

The most revealing fix, though, has to do with James Lennox. At the height of the celebrations after the exploding rock, Stuckmore, the giant to whom Lennox owes money, reappears. He rushes across the ice. Lennox, trapped, braces for an assault. Instead of attacking him, however, Stuckmore gives him a big hug and forgives his debt. He explains: "I can trace my lineage back through twelve generations of curling men, and even if Yount is gracious in defeat, his shiny suits and lumpen cheerleaders represent all that is corrupt in God's greatest game" (1:33:00). Forgiving the debt turns out to be Stuckmore's thanks for Lennox's role in helping to preserve the traditional, non-commercial version of curling to which he—like so many others—remains attached.

The transformation of Stuckmore is as extreme as the transformation of Annie Brown. With its over-the-top nature, the film's satire has a way (along with all the other life fixes at the end of *Men with Brooms*) of sending up the idea that a great sporting victory can transform a life. But the satire, like all satire, is double-edged. While it makes fun of the magical potential sometimes ascribed to sport, it doesn't discount this potential entirely. If there is a serious message at the end of the film, it is much like the message implied by the ending of *The Black Bonspiel*: there is something strange and beautiful in the human need to play, and when we create games, we take what is ordinary and create something potentially extraordinary. Though sport cannot give us magical solutions or the immortality craved by Faustus, it does have the power, like literature, to stir our emotions and imaginations—and to create a bit of life-affirming fun. Perhaps the most serious moment in either *The Black Bonspiel* or *Men with Brooms* is when Cutter describes to Amy the potential in a curling rock. Let me end by quoting his speech in full: "Forty-two pounds of polished granite with a beveled underbelly and a handle a human being can hold. And it may have no practical purpose in itself, but it is a repository of human possibility, and if it's handled just right, it will exact a kind of poetry" (23:00).

Abbott, George, and Stanley Donen, dirs. 1958. *Damn Yankees*. Burbank, CA: Warner Bros. Based on the 1955 musical *Damn Yankees* by George Abbott and Douglas Wallop, music by Richard Adler, lyrics by Jerry Ross.

Armstrong, Karen. 2006. *A Short History of Myth*. New York: Vintage Books.

Atwood, Margaret. 1972. *Surfacing*. Toronto: McClelland & Stewart.

Bamford, Allison. 2020. "Scotties' Skips Pleased with Prize Money Boost: 'We're Now Equal with the Men.'" *Global News*, February 21, 2020. globalnews.ca/news/6581454/scotties-skips-prize-money-boost-equality/.

Benét, Stephen Vincent. (1936) 1937. "The Devil and Daniel Webster." *Saturday Evening Post*, April 24, 1936. Reprint, New York: Farrar & Reinhart.

Bowser, George, and Rick Blue. 2003. "The Curling Song." In *The Illustrated Canadian Songbook (with CD)*, by Bowser & Blue. Toronto: McArthur & Company, 47.

Canadian Curling Association. 2022. *Rules for General Play (2022–2026)*. Orleans, ON: Canadian Curling Association. https://www.curling.ca/about-curling/getting-started-in-curling/rules-of-curling-for-general-play/.

Gross, Paul, dir. 2002. *Men with Brooms*. Toronto: Alliance Atlantis.

Hansen, Warren. 1999. *Curling: The History, The Players, The Game*. Toronto: Key Porter.

Luciani, Kim. 2021. "2021 Masters Prize Money: Here's a Breakdown of How Much Money Players Can Win." *The Masters* (blog), April 10, 2021. www.augusta.com/masters/story/news/2021-04-10/masters-tournament-2021-payout-prize-money-breakdown-purse.

Molson Canadian. 2010. "Made from Canada" (commercial). First aired February 12, 2010. YouTube video, 1:00. www.youtube.com/watch?v=X_yW4-cgG4g.

Malamud, Bernard. 1952. *The Natural*. New York: Harcourt, Brace & Company.

Marlowe, Christopher. (ca. 1590) 1933. *The Tragical History of Dr. Faustus*. In *English Drama, 1580–1642*, edited by C. F. Tucker Brooke and Nathaniel Burton Paradise, 167–91. Boston: D. C. Heath.

Mitchell, Ormond, and Barbara Mitchell. 2009. "Introduction." In *The Devil Is a Travelling Man: Two Plays by W. O. Mitchell*, edited by Ormond Mitchell and Barbara Mitchell, 1–20. Don Mills, ON: Oxford University Press.

Michell, W. O. 1947. *Who Has Seen the Wind*. Toronto: Macmillan Company of Canada.

Mitchell, W. O. 1993. *The Black Bonspiel of Willie MacCrimmon*. Toronto: McClelland & Stewart.

Novak, Michael. (1967) 1988. *The Joy of Sports: End Zones, Bases, Baskets, Balls, and the Consecration of the American Spirit*. New York: Hamilton Books.

Oriard, Michael. 1982. *Dreaming of Heroes: American Sports Fiction, 1868–1980*. Chicago: Nelson-Hall.

Pezer, Vera. 2003. *The Stone Age: A Social History of Curling on the Prairies*. Calgary: Fifth House Publishing.

Redmond, Gerald. 1988. "Curling." In *The Canadian Encyclopedia*. 2nd edition, edited by James H. Marsh, 555–56. Edmonton: Hurtig Publishing.

Werenich, Ed. "Curling Debuts as Olympic Demo Sport." Interview with Nancy Lee. *CBC Radio*, April 12, 1987. cbc.ca/player/play/1467724377.

Part II
Colonialism and Nature

5

Eva-Maria Müller

Sporting Mountain Voice
Alpinism and (Neo)colonial Discourse in Thomas Wharton's *Icefields* and Angie Abdou's *The Canterbury Trail*

Mountaineering is "the most literary of sports"; indeed, according to Bruce Barcott, it is an activity that "compels its participants, from the international star to the weekend scrambler to turn each personal quest into a public tale" (1996, 65). It is, as sport historian and mountaineer Zac Robinson explains, a practice that "has more than rested on its literary laurels since the mid-1800s" when the sport emerged from Victorian Britain (2015, 105). Historically, literature allowed the growing sport to share its scientific results, negotiate its rules, mark athletic achievements, and express structures of feeling. Literature now permeates the mountaineering practice. Aspiring climbers read their way into mountains; they fill their time waiting with books and speak of their favourite books almost as enthusiastically as their favourite climbing routes. Alpine club journals are thick with tales of ascent, and the sport has its own section in bookstores, its own annual book festivals. The most acclaimed athletes in the sport are also the genre's bestselling writers. Mountaineering consolidates itself as a community of readers (Barcott 1996; Hansen 1995, 1996; Robbins 1987; Robinson 2015,

This chapter was written with support from the Austrian Science Fund (FWF), grant number P 32994-G. It is based, in part, on Eva-Maria Müller, "Rewriting Alpine Orientalism: Lessons from the Canadian Rockies and Austrian Alps" (2019).

105; Slemon 2008, 239; 2017). In short, narratives drive mountaineering and mountaineering drives narrative expression.

In addition to being the sport most strongly roped to the written word, it is, perhaps, also the one most strongly associated with imperialism. In his pioneering essays, Peter H. Hansen notes that mountaineers readily "employed the language of empire to justify their climbing" (1995, 320), and that mountaineering in large part served Victorian Britain as a form of recreation that fostered "the cultural re-creation of Britain as an imperial nation" (49). Both the adoption of imperial and Orientalist discourse in mountaineering literature and the appropriations of projects of power, supremacy, and control in the practice of mountaineering itself are of ongoing interest in the study of postcolonial mountain literature, undertaken by scholars such as Stephen Slemon (2000, 2008, 2017) and, more recently, Amrita Dhar (2019) and myself (Müller 2019). Slemon argues that classic mountaineering literature in the colonialist mode is characterized by a focus on first ascents and new routes, a fetishization of arrival points as unpeopled, the denial of guides' generative agency in climbing expeditions, and "the narrative need for death" (2000, 57) that sits at the figurative centre of the genre. These texts have, as Rachel Hunt argues, governed the space of academic literature on mountaineering for long enough (2019, 1–2).

Two contemporary Canadian novels that challenge the imperial legacies of mountain sport are Thomas Wharton's *Icefields* (1995) and Angie Abdou's *The Canterbury Trail* (2011). *Icefields* is a historical novel set between 1898 and 1923 in the area that today is Alberta's Jasper National Park. It offers a fictionalized account of early explorations of the park by Norman Collie, Hugh Stutfield, Arthur P. Coleman, and Charles Thompson in which mountain sport (except for an elusive excursion into hunting) almost exclusively means traditional alpinism. *The Canterbury Trail*, by contrast, is a dark comedy about a modern mountain pilgrimage to the backcountry hut of Camelot in Coalton, a fictionalized version of Fernie, British Columbia's skiing mecca. Inspired in many ways by Geoffrey Chaucer's classic tale, *The Canterbury Trail* incorporates a number of practices that involve moving up and down mountains, including ski touring, snowboarding, snowmobiling, telemarking, hiking, biking, and snowshoeing. Despite their differences, both novels expose the ties between (neo)colonialism and mountain sport and rewrite the traditional mountaineering narrative to imagine alternatives for what it means to move through mountain space. In complex acts of decolonization, each novel exposes and attempts to counter the imperialist and Orientalist discourses that are so much a part of the traditional mountaineering narrative, modelling instead a more authentic relationship with mountains—one that allows the mountains to speak.

ICEFIELDS AND COLONIAL DISCOURSE

Thomas Wharton's *Icefields* opens in 1898 with Doctor Edward Byrne falling into a crevasse on Arcturus glacier. The accident occurs during the fictionalized Royal Geographical Society expedition led by British mountaineers Norman Collie and Hugh Stutfield. In the novel, as in Stutfield and Collie's own records (1903, 13), this expedition set out to the Canadian Rockies in search of Mount Brown, a peak of which little was known except that it was situated on the trading route of the Hudson Bay Company and estimated to be 16,000 feet:

> The goal is Mount Brown, Collie had said. *Find it, or prove it a hoax. It's been on every map in the empire for sixty years as the highest on this continent. And no one even knows if it really exists. So far no one has thought to go and verify the one lone sighting that got it on the maps in the first place.* He was determined to rediscover the lost giant and, if possible, to be the first to reach its summit. (*Icefields*, 18)

This linking of mountaineering—to reach a summit, to aim for a goal—and imperial practice—to see and discover, to arrive first, and to map—carries on throughout *Icefields*. The novel repeatedly builds a connection between climbing and the project of power and control: it portrays the Royal Geographical Society's climbers as "discoverers" and, in the second narrative strand, follows the colonialist Lord Sexsmith, modelled on James Carnegie, Earl of Southesk, on his hunting trips and climbing attempts. Over the course of almost a century, Sexsmith, like Collie and his fellow mountaineers, climbs in service of Empire.

Icefields, as Pamela Banting notes, is a narrative of obsessions (2000, 67). It engages with a fixation on imperial expansion, entrepreneurial opportunities, and alpinist heroism, and it highlights the imaginative power of mountains and their natural energy. The novel, which uses tall tales, myths, fairy tales, and dream visions to reflect the enlarged spatial repertoire of mountains (Hepburn 2001, 73), uncovers the multi-layered fascination with alpine space through the English Doctor Byrne. Waiting to be rescued from his fall, Byrne sees an angelic figure in the ice. For the next twenty-five years—from 1898 to the novel's close in the summer of 1923, when the ice that trapped him reaches the end point of the glacier—Byrne seeks to make sense of his apparition. He follows the glacier's movement with the scientific, spiritual, and Romantic obsession that characterizes many nineteenth- and early twentieth-century mountaineers. The narrative is structured according to glacial anatomy, with each of the novel's five main sections named after a specific phase of glaciation, laying bare the development of the many histories embedded in the region. Over the course of the novel, numerous peaks are scaled (some allegedly for the first time), trails and railroads are constructed, hotel facilities are built, glacier water is sold off, mountains and people are touched by the fate of World War I, and Jasper Park is established. Wharton's novel taps deeply into the history of mountaineering, exploration, and tourism in the Jasper region; reflects on the cultural history of mountains; and offers an alternative to the traditional mountaineering story that challenges the inventory of knowledge production available to the imperial alpinist.

As the novel connects mountain sport with imperialism, it has us see that the knowledge of alpine space acquired by nineteenth-century mountaineers is shaped by the already established system of knowledge about other colonial destinations: they see in mountains an "island in the ice" (153), a "tropical jungle" (196), an "Asiatic temple" (28), and a range of "Olympian palaces" (206). Such lines of comparison—instances of Orientalist appropriation—exhibit the proclivity of nineteenth- and early twentieth-century mountaineers to apply what they already knew about sites of British colonial desire to new locations encountered on their climbs in the Rockies (Tiffin and Lawson 1994, 2).

Climbing in nineteenth-century Canada was very much a mode of knowledge production, and for the Canadian Rockies to successfully enter the European knowledge apparatus, as Chris Tiffin and Alan Lawson argue, they had to first be rendered unfamiliar (1994, 2). By referring to the alpine space in terms of "a new world" (*Icefields*, 49), "the edge of the earth" (228), and a "true terra incognita" (99), Wharton's novel exposes the common practice of casting mountains as unfamiliar so that mountaineers appear victorious in their quest. This discourse of negation that repeatedly asserts absence serves to clear mountain space for alpinists. It allows athletes, like Collie and Stutfield in *Icefields*, to turn the Canadian Rockies into an "imaginatively malleable space" full of unbounded possibility (Macfarlane 2003, 175): only when mountaineers portray the mountains they ascend through a "consciousness of absence"—a commonly deployed rhetoric of empire according to David Spurr (1993, 2)—can they be first. Wharton's Collie and Stutfield return from their expedition to the icefield "smiling, pleased with the morning air" not merely because they have had a good day on the icefield but precisely because they are the "first human beings ever to see it" and "definitely to have traversed it" (*Icefields*, 50).

The degree to which the assertion of coming first and the construction of absence are related to an imperial violence that involves the negation and forcible removal of First Nations in the Jasper region becomes apparent in the section titled "Moraine," which brings together various fractions of place-based mountain history. The transformation of Jasper from an outpost of Empire to a pleasure ground for travellers required an imperial elision of First Nations claims that culminated in the first decade of the twentieth century with the federal government removing First Nations and Métis people living in the park and withdrawing Stoney and Cree rights to their local hunting grounds in the mountains (Müller 2019, 14). This displacement of First Nations and the subsequent reassertion of pristine wilderness allowed for the Jasper region to be populated afresh by paying guests—"travellers, mountain climbers, and seekers after solitude" (*Icefields*, 62). It is worth pointing out here that James B. Harkin (1914), first commissioner of the Parks Branch, turned to the writings of alpinists like Collie and Stutfield (but also, for example, James Outram, Walter Wilcox, A. P. Coleman, and Tom Longstaff) to conserve the notion of being alone amidst "the virginal beauty" (*Icefields*, 62) of the Canadian Rockies. This kind of deterritorialization is motivated by a conflation of colonial and commercial interest (Pratt 2008, 132). "Only those who had sanctioned business within the boundaries, guides and trailblazers . . . were allowed"; all others were obstacles in the mission to exploit "to the full the resources at hand" (*Icefields*, 74, 101), exhibiting the reliance of the ongoing business of mountains and mountaineering on a cultivation of absence. In another key act of decolonialization, *Icefields* gestures towards the imperial violence bolted deeply into the founding pillars of the park by referencing the non-place previously inhabited by First Nations and Métis communities: white settlers "got compensation or deeds to land" outside the park's boundaries, while First Nations were "driven off with guns" (74).

Icefields further dramatizes the colonial literary playbook in the Canadian Rockies when its mountaineers engage in the systematic discipline of knowing alpine space through inscription. Mary Louise Pratt demonstrates that the mid-Victorian paradigm of "being first" does not exist, even within the ideology of discovery and a politics of dispossession, unless the explorer returns home and "brings it into being through texts": journals, letters, reports, or something as simple as a name on a map (2008, 200). In Wharton's novel, the majority of British climbers perceive the mountains as a "blank, wordless space in the atlas" (29) that only become "place" through Western inscription. Lord Sexsmith, when not reading from a tapered volume of Shakespeare's plays, names the places he encounters with England in mind: "I'll call it little Albion" (38). Collie and Stutfield hurl names at the giants that circle the icefield: "Arcturus, Diadem, the Brothers, Parnassus" (59). Byrne keeps a daily journal and is rarely seen without his calfskin notebook. Hal Rawson, a poet turned packer, is eager to "make up stories" about what he finds on the glacier (193). Freya Stark, a climber, "wants to write a book about her climbs in Jasper" (187), and a new "patriotic fever of naming" quite literally changes Jasper after World War I (217). In the novel's final section, "Terminus," the local entrepreneur Trask checks "the names of glaciers in illustrated guidebooks" and gazes in awe at a world that is "no longer a blank space" (247).

What distinguishes *Icefields* from historical mountaineering reports of imperial appropriation is that it portrays the inherent violence of these colonial inscriptions. As colonial discourse is exposed, it is defined as a "record of damage" (184) and unmasked as arbitrary, inaccurate, and futile, with the novel indicating, for example, that the "region has had a lot of names" (68), and that the maps, hand drawn in the early, unnumbered pages of the book, are "not to scale." At one point, an act of immersion refuses the discursive violence of naming that claims power and knowledge. When Byrne falls into the crevasse on Arcturus glacier, he gains insight rather than control, and sees "no reason to give this body of water a name," referring to an ephemeral pool that appears on the glacier on warm days and disappears in the cold of night: "As the glacier flows forward, its topography will inevitably change, and the lake will vanish" (150). Thus, the novel ignites a reconsideration of the relationship between mountain and mountaineer that moves beyond imperialist inscription. The fallen alpinist ends up abandoning any colonialist desire to fixate the glacier in practices of naming or mapping and gradually gives in to the mountain's intangibility. Delving deeper into postcolonial revision and Byrne's own psychological landscape, one could argue that the glacier occupies him more than he can ever occupy the ice. Thus, the inscription that occurs is one embedded in Byrne's name, a man who is, as Françoise Besson explains, burnt and reborn as a result of his contact with the ice (2011, 219). In this sense, Besson concludes, Byrne's treatment of Arcturus moves away from colonial mastery and toward "a new awareness of life as revealed by Nature" (220).

Another instance exposing the instability of colonial power over mountain nature is revealed in one of the many journal entries that appear through the novel. Elspeth Fletcher, a young Scottish woman who works in Trask's chalet, observes nature's transformation of Byrne as he sits in the pool and lets the snow pile up on his head, "an absurd crown" (220). By inviting comparison between king and climber, *Icefields* calls forward the colonialist mode of mountaineering while disempowering its (fleeting) symbols of sovereignty. Through this deconstruction of power, the novel locates what Ashcroft, Griffiths, and Tiffin call "a crack in the certainty of colonial dominance" (2013, 155), whereby the irony of a crowned alpinist does more than mock the climber who assumes victorious postures in mountain nature: it challenges the entire practice of imperial mountaineering. Thus, when contemporary mountain novels that, like *Icefields*, are critical of tourism use colonial discourse in their stories—whether highlighting textual control, conceptual emptying, or Orientalist rhetoric—they write back to the colonial legacies of mountaineering and its literature.

(NEO)COLONIAL ECHOES IN *THE CANTERBURY TRAIL*

Set in the twenty-first century and published sixteen years after Wharton's *Icefields*, Angie Abdou's *The Canterbury Trail* (2011) operates in a similar manner to Wharton's *Icefields* in its treatment of colonial discourse. The novel follows fourteen mountain pilgrims (and their dogs) who set out in separate groups along the Canterbury Trail to Camelot, a backcountry hut, for a final day of spring powder. The pilgrims are devotees of different mountain sports: skiers, snowboarders, snowmobilers, snowshoers, mountain bikers, and hikers. They also come from a range of social groups and classes. Abdou's cross section of ski-town society includes a ski bum, a redneck, a trustafarian, an urbanite, a French Canadian inamorata turned second wife, a mother-to-be, a hippy, an environmentalist, a rad chick, a retired teacher, a miller, a foreigner, a developer, and a self-proclaimed local. All end up in the same place and are trapped not just on an avalanche slope but in their own competitiveness. In addition to their athletic feats, they compete over their status in town, the fanciness of their gear, their visions for the region, their hard drinking, their sex appeal, and their ability to tell the perfect mountain story. Their obsession with outdoing the heroic tales of their compatriots nips in the bud any possibility of establishing a connection to the mountain or to their fellow human beings. Abdou's novel subverts colonial traditions of the classic mountaineering narrative and reworks mountains and movement into new forms of expression while spoofing a number of mountain-athlete stereotypes for good measure.

Each of the fourteen characters in *The Canterbury Trail* carries a different set of desires up to Camelot and is affected differently by mountains. Alison Batz, a modern-day Wife-of-Bath on skis, is a ribald forty-something Toronto journalist who perpetuates colonial rhetoric with her interest in selling a story. In Camelot, she longs for the time when a trip to the mountains meant the luxury of a Canadian Pacific Railway hotel and getting up close and personal with a rustic mountain man. In true Alpine Orientalist manner, she reads sexual promise and unlimited sensuality into the mountains (Said 1979, 188) and wants to capture a slice of mountain life "to package up and take home with her to sell" (*Canterbury*, 94). Alison's perception of mountains as a sexual playground is shared by Shanny, a young snowboarder who works at the front desk of the local gym and uses every opportunity to show off her perfect backside. For Shanny, the mountain is a site of sexual fantasy that allows her to explore homoerotic curiosities while trying to imitate male behaviour. Over the course of the novel, it becomes difficult to distinguish which she enjoys more, "the pure exhilaration of the downhill ride" (70) or her own masking in mountain masculinity. Meanwhile, Cosmos and Ella, a Bear-Aware gay couple, worship mountain nature like a divine mother. They snowshoe to Camelot to escape from their problems only to encounter a drunk ex-husband with his French Canadian second wife and their Swedish friend in tow. Then there are Michael and Lanny, a realtor and a miller who long for one last guys' weekend before Michael's wife gives birth; and Antonio (alias Loco) and SOR, another couple of mates who compete over their local status as much as over their athletic abilities.

Three of the fourteen characters stand out and on the margins of the already heterogenous cast of Abdou's tale: F-Bomb, who sets out with Loco and SOR, is a quiet and frequently misunderstood ski bum and the only Indigenous (specifically, Cree) character in the narrative. He is, in a sense, silenced like the Sherpa figures omitted from traditional mountaineering accounts. Heinz, the sign-maker who named the Canterbury Trail, is not a pilgrim in the strict sense. Referred to as "the hermit," he retreats to the mountains following the loss of his wife. Year after year, Heinz immerses himself in nature and increasingly behaves like a conqueror charting a mountain wilderness. The character who is most conspicuous is Janet. Six months pregnant, she insists on joining Michael and his friend. She is the only pilgrim who does not perpetuate colonialist practices or rhetoric and has a realistic understanding of what it means to stay in a backcountry cabin with thirteen other people during the end of the ski season (Müller 2019, 44). Janet and her unborn baby are also the only ones to survive the avalanche that ends the lives of all the other characters who encroach upon the mountain, just as it ends their continuous quarrelling over the ownership and meaning of those mountains.

The diverse characters create conflict and tension and add humour to Abdou's novel. But their diversity also reminds readers of the multi-layered approaches to alpine space. Like Wharton's *Icefields*, *The Canterbury Trail* demonstrates how Romantic, economic, gender, wilderness, and colonial discourses overlap when sports and mountains meet. Most of the characters on the pilgrimage embody a dominant approach to mountains, and all of them (except for Janet) are additionally implicated in the colonial mentality of mountaineering, despite their societal difference, through their imitation of imperial rhetoric and activities. They refer to themselves as "blood-thirsty warriors" (7) and "captain[s]" (122) in a simulation of alpine conquest that, in the long run, establishes a relationship in which the characters are rulers and the mountain is the ruled. Setting off a series of coronations, the novel foregrounds the imperial implications of mountain sport by turning to a literary tradition that reaches back to Giovanni Boccaccio's *Decameron* (written c. 1349–1353), in which each of the ten characters, who are fleeing plague-ridden Florence, take turns being king or queen for a day.

This royal storytelling status is reflected in the structure of *The Canterbury Trail*. In the first part of the novel, chapters are named after individual characters. In addition, at the level of content, the novel engages with the imperial implications of twenty-first-century mountain sport. The first king introduced to the reader is Heinz. He becomes sovereign by obsessively charting, mapping, and naming "his kingdom of forest trails" (5):

> At first, he just wandered—finding the quickest way to mountaintop, then the most scenic, then the most likely to spot wildlife, then the path with a well-placed swimming spot or a nicely shaded nook for an afternoon nap. Eventually, he began marking his routes—more to leave evidence of his existence than to save himself from getting lost. By then he knew the way—*all* the ways—but naming a certain incline or a particular creek-crossing gave him an inexplicable satisfaction. He didn't want to name the squirrels and birds. He didn't need a "Chip" and a "Chirp," and he had no interest in being the crazy old hermit who deluded himself that the animals were his friends. Instead he named the land. (4)

Heinz retreats to the mountains using the open formalism "all" as an empty placeholder "for the unknown and imaginable" (Greenblatt 1991, 60), and names the places he encounters. A few chapters later, his rule is challenged by the snowboarder Shanny who imagines herself "the Queen of the Jujubes," not in Heinz's kingdom but in "her Candied Kingdom" (*Canterbury*, 68). Their regal (self)-ascriptions together with the use of possessive pronouns reveal a proprietary rhetoric in contemporary mountain discourse that parallels its imperialist ideas and appetites. The futile arbitrariness with which humans have sought to control landscapes is revealed through competing claims, from various perspectives and repeated even into the twenty-first century, while engaging in mountain sport (Müller 2019, 69). Just as imperial pretensions are challenged via the symbolism of a melting crown in *Icefields*, the regal status of the characters in *The Canterbury Trail* is short-lived: Heinz's signs are overwritten by weekenders, and "the hum of snowmobiles" quickly shatters Shanny's illusion "that this mountain is hers to consume in its frosting-covered entirety" (69).

Although the characters are mostly after-work athletes on a leisurely quest up the mountain, they seek Camelot as if it were a trophy in the Great Game. Instead of holding "the last bastion of the British Empire" (*Icefields*,

215) or drawing up imperial maps like their literary predecessors in *Icefields*, they use a pocketknife to carve traces of themselves into the hut's furniture, let their dogs "mark territory" (*Canterbury*, 191), and possessively strew wet clothing and sweaty socks across beds in twenty-first-century versions of leisurely appropriation (118). In one of the novel's final chapters, Janet observes that the group's conflicts are generated in a somewhat colonial manner, with "each claiming the land as their own, insisting upon the right to name it, the power to decide how to use it" (240).

To leave us no doubt about the discursive similarities between contemporary alpinist aspirations and colonial endeavours, the novel evokes the spectre of Columbus. In a moment that highlights the relationship between colonial history and the imperialism of new commerce, those who participate in mountain sport, as well as those who invest in its destination, are cast as Columbus-like figures who treat the place as if it "sat empty before they arrived" (9). Opportunities for mountain sport—"the new golf course, the ski hill upgrades" (9)—drive real estate and change the socioeconomic set-up of a mountain town. For the ski bums in *The Canterbury Trail*, this means that they can only afford to live in a rundown miner's shack "with a sinking foundation" (9). Thus, the novel interrogates the reciprocity between mountain sport and (neo)imperialism and hints at questions of belonging and uprootedness. It does so most notably through the character of F-Bomb who, otherwise rendered silent, points out the business with "million-dollar views" (9).

F-Bomb, embodying the conversational taboo inherent in his name, is undoubtedly the character most defeated by (neo)colonial forces. The notion of silence is an important one throughout Abdou's novel and reaches its peak in this character. F-Bomb's self-censorship in not talking about his Cree heritage is a consequence of the colonial environment. These absences in his narration highlight the omission of First Nations among the pilgrims: "F-Bomb talked about his grandmother, about his family's past in the valley . . . never once saying that he was an Indian—everyone toeing around the word like it was a curse" (103). First Nations people and history are only articulated in F-Bomb's thoughts, leaving them absent from dialogue yet still visible on the page (Müller 2019, 74). Readers are additionally reminded of the absence of Indigenous peoples in mountaineering projects when Alison, unaware of First Nations history in the Canadian Rockies, "wondered if he [F-Bomb] was Hispanic or something" (*Canterbury*, 33).

In the novel, the silencing of First Nations in Canadian mountaineering is most palpable in the often one-sided interactions between F-Bomb and Loco. Feeling that his local status is threatened by F-Bomb, Loco silences his friend, arguing that F-Bomb's "connections were to the Coalton of *yesterday*, not of *today*" (103). This consignment of First Nations knowledge to the past is, according to Johannes Fabian (1983), a common practice of colonial discourse.[1] In a key act of decolonization, the novel points out (directly and indirectly) the muting of alpine Others in mountaineering (hi)stories as well as the cultural violence of dispossession and the commodification of First Nations bodies in the colonial discourse of mountaineering.

In addition to exposing conflict deriving from the muting of alpine Others in colonial history, *The Canterbury Trail* engages with conflicts deriving from continued colonial practices through narrative competition between all pilgrims. Each of the characters is implicated in colonialism and so preoccupied with seeing a rival in the people with whom they share the mountain that a well-intentioned sharing circle, suggested by Ella and Cosmos, soon turns into a "story contest" in which the language of sport lends itself to expressing claims of power (198). The characters discuss the rules of the story contest and name its judge. It isn't long before the cabin turns into a fighting pit and the weekend athletes charge at each other like "Olympic boxers" (171). What the novel also demonstrates—in the final failure of the contest itself—is that new forms of articulation and interaction can emerge once the game is no longer about winning. Ultimately, none of the characters abide by the rules of the contest and none of them emerge as the winner. In fact, *The Canterbury Trail* radically disables the idea of winning by casting all characters as losers: Janet loses her husband and all the others lose their lives in a deadly avalanche. In this way, Abdou writes a mountain sport novel that, like her swimming-wrestling story *Bone Cage* (2007), is about something other—or Other—than the athletic quest. It is about the possibilities that emerge once literature moves sport out of bounds, and, more specifically, considers mountains not simply as a playground but as bodies capable of telling a story.

---

1 In a later novel, *In Case I Go* (2017), Abdou returns to the fictional terrain of Coalton to explore how mountain territory is haunted by the colonial treatment of First Nations.

Icefields and *The Canterbury Trail* tread a bifurcated path in their decolonization of the imperial mountaineering story, in a textbook version of "writing back" (Ashcroft, Griffiths, Tiffin 1989). The novels expose the inherent colonial discourse in the language and practice of mountain sport and, in their attempt to let mountains speak, they carve out spaces in which to remould our notions of moving in mountain space. *Icefields* achieves this in a careful retooling of imaginative, narrative, and scientific perspectives, by casting the glacier as a body in motion. From the moment Byrne sees the figure of the angel in the crevasse, the ice changes, and all efforts fail to scientifically explain the apparition with the glacier's unsteady forward motion. Arcturus glacier "groans, cracks, thunders, and rears up a cathedral" (*Icefields* 161); it "crumbles" (252), "collapses" (208) and emerges (261); it descends (170) and flows (133), and makes Byrne's winged story difficult to capture. *Icefields* casts the glacier and the stories it provokes as entities in motion. It renders the mountain alive and echoes a scientific principle that interprets mobility as one of the central characteristics of life. "The ice is alive" (193), the novel asserts more than once, and it is this liveliness that positions Arcturus as the main protagonist in *Icefields*. In an interview with Aritha van Herk, Wharton explains that "the landscape is kind of the main character, the centre; the [human] characters are almost what one could call fields of force, or objects within a field, interacting" (in Banting 2000, 68). Accordingly, it is Arcturus, more than the ambitious alpinists, who moves the narrative forward (72).

The novel's insistence on the mountain as a living being is supported by the narrative structure of *Icefields*, in which glacial movement overlaps with narrative development. As mentioned earlier, Wharton structures his novel according to glacial anatomy and characterizes each of the novel's five main sections as a specific phase of glaciation. As *Icefields* takes readers from the névé to the moraine, the nunatak, the ablation zone, and the terminus, it traverses Gustav Freytag's (1900) structural pyramid of exposition, rising action, climax, falling action, and denouement (see also Martineau 1998; Banting 2000; Omhovère 2005; Willard 2018). In this way, Arcturus is simultaneously a natural *and* narrative force, and the story that unfolds between the accumulation and ablation zone is very much "the glacier's writing" (*Icefields*, 143).

Echoing in certain ways Jay Schulkin's assertion that sport "lies in the continuous fluidity between biology and culture" (2016, 2), *Icefields* mediates between the mountains we climb and those we read about. Although the narrative is structurally and textually pushed forward by glacial anatomy, the description of each section is not a systematic observation that orders mountains into scientific epistemes but rather a testimony to the power of imaginative narrative expression. In this sense, the novel engages in more than the "playful fictionality" described by Joel Martineau (1998, 44), who compares dictionary definitions of glacial zones with those provided in *Icefields*. When the novel opens with a description of névé as a "plain of snow and ice from which the glaciers descend" that "must be imagined" (1) instead of seeing it as "partially compacted granular snow that is the intermediate stage between snow and glacial ice" (Editors of the *Encyclopaedia Britannica*, 1998), it subverts standardized definitions perpetuated by scientific and colonial claims of power/knowledge over mountains. *Icefields* renders the glacier something that continuously escapes control and evokes a notion of (alpine) wilderness that, in Don McKay's words, is "the capacity of all things to elude the mind's appropriation" (2002, 21).

The mountain in *The Canterbury Trail* likewise escapes traditional patterns of representation by deploying the natural catastrophe of an avalanche to disrupt established orders. In the final part of the novel and on the second morning of their skiing weekend, most of the pilgrims are out with their skis, snowboards, snowmobiles, or snowshoes. Many of them find themselves on one side of an avalanche slope. As they begin the traverse, the mountainside suddenly gives way. Heinz, watching the scene from his hut,

> hears a booming explosion, as if the mountain has stomped its foot in approval. Then right before his eyes, a giant crack opens across the mountain's face, a grinning fracture from one side of the bowl to another. While he sits and contemplates that toothless gaping mouth—and it is, ever so faintly, pointing upwards—he swears he hears the mountain sigh, a swooshing breath of utter contentment. (274)

The mountain is depicted as a body capable of motion (dare I say, also emotion) and the avalanche as an auditory event. The avalanche is heard before it is seen or felt: Heinz hears it as a sigh; Lanny "hears the hollow *whumpf*" (267); Alison "hears the *toasssss*" (268); and to SOR, the avalanche "sounds like goodbye. It sounds like dirt shoveled onto his coffin" (270). To the pilgrims, the fatal end of the avalanche is as clear as its auditory force. By being so attentive to the acoustic dimension of the catastrophe, which thunderously breaks into the silence of athletic ambition, social rivalry, and neocolonial order, the novel provokes a sensitization to the voice of mountains. F-Bomb, accustomed to the role of the listener, "knows right away that it's a big fucking avalanche"—a "life-ender"—and interprets its sound as a form of alpine articulation: "[H]e knows the mountain has spoken" (271).

As Abdou (2011b) confirms in an interview, the avalanche heralds the mountain as the main character of the novel. By weaving a number of interpretive models into its representations, she fires her ultimate salvo against the (neo)colonialist discourse of possession in the mountaineering narrative.[2] The avalanche is cast as an event for the ears, matching the pilgrims' deafness towards mountain voices with its own deafening roar. The avalanche is also a continuous speech act, not a single utterance, that traverses literary genres as it counters colonial erasure with a wealth of local mythology (Fernie's Ghostrider and Grizz legends, for example). The avalanche turns the alpine landscape into the personified nature of mountain myth that—all ear, all eye, all body—paves its way through snow to knock loose the mountains of colonial discourse embedded in twenty-first-century mountain sport. And, finally, there is an experience of delimitation that is far from being destructive because it lends the strong-voiced element something of the dynamic of a creative motor (Utz 2013, 138).

"Death is creative, not destructive," wrote Helen Tiffin (1978, 148), setting the foundation for postcolonial scholarship's hopeful treatment of endings. In a similar vein, Abdou's avalanche, albeit a catastrophe and, as such, a "calamitous, destructive, horrible and tragic event" (Nünning 2012, 67), is also a turning point where "an old order is lost and a new one has yet to arrive" (Brown 1997, 8). Such a catastrophic turning point, says Marshall Brown, is "both a moment of balance and a moment of unbalance, of decision and of indecision, of determination . . . and of indetermination" (1997, 10). This fragile yet highly productive moment is what Dipesh Chakrabarty calls the "'not yet' of the actual," (2000, 250), and it is embodied

---

2 My interpretation of the avalanche rests on Peter Utz's (2013) interpretation of avalanches in Swiss art and literature in *Kultivierung der Katastrophe: Literarische Untergangsszenarien aus der Schweiz*.

in *The Canterbury Trail* by Janet's unborn child. In the closing scene, Janet, unaware of the fatalities and sitting in front of the cabin stove, "rub[s] her hands across her belly" (275). Until officials knock at Camelot's door to confirm the news of the avalanche, Janet "knows nothing" (276), and her waiting invites us to imagine "an ending—a future—Otherwise" (Müller 2019, 84). With this image, *The Canterbury Trail* gifts mountains not just with a voice of their own but with the ideal figure of a promising post-colonial future that, according to Bill Ashcroft, is the unborn child (2012, 9). Abdou's attempt to let mountains speak is thus as much a celebration of CanLit's theme of survival as it is a powerful symbol of postcolonial hope. The impending birth transcends the death that looms over classic mountaineering narratives just as it looms over those who participate in colonialist athletic ventures.

* * *

Against the "narrative need of death" in the classic mountaineering story (Slemon 2000, 57), *Icefields* and *The Canterbury Trail* set a wealth of literary manoeuvres. Abdou's and Wharton's novels demonstrate that literature that writes back to the colonial implications of the traditional mountaineering narrative is rich in opportunities to renegotiate the relationship between "mountains" and "movement." Such literature exposes the workings of imperial discourse in the mountaineering project; upsets colonialist claims brought against mountains and mountain communities; expresses an awareness for mountains as living, speaking entities; and articulates meaningful encounters between mountains and mountaineers. It also shows that this openness involves a seismic shift of narrative attention from uphill to downhill, from the traditional mountaineering novel that charts a summit-oriented assault line (Slemon 2000, 58) to a downward perspective that upsets the (neo)colonial implications of mountain sport literature. Abdou's and Wharton's novels write back to (neo)colonial implications of mountain sport most effectively when they write *down* their articulations of alpine voice: *Icefields* lets the mountain speak in the descending flow of glacial ice and *The Canterbury Trail* activates mountain voice with the sound of an avalanche barrelling downward. Thus, these books remind us that the most moving mountain story may lie far beneath the celebrated heights of alpinist quests and unfold its greatest reward when we lose or fall.

Abdou, Angie. 2007. *The Bone Cage*. Edmonton: NeWest Press.

Abdou, Angie. 2011a. *The Canterbury Trail*. Victoria, BC: Brindle & Glass Publishing.

Abdou, Angie. 2011b. "The Canterbury Trail—Interview with Angie Abdou." Interview by Kim McCullough, May 24, 2011. http://kimmccullough.ca/the-canterbury-trail-interview-with-angie-abdou/.

Abdou, Angie. 2017. *In Case I Go*. Vancouver: Aresenal Pulp Press.

Ashcroft, Bill. 2012. "Introduction: Spaces of Utopia." *An Electronic Journal* 2 (1), 1–17.

Ashcroft, Bill, Gareth Griffiths, and Helen Tiffin. 1989. *The Empire Writes Back: Theory and Practice in Post-Colonial Literatures*. London: Routledge.

Ashcroft, Bill, Gareth Griffiths, and Helen Tiffin. 2013. *Postcolonial Studies: The Key Concepts*. 3rd ed. New York: Routledge.

Banting, Pamela. 2000. "The Angel in the Glacier: Geography as Intertext in Thomas Wharton's *Icefields*." *ISLE: Interdisciplinary Studies in Literature and Environment* 7 (August): 67–80.

Barcott, Bruce. 1996. "Cliffhangers: The Fatal Descent of the Mountain-Climbing Memoir." *Harper's Magazine*, August 1, 1996.

Besson, Françoise. 2011. "Botany as the Path to Awareness, or the Flower as Grail in Thomas Wharton's Icefields." *Ecozon@: European Journal of Literature, Culture and Environment* 2 (2): 211–27.

Brown, Marshall. 1997. *Turning Points: Essays in the History of Cultural Expressions*. Redwood City, CA: Stanford University Press.

Chakrabarty, Dipesh. 2000. *Provincializing Europe: Postcolonial Thought and Historical Difference*. Princeton: Princeton University Press.

Dhar, Amrita. 2019. "Travel and Mountains." In *The Cambridge History of Travel Writing*, edited by Nandini Das and Tim Youngs, 345–60. Cambridge: Cambridge University Press.

Editors of the *Encyclopaedia Britannica*. 1998. "Firn." In *Encyclopaedia Britannica Online*. Last modified November 19, 2014. https://www.britannica.com/science/firn.

Fabian, Johannes. 1983. *Time and the Other: How Anthropology Makes its Object*. New York: Columbia University Press.

Freytag, Gustav. 1900. *Freytag's Technique of the Drama: An Exposition of Dramatic Composition and Art*. Chicago: Scott Foresman & Company.

Greenblatt, Stephen. 1991. *Marvelous Possessions: The Wonders of the New World*. Chicago: University of Chicago Press.

Harkin, James B. 1914. "Memorandum re National Parks, Their Values and Their Ideals," 14 March 1914. James Bernard Harkin fonds, MG30 E169, vol. 2. Library and Archives Canada.

Hansen, Peter H. 1995. "Albert Smith, the Alpine Club, and the Invention of Mountaineering in Mid-Victorian Britain." *Journal of British Studies* 34 (4): 300–24.

Hansen, Peter H. 1996. "Vertical Boundaries, National Identities: British Mountaineering on the Frontiers of Europe and the Empire." *Journal of Imperial and Commonwealth History* 24 (1): 48–71.

Hepburn, Allan. 2001. "'Enough of a Wonder': Landscape and Tourism in Thomas Wharton's *Icefields*." *Essays on Canadian Writing* 73 (March): 72–92.

Hunt, Rachel. 2019. "Historical Geography, Climbing and Mountaineering: Route Setting for an Inclusive Future." *Geography Compass* 13 (4): 1–9. https://www.doi.org/10.1111/gec3.12423.

Macfarlane, Robert. 2003. *Mountains of the Mind*. New York: Pantheon Books.

Martineau, Joel. 1998. "Landscapes and Inscapes in Thomas Wharton's *Icefields*." *Open Letter* 2: 41–50.

McKay, Don. 2002. *Vis à Vis: Field Notes on Poetry and Wilderness*. Kentville, NS: Gaspereau Press.

Müller, Eva-Maria. 2019. "Rewriting Alpine Orientalism: Lessons from the Canadian Rockies and Austrian Alps." PhD diss., University of Gießen.

Nünning, Ansgar. 2012. "Making Crises and Catastrophes: How Metaphors and Narratives Shape Their Cultural Life." In *The Cultural Life of Catastrophes and Crises*, edited by Carsten Meiner and Kirstin Veel, 59–88. Berlin: DeGruyter.

Omhovère, Claire. 2005. "The Melting of Time in Thomas Wharton's *Icefields*." In *History, Literature, and the Writing of the Canadian Prairies*, edited by Robert A. Wardhaugh and Alison C. Calder, 43–62. Winnipeg: University of Manitoba Press.

Pratt, Mary Louise. 2008. *Imperial Eyes: Travel Writing and Transculturation*. 2nd ed. London: Routledge.

Robbins, David. 1987. "Sport, Hegemony and the Middle Class: The Victorian Mountaineers." *Theory, Culture & Society* 4 (4): 579–601.

Robinson, Zac. 2015. "Early Alpine Club Culture and Mountaineering Literature." In *Mountaineering Tourism*, edited by Ghazali Musa, James Higham, and Anna Thompson-Carr, 105–17. London: Routledge.

Said, Edward. 1979. *Orientalism*. New York: Vintage Books.

Schulkin, Jay. 2016. "The Concept of Sport." In *Sport: A Biological, Philosophical, and Cultural Perspective*, edited by Jay Schulkin, 1–11. New York: Columbia University Press.

Slemon, Stephen. 2000. "Climbing Mount Everest: Postcolonialism in the Culture of Ascent." In *Postcolonizing the Commonwealth: Studies in Literature and Culture*, edited by Rowland Smith, 51–73. Waterloo, ON: Wilfrid Laurier University Press.

Slemon, Stephen. 2008. "The Brotherhood of the Rope: Commodification and Contradiction in the 'Mountaineering Community'." In *Renegotiating Community: Interdisciplinary Perspectives, Global Contexts*, edited by Diana Bryon and William D. Coleman, 235–71. Vancouver: UBC Press.

Slemon, Stephen. 2017. "The Literature of Ascent." *Alpinist*, March 15, 2017. www.alpinist.com/doc/web17w/wfeature-literature-of-ascent.

Spurr, David. 1993. *The Rhetoric of Empire: Colonial Discourse in Journalism, Travel Writing, and Imperial Administration*. Durham: Duke University Press.

Stutfield, Hugh Edward Millington, and John Norman Collie. 1903. *Climbs and Exploration in the Canadian Rockies*. London: Longman.

Tiffin, Chris, and Alan Lawson, eds. 1994. *De-Scribing Empire: Post-Colonialism and Textuality*. London: Routledge.

Tiffin, Helen. 1978. "Towards Place and Placelessness: Two Journey Patterns in Commonwealth Literature." In *Awakened Conscience: Studies in Commonwealth Literature*, edited by Closepet Dasappa Narasimhaiah, 146–63. New Delhi: Sterling Publishing.

Utz, Peter. 2013. *Kultivierung der Katastrophe: Literarische Untergangsszenarien aus der Schweiz*. Munich: Wilhelm Fink Verlag.

Wharton, Thomas. *Icefields*. 1995. Edmonton: NeWest Press.

Willard, Cory. 2018. "Glaciers, Embodiment, and the Sublime: An Ecocritical Approach to Thomas Wharton's *Icefields*." In *Writing the Body in Motion*, edited by Angie Abdou and Jamie Dopp, 71–92. Edmonton: Athabasca University Press.

"Climbing It with Your Mind"

An Interview with Thomas Wharton

This interview was conducted in writing between February 15 and March 26, 2021, from Thomas Wharton's home in Edmonton, Alberta, and Eva-Maria Müller's home in Innsbruck, Austria.

EVA-MARIA MÜLLER: In your novel *Icefields* (1995), as well as in *The Logogryph* (2004), mountains feature as places that harbor stories. *Icefields* also gives a sense of the many different ways in which humans can tap into these stories, for example, by hiking, climbing, hunting, observing, recording, living, and listening to mountains. Could you talk a little bit about the relationship between the athletic and more intangible ways of accessing mountains and their stories?

THOMAS WHARTON: Mountain landscapes draw me in as challenges to be met in a physical sense, but they're also aesthetic and imaginative experiences. They call to me in a way that no other landscape does, as if it's in the mountains that I get closest to who or what I really am. If one wants to call that spiritual, that's fine by me, but I just find that all of these aspects of what I feel in the mountains are pretty much inseparable. Is it possible for an experience to be purely physical? I don't think so. The mind and the spirit, for lack of a better word, are fully involved in everything we do as human beings. Climbing a mountain with your body can only mean you're also climbing it with your mind, your will, your imagination, your desires and hopes and fears.

I think it was probably a desire to try to understand how and *why* mountains make me feel that way that led me to write my first novel. As a writer, I'd been searching for a subject matter and a story I could call my own, some territory I could write my way into that hadn't already been claimed by other writers. When I started writing about the mountain and glacier landscapes of the Canadian Rockies, I realized this was it: this was my imaginative homeland, the place I needed to write about. The strange, seemingly supernatural event that Doctor Edward Byrne has when he falls in the glacier at the beginning of the novel captures something of my own experiences. And having him as my protagonist, exploring the icy landscapes, he could become a kind of surrogate for my own need to say everything I could possibly say about this particular landscape and how compelling and meaningful it is to me.

EM: In your 1998 essay "The Country of Illusion" you recount your own Doctor Byrne moment when you slipped and fell hiking in Maligne Canyon in Jasper Park and explain that it triggered your fascination with narrative expression and the possibilities it holds for alternative endings. *Icefields* begins with Doctor Byrne falling into a crevasse where, hanging upside down, he sees an angelic figure in the ice. Over the course of the novel, a number of other characters and objects also fall. Curiously, though, in one way or another, they all return—and they return changed. Are these returns, together with Byrne's alpinist failure, a reflection of how you locate a transformative capacity, an inherent value, as it were, in falling? And if so, what can it teach us about our relationship to the natural world, the command we have over our bodies, and the slippery practice of the literary sport?

TW: That's a good question. I honestly hadn't noticed there was so much falling in the novel, but now that you point it out . . . ! I think I'm fascinated by falling simply because I'm terrified of it. I've never been much of an alpinist because I learned very early on that I simply don't have the nerve for scaling heights, even secured with a rope. I admire and envy people who can tame this primal fear and accomplish incredible feats, but in general I'd much prefer to read about mortal danger in a climbing memoir than face it myself. Some of the most haunting passages in mountain literature for me have been descriptions of falling, fatal or otherwise.

EM: Falling is just one of the many movements that run through your writing. In *Icefields* we encounter a glacier that rolls forward, mountaineers who traverse icy plains, travellers who cover long distances to get to Jasper—and then there is the movement of the story. How do you navigate these forms of motion? Do you see them moving in the same way or differently? And does writing about these distinctive movements contribute to your understanding of the bodies of mountains, humans, and texts?

TW: I see story and movement as intimately connected. We are animals, of course, and all animals have a strong seeking drive that impels movement. In evolutionary terms, moving through one's environment originated as a survival mechanism, so that animals could find food and shelter, and escape becoming food themselves, but in humans and probably in other mammals and in birds, there's a large component of curiosity and pleasure involved in goal-directed movement. There's a need to move, but also the enjoyment of it for its own sake. I think this is at least a partial explanation for why human beings derive so much pleasure from stories. Traditional stories—myths, legends, epics—are almost always goal-directed. So many of these old tales involve heroes setting out from somewhere on a quest and returning somewhere. I think humanity cherished and retold these stories over the millennia at least partly because a story involving people in motion towards a goal provides some of the same psychological gratification and reward that actual goal-oriented movement does.

Hiking in the mountains, or even just taking a walk in my own neighbourhood, is good physical exercise, but it's also psychologically enriching, and always feels just a little bit like a "hero's journey," especially during this pandemic when I spend most of my time cooped up at home. I've always thought it must be significant somehow that my settler ancestors were people who travelled huge distances, from their homelands to an unknown country, to make a new life for themselves. I'm a product of people that had that desire for movement and adventure, and I know I have it too, though I'm not accustomed to the same hardships they were. Increasing prosperity allowed my generation to take trips all over the world quickly and in relative ease. So maybe that desire for movement gets satisfied pretty easily in our world, but the experience of struggle and risk doesn't, and that's why the mountains call to so many people.

As for glaciers, I think we're psychologically habituated to see intention and goals even in the movement of inanimate things. That's why the poet Shelley says in his poem "Mont Blanc," "the glaciers creep / Like snakes that watch their prey" (lines 100–101). We see movement, even the slow epochal movement of a river of ice, and we have to find a story in it.

EM: That's interesting and it makes me wonder whether what you are saying about the glacier's movement might also apply to the writing process. You are not just a writer but also a teacher of writing. Do you encounter moments when writing itself feels like a "slow epochal movement" and what is your advice to all those who find themselves in the writer's equivalent of hanging upside down in a crevasse?

TW: One of my writing mentors, Robert Kroetsch, had a lot of great advice for writers. He said once, "Remember storytellers, just to attempt the impossible is victory enough." I like to remind myself about that whenever I've reached a point in my writing, or my writing life, where I seem to have hit a wall: I'm blocked in some way by a creative challenge I can't solve, or a story I've poured my heart and soul into gets rejected for the thirtieth time, or I just feel like giving up and doing something, anything, easier than writing. Kroetsch's words remind me that it's in the doing that the true fulfillment and reward comes, not in the results of the effort. If you have a vocation, a gift, a love of something difficult, whether it's mountain climbing or writing or whatever, when you're immersed in it fully, you know who you are. Or, rather, you forget who you are and you simply become what you do. After you leave that heightened creative state, the critical voice within returns and tells you how well or poorly it thinks you've done. And the world gets its turn to evaluate your performance too, and sometimes they'll acclaim it, and sometimes they'll ignore it. But no one and nothing can take away the joy that comes from doing the thing itself, expressing the gift, the vocation, and giving it everything you have.

WORKS CITED

Shelley, Percy Bysshe. 1970. "Mont Blanc (1817)." In *The Complete Poetical Works of Percy Bysshe Shelley*, edited by Thomas Hutchinson, 206–211. Oxford: Oxford University Press.

Wharton, Thomas. 1995. *Icefields*. Edmonton: NeWest Press.

Wharton, Thomas. 1998. "The Country of Illusion." In *Fresh Tracks: Writing the Western Landscape*, edited by Pamela Banting, 304–10. Victoria, BC: Polestar.

Wharton, Thomas. 2004. *The Logogryph*. Kentville, NS: Gaspereau Press.

6

Misao Dean

A "Most Enthusiastic Sportsman Explorer"

Warburton Pike in *The Barren Ground*

Warburton Pike was a sportsman. But he did not think of sports the way that the other contributions to this volume would define the word. He did not play team sports or field sports (which he might have called "athletics"); he was not a fan or a coach or a swimmer. Warburton Pike was a hunter, a man who travelled in search of unique hunting opportunities, and who sought trophy heads, animal skins, and specimens for the taxidermist. His two published books, *The Barren Ground of Northern Canada* (1892) and *Through the Sub-Arctic Forest* (1896), considered classics of Canadian travel writing, describe his trips through northern British Columbia, Yukon, the Northwest Territories, and southern Alaska in search of nothing more serious than "sport," the leisure pastime of killing caribou, deer, moose, and musk-ox, with a side order of geese, ducks, grouse, and other "game."

Described this way, Pike's idea of "sport" perhaps does not seem very sporting to a twenty-first century reader, evocative perhaps of Donald Trump Jr.'s controversial hunting expeditions, or the practice of "canned hunting," in which specially raised animals are provided to hunters for a guaranteed kill. But Pike's idea of "sport" resists simple identification with the trophy hunting of today. Instead, the practices of hunting in northern Canada during Pike's lifetime required intense physical fitness, strength, and endurance, knowledge of guns and of camping equipment, multilingualism, and willingness to risk discomfort, or even starvation. Unlike the hunters who followed him, who travelled with luxuries like whiskey and sleeping cots, Pike frequently ventured into territory that was little known to Europeans and carried little more than his blankets, his guns, some tobacco, and tea.

Pike did resemble contemporary "sport" hunters in that an essential part of his experience was telling the story afterwards. For Pike, the equivalent of the hunter's selfie was the hunting story, with the necessary evocation of an audience for his achievement through "the remembrance of the chase, its recollection, and its retelling" (Jones 2015, 12). In *The Barren Ground of Northern Canada* Pike creates a hunting and travel narrative that, like many similar books of its time, includes natural history, commentary on Indigenous hunting practices and a one-on-one confrontation with a male trophy animal. But *The Barren Ground* stands out among its contemporaries for its elegant and concise Neo-Romantic descriptions of landscape and its modest, reticent, good humoured, and open-minded narrator. While he sometimes defies the advice of his Indigenous guides and debunks the more romantic notions many Europeans had about "Indians," the narrator more often acknowledges their superior knowledge of animal habits, ranges, and breeding cycles. As Peter Murray writes in *Home from the Hill: Three Gentlemen Adventurers*, Pike's books seem "remarkably free of the patronizing racism toward Indians that most of his countrymen in Canada exhibited at that time" (1994, 13).[1]

Pike seems to have considered his trips to be personal adventures rather than the expression of a national destiny for Canada or for the "Anglo-Saxon race," as many of his contemporaries did (see Loo 2006; Rico 2013; Harraway 1989). In his writings, while he occasionally offers opinions on proposals for local or national game regulation, he never offers visions of future development or "civilization" of the Indigenous spaces he visits; instead he writes that the land should be "entirely given up to what it was evidently intended for, a hunting-ground for the Indian" (*Barren Ground*, 1). However, the paratexts that accompany the book reveal a more nationalist vision for the North: *The Barren Ground* contains as an appendix George M. Dawson's article "On Some of the Larger Unexplored Regions of Canada," which Dawson wrote as a member of the Geological Survey of Canada. Pike writes that this appendix "shows more plainly than any words

---

1 All of the information given about Pike's biography is drawn from Murray (1994), and I am very grateful to have all of this hard work done for me.

of mine could tell how much more yet remains to be done before this great portion of the British Empire is known as it ought to be" (303). In this way *The Barren Ground* demonstrates the contradiction at the heart of Pike's book, which advocates for leaving Indigenous Peoples and their lifeways intact, while taking for granted Crown sovereignty and his own right, as a citizen of the empire, to make use of both people and resources.

In pursuing the "sport" of hunting, Pike was to a certain extent behaving as a typical white Englishman of his class. Pike was born in 1861 in Dorset, one of four sons in a wealthy family who made a fortune mining the clay that was used to make Wedgewood china. His parents died when he was young, and he was raised by servants, attending Rugby School and Brasenose College at Oxford before dropping out when he came into his inheritance at age twenty-one. Like other upper-middle-class young men of his time, Pike would have hunted as a matter of course; weekends spent shooting grouse were a popular way for wealthy people who had recently bought country estates to show off for their friends and claim a faux aristocratic status (see Squires 2017, 294–96). Monica Rico (2013) and Tina Loo (2006) have analyzed the way that hunting was a reinscription of the moment of imperial conquest, as well as a recursive practice of gendered masculinity in self-conscious opposition to the perceived limitations of urban life at the turn of the century. As a well-to-do young man just come into his inheritance, Pike would have considered big game hunting both an appropriate and a challenging way to spend his time.

After Pike left school in 1882, the opportunities for both hunting and investing became an excuse for knocking around "America" for a couple of years with his elder brother Marmaduke. As Rico points out, "During the 1880s the American West drew British younger sons, family black sheep and miscellaneous wellborn young men at loose ends. . . . These men dreamed of making fortunes as ranchers and returning to Britain to resume their lives of privilege" (2013, 48). Pike and his brother were persuaded to invest in timber leases in British Columbia in 1883, and made their way to Victoria, at the time the only urban community in British Columbia, to investigate. Like others of his time and class, Pike "linked the pleasures of the big game hunter and the rewards of the entrepreneurial investor" (Rico 2013, 55), and expected to find both in the congenial society of Victoria, whose upper crust was dominated by English expats and "remittance men." Pike purchased most of the available land on Saturna and Mayne, islands located in the Gulf waters between Victoria and Vancouver, and built a substantial home in Oak Bay, then a rural suburb of Victoria.

Colonial Victoria had originally been settled by Hudson's Bay Company officers and their mixed-race Scottish and Indigenous families, who had formed the elite of the colony in the mid-nineteenth century. The original governor on behalf of the Hudson's Bay Company, James Douglas, was himself a mixed-race man born in Guyana; his wife Amelia Connolly Douglas was Métis. But by the 1880s, many of these men had retired; the colony had become a province, and their place was taken by recent immigrants from Britain and the United States who, like Pike, came to the province to take advantage of more modern economic opportunities. These men made substantial livings through becoming "first on the ground" in shipping, mining, logging, and land speculation in the developing province, and benefited from the inside knowledge that their political connections provided. Hunting was one of their most common leisure pastimes. Pike set up a bachelor household with English friend Charles Salusbury Payne, and almost immediately commenced the series of wilderness adventures that would form the basis of his books. In 1885 he travelled by canoe to the headwaters of the Athabasca River on the eastern slopes of the Rocky Mountains (the current location of Jasper National Park), and explored the area at the east end of Tête Jaune Pass near Mount Robson. On the basis of this positive experience, he undertook the two much longer journeys, one to the Barren Ground in 1889 and another up the Stikine River to Dease Lake and back to the coast via the Yukon River in 1892, trips he would later recount in his books.

As Karen R. Jones argues in *Epiphany in the Wilderness*, an intrinsic part of the sport of hunting was its narrativization, whether in the form of oral stories for fellow hunters or published narratives for general readers. Jones points out that big game hunting in North America is a performance of class, national, and gender identity specifically for an audience, and "the act of storytelling—of ritually performing the hunt as a way of creating, consolidating, and evoking a frontier identity—was shared by all" (2015, 11). Within these narrative tropes of "self-discovery, proving and renewal, conquering 'virgin land,' and competing with faunal 'monarchs'" (36) were common characteristics, as well as "referents of scientific and explorer acumen, natural history appreciation, self-awareness of the gravitas of the moment, and a performative bent: a full roster of passionate manhood"

(41). Pike is characteristically modest in his self-presentation as the narrator of *The Barren Ground*, asking the reader's indulgence for "faulty style, and the various errors into which a man who has spent much time among the big game is sure to fall when he is rash enough to lay down his rifle and take up the pen" (*Barren Ground*, viii). But he nonetheless provides a model of many of Jones's conventions, including natural history information and Neo-Romantic landscape description.

Pike's trip to the place he calls "the Barren Ground" was prompted, he writes in the preface to the book, by the rumours he heard about the musk-ox, "a strange animal, a relic of an earlier age, that was still to be found roaming the Barren Ground, the vast desert that lies between Hudson's Bay, the eastern ends of the three great lakes of the North, and the Arctic Sea" (v). He recounts that few Europeans had seen the musk-ox, and no big game hunters had managed to find them. "This, then, was the sole object of my journey; to try and penetrate this unknown land, to see the Musk-ox, and find out as much as I could about their habits, and the habits of the Indians who go in pursuit of them every year" (vi). Pike was at pains to clarify that his trip to the Barren Ground was only "an ordinary shooting expedition, such as one might make to the Rocky Mountains or the interior of Africa" (v), and not a scientific or geographic expedition. But he was being modest: on his trip he travelled deeply into Indigenous territories by way of a portage that was later named after him, and he became one of few Europeans who had seen the Barren Ground musk-ox. Since he considered Samuel Hearne the only European before him who had made a successful trip to the Barren Ground, he decided "to follow Hearne's example, and trust to the local knowledge of Indians to help me," since "they are possessed of a thorough knowledge of the movements of the various animals at different seasons, and thus run less danger of starvation than strangers, however proficient the latter may be in driving dogs and handling canoes" (vii). He travelled by train to Calgary, then by buggy to Edmonton and Athabasca Landing, and by steamer down the Mackenzie to Fort Resolution on Great Slave Lake. There he contracted with Joseph "King" Beaulieu (1836–1916), a well-known Métis guide and sometime employee of the Hudson's Bay Company, to take him on the seasonal trip to the Barren Ground to hunt caribou and musk-ox. "In following out this plan" Pike says, he "naturally passed through a great deal of new country, and discovered, as we white men say when we are pointed out some geographical feature by an Indian who has been familiar with it since childhood, many lakes and small streams never before visited except by the red man" (vii). Pike's hand-drawn maps became a touchstone for European explorers, naturalists, geographers, and hunters who followed him up Pike's Portage at the eastern end of Great Slave Lake, from Harry Lake to French Lake, Acres Lake, Kipling Lake, Burr Lake, and finally to Artillery Lake and the beginnings of the tundra.

Pike's guide, King Beaulieu, was a Métis man from a prominent family whose grandfather Francois "Old Man" Beaulieu (Francois Beaulieu I) had travelled with Alexander Mackenzie to both the Arctic Ocean (in 1789) and the Pacific Coast (in 1793), and whose father (Francois Beaulieu II) had guided Sir John Franklin.[2] Well-known as a guide and successful hunter, King Beaulieu had founded a Hudson's Bay trading fort in 1868 at Fond Du Lac on the eastern arm of Great Slave Lake, near the present-day Dënesųłıné community of Łutsël K'é, though by the time he met Pike the post had been closed. Beaulieu was literate and spoke French with Pike, though Pike reports learning a few words of Chipewyan (Dënesųłıné) from Beaulieu family members over the course of the months they travelled together.

Pike's representation of Indigenous people in *The Barren Ground* is a complex one that combines common racist stereotypes with astute judgement of individuals and defense of Indigenous hunting practices and lifeways. At the beginning of *The Barren Ground*, he describes King Beaulieu:

> Nobody could give him a very good character, but as he was known as a pushing fellow and first-rate traveller, besides having made a successful musk-ox hunt in the previous year, I concluded that my best chance lay in going with him. Certainly, with all his faults, I must say that he was thoroughly expert in all the arts of travel with canoes or dog-sleighs, quick in emergencies, and far more courageous than most of the half-breeds of the Great Slave Lake. (18)

2 There is some disagreement in the various sources available to me about whether King Beaulieu was the son, or grandson, of the Francois Beaulieu who guided Mackenzie. The information given is from The NWT Metis Nation website, https://nwtmetisnation.ca/communities/fort-resolution/. See also Mandeville (2009).

He continues: "When I was alone with him I found him easy enough to manage; but his three sons, who accompanied us, are the biggest scoundrels I ever had to travel with, and as they seem to demoralize the old man when they are together, the united family is a bad combination" (18). Here Pike is magnifying his authority over his guides: like Hearne, Pike was travelling with an established Indigenous family group and completely reliant upon them. He would have had little power to "manage" his travelling companions, other than King Beaulieu's sworn word and his promise "to do everything in his power to ensure the success of the expedition" (18). Pike's condemnation of Beaulieu's sons is explained by their helping themselves liberally to his supplies, beyond what Pike felt he had agreed, while he and King Beaulieu were absent from the winter camp near Great Slave Lake in the Barren Ground. The Indigenous ethic of sharing may explain their actions, or they may indeed have felt they deserved payment in addition to what was agreed; in any case, Pike has little complementary to say about Beaulieu's sons throughout the book.

Another common cause of conflict between European hunters and Indigenous guides was their refusal to abide by the ethics that hunters use to construct their sport as "fair" to animals. "Sport," as Pike understood it, was governed by a code of conduct—"rules," as it were—for hunting specific animals such as deer, moose, and bear, designated as "game." As Monica Rico recounts in *Nature's Noblemen: Transatlantic Masculinities and the Nineteenth-Century American West*, "big game hunters created a whole ideology designed to make the process as arduous as possible" (2013, 174). Big game hunters were to focus on mature male animals in the prime of health and leave female and young animals alone; they were supposed to kill specific identified animals quickly and cleanly, and have sufficient knowledge of the animal's habits and anatomy to enable them to kill with one well-placed shot: "Trapping, baiting, and in any way increasing the pain and suffering of the hunted animal were all considered ungentlemanly" (174). William Hornaday, a pioneer of US wildlife conservation and the first director of the Bronx Zoo, articulated a similar "Sportsman's Creed" for US hunters, which stated that "ethical hunters did not engage in 'wanton slaughter,' going into the woods or mountains with guns ablazing and mowing everything on four legs: they exercised restraint and avoided 'waste'" (Loo 2001, 307). Instead, an ethical hunt required the hunter to approach the animal on foot and give it a fair chance to escape; hunting carried out over difficult terrain was more admirable, and trophies that required extensive travel or mountaineering, such as mountain sheep or goats, were prized. "The greater the difficulty, the greater the achievement, and the greater the man who was successful" (Loo 2001, 307; see also Altherr and Reiger 1995).

Unlike many subsequent hunters (see Dean 2007; Jones 2015), Pike seems to have felt no responsibility to impose this code on his travelling companions, or to condemn either their hunting practices or their way of life. He notes the ways that Indigenous hunters violate the "Sportsman's Creed" by shooting indiscriminately into herds of caribou, shooting animals while they are swimming and unable to get away, and shooting many more animals than can be practically consumed. Yet his experience of starvation while travelling with the Beaulieus seemed to convince him of the necessity of these practices. He even participates in a summer hunt of breeding females and calves. "Cruel work, this shooting in the summer-time," he comments, "but it was necessary to keep the camp in meat" (*Barren Ground*, 174). Pike notes the "improvidence" of the Beaulieu family as they gorge whenever they have access to fresh meat, repeating the common complaint of Europeans that Indigenous families refuse to plan for future periods of famine: "Starvation will always be one of the features of a Northern Indian's life, owing to his own improvidence; his instinct is to camp close on the tracks of the caribou and move as they move; a permanent house and a winter's supply of meat are an abomination to him" (50). Yet Pike himself takes part in this "improvidence" when, after travelling for many days without food, he gorges on the delicacies of caribou tongues and loins and acknowledges the impossibility of preserving and carrying the leftover food.

The Barren Ground of Northern Canada does occasionally indulge in what Mary Louise Pratt (1985) calls "othering discourse," a

> very familiar, widespread, and stable form of "othering." The people to be othered are homogenized into a collective "they," which is distilled even further into an iconic "he" (the standardized adult male specimen). This abstracted "he"/"they" is the subject of verbs in a timeless present tense, which characterizes anything "he" is or does not as a particular historical event but as an instance of a pregiven custom or trait. . . . Through this discourse, encounters with an Other can be textualized or processed as enumerations of such traits. (1985, 120)

Pike applies these grammatical strategies abundantly, describing both Indigenous Peoples, as well as animals, in the "timeless present" of traditional anthropology, or what Anne McClintock might describe as its "anachronistic space" (1995, 30). For example, he describes the Yellowknife people he has met with distancing generalizations and the tropes of anachronistic space: "They are rather a fine race of men, above the average of the Canadian Indian, and, as they have had little chance of mixing with the Whites, have maintained their characteristic manners till this day; they are probably little changed since the time when the Hudson's Bay Company first established a trading-post on the Big Lake a hundred years ago" (*Barren Ground*, 120). The section from pages 119 to 122, with its sweeping judgements of Yellowknife women ("The women are, as a rule, not quite so hideous as the squaws of the Black-feet and Crees; they are lax in morals, and accustomed to being treated more as slaves than wives" [121]) and its complaints of "Indian" temperament ("a curious mixture of good and bad, simplicity and cunning; with no very great knowledge of common honesty, thoroughly untrustworthy, and possessed with an insatiable greed for anything that takes their fancy" [120]), have a racist flavour reminiscent of Hearne's *Journey*. Yet elsewhere in the book, particularly when he writes of individuals, Pike writes differently. Recounting a stay in a Yellowknife camp, he speaks well of his hosts and the sense of comfort he feels. While he complains that the "lodges" (skin tents) of his hosts are "infested with the vermin from which these people are never free" he also finds "an air of warmth and plenty about it" (71) and declares "there is no better camp than a well-set-up lodge (skin tent) with a good fire crackling in the middle" (37). He praises King Beaulieu and counts the Yellowknife man Saltatha, another man in the hunting party, among his friends. Yet he admits that, despite his many months of travelling with them and with the Beaulieu family, he does not understand Indigenous people as a whole. Unlike many of his European contemporaries, who claim to know Indigenous cultures and motives with no evidence of either, he suggests that the Indigenous "mind runs on different principles from that of a white man, and till the science of thought-reading is much more fully developed, the working of his brain will always be a mystery to the fur-trader and traveller" (122).

The Barren Ground is often praised for its spare, matter of fact style, and indeed the book focuses on conveying information that would be of interest, or of use, to the sportsman. Like many travel books, it begins with a list of necessary gear he carries from Edmonton: field glasses, "ammunition for a 12-bore Paradox and a 50–95 Winchester Express, besides a pair of large blankets and a little necessary clothing" (1). The Paradox was a classic hunting rifle whose ability to shoot both bullets and shotgun shells made it highly flexible in the bush; later in the book, David, an orphan boy who attaches himself to the hunting party, uses the Paradox to bag his first musk-ox, first expending all his bullets in the chase, then shooting stones, and finally killing the animal by firing the ramrod. The 50–95 Winchester was an up-to-date hunting rifle designed for big game hunting in Africa, India, and the western United States and was popular in England and North America. In addition, at Fort Resolution Pike purchased "a couple of sacks of flour and fifty pounds of bacon," and by the time he left for the Barren Ground he had equipped the party with

> a good supply of tea and tobacco, though it proved after all
> insufficient, plenty of ammunition for the three Winchester rifles,
> and powder, shot, and ball for the muzzle-loading weapons of the
> party; we had also nets and a few hooks and lines, matches, nee-
> dles, and awls to be used in the manufacture of moccasins and the
> deer-skin clothes so essential for winter travel; knives of various
> shapes and sizes, scrapers for dressing skins, and a small stock of
> the duffel imported by the Company for lining mittens and wrap-
> ping up the feet during the intense cold. (23)

The group left in three canoes "crowded with men, women and children, amounting in all to over twenty souls" (23) and including fifteen dogs.

Pike's party began by heading toward the "Inconnu Fishery" (located near Thaltheilei Narrows). They moved slowly to accommodate the wind on Great Slave Lake as well as the necessity of hunting and fishing along the way. Pike provides an impromptu natural history of the "game" fish in the lake and various methods of catching them. This section inaugurates his method, used throughout the book, of interspersing descriptions of the progress of the group toward the Barren Ground with accounts of the local fauna, their habits, ranges, abundance, and suitability for hunting. For example, he describes a successful day's hunting for geese in the forest south of the Barrens:

Along the foot of the sandy ridge . . . were many small lakes partially thawed, and here the snow geese, or white "wavies," were resting in thousands, waiting till the warm weather should have melted the snow from their feeding-ground along the sea-coast. We could have made enormous bags of them, as they were tame and disinclined to leave the open water; but we were sparing with our ammunition, as we might want it badly later on. Great numbers were killed, however, and their prime condition told of the good feeding-ground they had left far southward. There were also plenty of large Canada geese, but the grey wavy, or laughing goose, the best of all for eating, is much scarcer. (161)

As he moves into the forest north of the Lake, he encounters caribou, and chapter four consists wholly of information about the caribou, its scientific names, ranges, breeding habits, best time of year for hunting (end of summer into September), usual predators (wolves, humans), and useful ways to tell young from old, and male from female specimens. After securing enough meat for present wants, the family group camps on Camsell Lake, and Pike, accompanied by King Beaulieu and several other men, continue north to look for musk-ox.

Pike encounters his first musk-ox on September 27, a "red letter day" (64). The book demonstrates "self-awareness of the gravitas of the moment" (Jones 2015, 41) by extending the description of Pike's first kill over numerous pages. As Jones argues, hunting narratives commonly frame the moment of the kill according to an established convention that Pike follows precisely. The animal is identified as a male with desirable characteristics such as large size, good condition, large head, prominent or even record horns, and healthy coat; the animal must be stalked, his demeanor studied with the goal of determining the perfect approach; and the moment of the kill is constructed as a direct confrontation with a knowing adversary, whose appearance represents a romantic concept of wilderness freedom and agency. Pike records that he encounters "a single old bull walking directly towards us." He continues, "We lay down in the snow, and I had a capital chance of watching him through the glasses as he picked his way quietly over the slippery rocks." The climax of the encounter occurs when the bull raises his head and looks directly at them, "with his neck slightly arched and a gleam of sunshine lighting up the huge white boss formed by the junction of the horns." This extended description figures the musk-ox adversary as desirable due to his prominent horns and "formidable appearance," and also fully aware of the enemy that will cause his death. Finally, the animal appears as if crowned "with his neck slightly arched and a gleam of sunshine lighting up" his horns—backlit, as it were, by the sunshine. Pike draws attention to the way that this scene functions as a climax and a justification for the whole narrative by stating that the animal was "a sight which went far to repay all the trouble we had taken in penetrating this land of desolation." The moment of the animal's death is almost anticlimactic: "His fate was not long in doubt, as my first shot settled him, and the main object of my trip was accomplished; whatever might happen after this, I could always congratulate myself on having killed a musk-ox, and this made up for a great deal of the misery that we afterwards had to undergo" (64–65).

Pike held that one of the frustrations of big game hunting in North America was the absence of established standards for trophy animals. In England, Rowland Ward and Co. taxidermists began in 1882 to write and distribute *Records of Big Game*, a serial publication that certified the specific measurements of a "record" animal, including length from nose to tail, height at the shoulder, depth of base of horn, width of horns, and so on. But there was no similar authority in North America, and when Pike later wrote about musk-ox hunting he resorted to the *Records of Big Game* measurements of a "fair average specimen" that had been transported to England for mounting (*Barren Ground*, 429). In later years the Boone and Crocket Club, the famous US men's club founded by Theodore Roosevelt in 1887, kept records of trophy animals in the western United States (as indeed they still do); Pike became an associate member in 1907. But in 1910 he pointed out that there was still no authority for specifically Canadian animals, which he considered an impediment to the promotion of hunting tourism in British Columbia (Pike 1910).

Throughout his accounts of travel in the North in *Barren Ground*, Pike sprinkles nuggets of information of use to hunters and other travellers who would follow him. "English is little spoken in any part of the North that I visited," advises Pike, and he describes guides translating from Indigenous languages into French for him (10). Pike declares his Paradox "the most useful gun yet invented for purposes of exploration" because it "shoots very true" with either ball or shot, though he thinks that a 20-bore with its lighter ammunition would be more practical if it were available (126). He advises against trying to carry provisions onto the Barren Ground in summer, because the "difficulty of transport is so great, and after the caribou are once found there is no danger of starvation" (160). He describes their outfit for the winter hunt and how they were fixed for provisions and ammunition; points out that they had to wrap their guns in fur, because if they touched the cold iron their fingers would stick; details the effects of having a frozen beard and eyebrows; describes what they ate and how they slept; and bemoans the inconvenience of the dogs, who not only slept on top of them but peed on packs and ate their gear.

Having declared that one of the goals of his trip was to learn about the "habits of the Indians who go in pursuit of them [the musk-ox] every year" (v), Pike also provides information about Indigenous hunting practices. He participated in a group hunt of musk-ox in which the animals were herded toward a river and shot while on the edges of the stream. He was surprised to discover after the hunt was over that the drivers were shouting directions to the musk-ox—"These animals are said to understand every word of the Yellow Knife language" (169–70)—and presumably were being offered the opportunity to give themselves to the hunters (on this point, see Houston 2004; Cruikshank 2005). When hunting caribou with a group, Pike explains that by custom the meat is shared equally, but the tongue and back fat belong to the man who made the kill; when hunting musk-ox, "it was a custom among the Yellow Knives to consider a band of musk-ox as the property of the discoverer, and only his personal friends were granted the privilege of killing them without payment of some kind" (102). Pike conforms to these practices without question despite his skepticism about their value, and somewhat ironically thanks his companions once he understands the significance of being offered a share of a musk-ox herd that he had not discovered himself (103).

Aside from the exoticizing effect of these details, they imply some of Pike's unstated attitudes toward Indigenous peoples and their futures. While he acknowledges the difficulty faced by European hunters in reaching the tundra, he nevertheless assumes that increased incursion of sport hunters into Indigenous territories is, if not desirable, at least inevitable, and so provides information to make these trips possible. While Pike elsewhere argues that Indigenous people have their own very effective ways of regulating hunting and suggests that attempts to assimilate them are wrong-headed, he does not doubt the claims of Canadian (imperial) sovereignty. Like many British hunters, he regrets the restrictive game laws that hamper "sport" in

England, where regulation reserves game animals for wealthy landowners, and he is happy to be hunting in a jurisdiction that considers game animals a public resource, available to all. Yet he seems oblivious to the consequences of development and settlement in Canada, which will in their turn result in Canadian game laws that will criminalize Indigenous hunting practices in the North within a generation.

Pike's pursuit of "sport" in *Barren Ground* is contextualized throughout the book with lavish landscape description that conforms broadly to the conventions of Neo-Romantic nature, describing prospects or "views" to mimic the composition of a Romantic landscape painting and emphasizing the ways that landscape views evoke emotions in the viewer. Pike's description of the "chutes" on the Peace River near Fort Vermillion begins with the foreground, where "the white broken water of the cascade showed in strong contrast to the broad blue stretches above and below"; the scene is framed by "several rocky, pine-covered islands" that "stand on the brink of the overfall" and in the background "the gloomy forest of black pines, relieved by a glimpse of the open side-hills of the Caribou Mountains." Pike comments: "I think the scene from the south bank is one of the most beautiful in the whole course of the loveliest of rivers" (220). In contrast, when he climbs "to the top of a high butte to have a look at the surrounding country" on the Barren Ground he describes "a good view of probably the most complete desolation that exists upon the face of the earth." He evokes the uncanny when he considers this winter range of the musk-ox: "[H]ere this strange animal finds abundance of its favourite lichens, and defies the cold that has driven every other living thing to the woods for shelter." From Pike's perspective, this Indigenous homeland deserved its characterization as "barren": "There is nothing striking or grand in the scenery, no big mountains or waterfalls, but a monotonous snow-covered waste, without tree or scrub, rarely trodden by the foot of the wandering Indian. A deathly stillness hangs over all, and the oppressive loneliness weighs upon the spectator till he is glad to shout aloud to break the awful spell of solitude" (107). These descriptions are examples of Pike's admirable style: direct, concise, well ordered, and expressive. Yet both of these descriptions, while representing "real life" experience, work to materialize Romantic theories about nature (see especially Glickman 1998; MacLaren 1984), judging the varied landscapes featuring jagged rocks, powerful water flows, and graceful trees to be picturesque, and representing the tundra, lacking these landscape features as well as signs of European inhabitation, as sublimely desolate and inhuman.

Pike's Neo-Romantic description of landscape is one component of the ideology of anti-modernism that justified trophy hunting for many in the late Victorian and early twentieth-century era. The Romantics of Wordsworth's era saw the natural world as a retreat from the sophistication and falsity of urban life; as industrialization grew and transportation and communication improvements seemed to speed up the pace of life, the Romantic view of nature was revived by the hunters and conservationists of Pike's era, who claimed "primitive" adventures in the natural world were a necessary antidote to the physical and mental effects of urban life. In the Neo-Romantic view, urban life also seemed incompatible with the traditional characteristics of the masculine self, such as independence, aggressiveness, and dominance—characteristics whose suppression supposedly resulted in ill-health and the feminization of men. Pike argues,

> [S]urely we carry this civilization too far, and are in danger of warping our natural instincts by too close observance of the rules that some mysterious force obliges us to follow when we herd together in big cities. Very emblematical of this warping process are the shiny black boots into which we squeeze our feet when we throw away the moccasin of freedom; as they gall and pinch the unaccustomed foot, so does the dread of our friends' opinion gall and pinch our minds till they become narrow, out of shape, and unable to discriminate between reality and semblance. (274)

Pike nods to this ideology throughout his book, claiming that outdoor life even under the harshest conditions promotes health (128), and commenting on the beauty of his surroundings.

In fact, Pike's book consistently declares how comfortable he is in the woods. These sections are some of the most striking in the book. While naturalists like Seton and hunters like Roosevelt claimed to love the natural world, accounts of their travels in the bush are filled with complaints about bugs, health, companions, diet, temperature, and equipment. In contrast, Pike seems almost ascetic, rolled in his blankets by the fire at all times of year, and matter-of-factly tackling any obstacles. Commenting on a December hunting trip with Hudson Bay–area commissioner James Mackinlay, "master" of Fort Resolution at the time, and Pierre Beaulieu, he states:

"We had everything we could want to make life pleasant in the woods, abundance of tea and tobacco, meat if we killed it, and no hardships; the cold was severe of course, but there was plenty of firewood, and it was our own fault if we could not keep ourselves warm" (136; given that the average temperatures in December in Łutsël K'é, a hundred and fifty miles south of Pike's trip, range from a high of minus sixteen to a low of minus twenty-four degrees Celsius, Pike's "of course the cold was severe" seems like an understatement). Pike gives the impression of a self-sufficient outdoorsman, whose consistent good humour in the face of rough travel and privation seems genuinely admirable. Clive Phillipps-Wooley, a British Columbian novelist who knew Pike well, described him as "the Boss" in *The Chicamon Stone*, a man of "seasoned strength" who could "cover his thirty-five or forty miles in a day, and as likely as not, if all were well, turn around at daylight next morning and 'lope' back" (1900, 98, 34).

After his initial success in killing his first musk-ox, Pike returned to the Camsell Lake camp to await the onset of winter weather. He made another successful trip to the Barren Ground with a Yellowknife family group by dog team and snowshoe. Returning (by way of the portage that was to bear his name) to Fort Resolution for Christmas, he lived happily in Mackinlay's household and in the summer participated in another hunt for caribou for the Fort. Leaving Fort Resolution late in the summer accompanied by Hudson's Bay Company officer Murdo Mackay, he attempted to reach Quesnel and transportation to the lower mainland, famously getting lost, along with his "Indian guides," between Hudson's Hope and Lake MacLeod. *The Barren Ground* tells the harrowing story of their eventual return to John Barrow's cabin at the east end of the portage:

> I pushed open the door, and shall never forget the expression of horror that came over the faces of the occupants when they recognised us. We had become used to the hungry eyes and wasted forms, as our misery had come on us gradually, but to a man who had seen us starting out thirty-two days before in full health the change in our appearance must have been terrible. There was no doubt that we were very near the point of death. (265)

Happily, he recovered, and returned to Victoria in the spring.

In an article published two years after *The Barren Ground*, Pike summed up what he had learned about the sport of shooting musk-ox: "In expeditions of this kind there is really no sport in the ordinary acceptance of the term," he wrote, because "the musk ox is so easily approached that one soon tires of the slaughter." The habit of musk-ox to defend themselves by standing and facing their enemies, no matter how useful against wolves and other predators, made them easy pickings for hunters equipped with rifles, "[b]ut it is never a certainty that the game will be forthcoming when most required for meat, and the knowledge that starvation, even to the last extremes, may come upon you at any time, goes far to counterbalance the tameness of the sport when once you have reached the land of plenty." The challenge of hunting musk-ox, Pike writes, is in their remoteness and difficulty of access, rather than in the experience of stalking, but this does not mean that musk-ox hunting is tame: "Sufficient excitement and danger will always be found in penetrating the little known desert of the north to satisfy the most enthusiastic sportsman explorer" (Pike 1894, 435).

Pike recounts his subsequent trip from Wrangell, Alaska, up the Stikine River into Northern British Columbia in his later book *Through the Sub-Arctic Forest* (1896). The book similarly includes numerous bits of information about hunting, the habits and prevalence of game animals, and the details of travel by canoe and on foot through Indigenous lands. His interest was piqued by the area, which was experiencing a prospecting boom; Pike staked a claim on the Thibault River, and subsequently ran a placer mine with money invested by many of his friends in Victoria. He set up a successful freight business and purchased a steamboat to run from Wrangell up the Stikine to Telegraph Creek, where he would meet the freight with a mule train and make the strenuous trip once again over the pass to Dease Lake. But the placer mine never more than broke even, and despite Pike's numerous attempts to open up the area by promoting a railroad from Telegraph Creek into the interior, his investments dwindled and by the time he died in 1915, he was broke. He had given up trophy hunting for photography, and become a fixture at Victoria's British-style men's club, the Union Club.

Pike's career as a "sportsman" was in many ways typical of his class and his era: like many well-to-do young men at the end of the nineteenth century, he drifted to North America in search of opportunities for hunting and investment. While he succeeded at the former, he was defeated by the latter. Nonetheless his books are an important achievement: *The Barren Ground* in particular constructs a persona who is modest, courageous, and physically indomitable, and a style of narration that foregrounds concrete detail, useful information, and carefully rendered landscape description, while also conforming to many of the tropes identified by scholars. The book concludes by quoting Saltatha's evocative comparison of the Barren Ground to heaven: "Is it more beautiful than the country of the musk-ox in summer, when sometimes the mist blows over the lakes, and sometimes the water is blue, and the loons cry very often? That is beautiful; and if Heaven is still more beautiful, my heart will be glad, and I shall be content to rest there till I am very old" (276). By ending with this memorable quotation, Pike evokes the wilderness sublime in the voice of his Yellowknife friend, restating the view that for those that are willing to brave its physical challenges, the Barrens are a rewarding experience for the sportsman.

WORKS CITED

Altherr, Thomas L., and John F. Reiger. 1995. "Academic Historians and Hunting: A Call for More and Better Scholarship." *Environmental History Review* 19 (3): 39–56.

Cruikshank, Julie. 2005. *Do Glaciers Listen? Local Knowledge, Colonial Encounters, and Social Imagination.* Vancouver: University of British Columbia Press.

Dawson, George M. 1892. "On Some of the Larger Unexplored Regions of Canada." In Pike, *The Barren Ground of Northern Canada*, 276–89. London: MacMillan.

Dean, Misao. 2007. "The Mania for Killing: Hunting and Collecting in Ernest Thompson Seton's *The Arctic Prairies*." In *Other Selves: Animals in the Canadian Literary Imagination*, edited by Janice Fiamengo, 290–304. Ottawa: University of Ottawa Press.

Glickman, Susan. 1998. *The Picturesque and the Sublime: A Poetics of the Canadian Landscape.* Montréal: McGill-Queen's University Press.

Harraway, Donna. 1989. "Teddy Bear Patriarchy: Taxidermy in the Garden of Eden, New York City, 1908–1936." In *Primate Visions: Gender, Race, and Nature in the World of Modern Science*, by Donna Harraway, 26–58. New York: Routledge.

Hearne, Samuel. 1802. *Journey from Fort Prince of Wales, in Hudson's Bay, to the Northern Ocean.* London: Joseph & James Crukshank.

Houston, John, dir. 2004. *Diet of Souls.* Mississauga, ON: Triad Films Productions and McNabb Connolly.

Jones, Karen R. 2015. *Epiphany in the Wilderness: Hunting, Nature, and Performance in the Nineteenth-Century American West*. Boulder: Colorado University Press.

Loo, Tina. 2001. "Of Moose and Men: Hunting for Masculinities in British Columbia, 1880–1939." *Western Historical Quarterly* 32: 296–319.

Loo, Tina. 2006. *States of Nature: Conserving Canada's Wildlife in the Twentieth Century*. Vancouver: University of British Columbia Press.

MacLaren, I. S. 1984. "Samuel Hearne and the Landscapes of Discovery." *Canadian Literature* 3: 27–40.

Mandville, Jeanette. 2009. "Beaulieu, Joseph." Winnipeg: Louis Riel Institute. Entry in the Gabriel Dumont Institute of Native Studies and Applied Research Biography and Essay Collection. https://www.metismuseum.ca/resource.php/11076.

McClintock, Anne. 1995. *Imperial Leather: Race, Gender and Sexuality in the Colonial Contest*. New York: Routledge.

Murray, Peter. 1994. *Home from the Hill: Three Gentlemen Adventurers*. Victoria, BC: Horsdal & Schubart.

Phillipps-Wolley, Clive. 1900. *The Chicamon Stone*. London: George Bell Publishers.

Pike, Warburton. 1892. *The Barren Ground of Northern Canada*. London: MacMillan.

Pike, Warburton. 1894. "Musk Ox." In *Big Game Shooting*. Vol I., edited by Clive Phillipps-Wolley, 428–35. London: Longman Green.

Pike, Warburton. 1896. *Through the Sub-Arctic Forest: A Record of a Canoe Journey from Fort Wrangel to the Pelley Lakes and Down the Yukon River to the Behring Sea*. London: Edwin Arnold.

Pike, Warburton. 1910. "The Big Game of British Columbia." *Victoria Colonist* 50 (406).

Pratt, Mary Louise. 1985. "Scratches on the Face of the Country; or, What Mr. Barrow saw in the Land of the Bushmen." *Critical Inquiry* 12 (1): 119–43.

Rico, Monica. 2013. *Nature's Noblemen: Transatlantic Masculinities and the Nineteenth-Century American West*. New Haven: Yale University Press.

Squires, Peter. 2017. "Hunting and Shooting: The Ambiguities of 'Country Sports.'" In *The Palgrave International Handbook of Animal Abuse Studies*, edited by Jennifer Maher, Harriet Pierpoint, and Piers Beirne, 289–311. London: Palgrave.

7

Gyllian Phillips

Getting Away from It All, or Breathing It All In
Decolonizing Wilderness Adventure Stories

Jolie Varela is the founder of "Indigenous Women Hike" and an advocate of hiking with awareness of Indigenous lands. In a 2018 interview in *Backpacker* magazine, she offers advice for anyone who engages in outdoor recreation: "I want all people who go to recreate to know where you are and to acknowledge where you are. When you go somewhere, you know there's a history. We were taken away from that land and put on a reservation. When you get to be in this beautiful spot, keep that in mind. I don't want people to be super bummed out, but just be aware. Google what tribe is indigenous to wherever you are" (in Johnson-Groh 2018). As both a non-Indigenous person and an avid hiker, trail runner, backpacker, canoeist, and Nordic skier, I have taken Varela's words to heart. I live and work in the traditional territory of the Nbisiing Anishinaabeg who are of Ojibwe and Algonquin descent. This is the land of the Nipissing First Nation and is covered by the Robinson Huron Treaty of 1850, which spells out the agreement between Canada and the Nbisiing Anishinaabeg on occupation and resource use. Whenever I am out on the land, and sometimes even in my backyard, I spend a little time thinking about how the Nbisiing Anishinaabeg people, since time immemorial, have walked the paths I walk and cared for the forests and lakes that I also love.

Because I enjoy outdoor sport, I also like reading about it. I especially like adventure stories, fiction and nonfiction, featuring (usually) lone travellers who venture into the woods or up mountains. One of the things I have noticed about these stories is that, if they have been written by and about settlers, they often lack acknowledgments like the one that Varela suggests recreational hikers should make. More than that, I have begun to wonder if these stories and their lack of acknowledgement actually serve to reinforce colonial attitudes towards land, even the wildest spaces. In this chapter, I think about the ways in which wilderness adventure stories by and about settlers, such as Jon Krakauer's *Into the Wild* (1996) and Cheryl Strayed's *Wild: From Lost to Found on the Pacific Crest Trail* (2012), express the motivation and the appeal of outdoor recreation. Reading these expressions through a postcolonial lens reveals the absences and displacements of Indigenous Peoples and histories in these works. In contrast, *Medicine Walk* (2015), a novel by Richard Wagamese (Ojibwe), revises the adventure narrative to reposition Indigenous characters and history into colonized landscapes, and in the process encourages a reconsideration of the relationship between human and land.

The three books under consideration here represent three distinct genres. *Into the Wild* is a journalist's account of the apparent death by starvation of a young traveller in Alaska, Christopher McCandless, who left only scanty records of his journey and motivations. *Wild* is a memoir by a woman who, hurting and addicted, and with little backpacking or athletic experience, solo-hikes a lengthy chunk of the Pacific Crest Trail. *Medicine Walk* is a novel about a young Indigenous man, Franklin Starlight, who takes his father, ill with terminal liver disease, into the backcountry to die and be buried. What these books have in common is their focus on a person or people, in all their complexity, on a journey characterized by physical and elemental challenges away from human-made places. The generic differences among these books generate some areas in which comparison is impossible and absolute contrast inevitable, but for my purposes, the key element they share is storytelling. Their stories are compelling, both in the sense that they engage and hold a reader's interest but also in that, in the case of *Into the Wild* and *Wild* at any rate, they compel readers to move out of the book and into what is commonly called nature (see Rane 2020; A. Williams 2015). Krakauer and Strayed represent a tradition of writing that has shaped Canadian and American attitudes both towards a notion of heroism in physical overcoming and towards a notion of wilderness. *Medicine Walk* takes both of these notional blueprints and reshapes them from the perspective of Indigenous dispossession. What settlers think of as "wild" is actually somebody's home.

WILD, INTO THE WILD, AND THE WILDERNESS ADVENTURE STORY

The idea of outdoor adventure is given a colonial frame through certain texts and stories. Kristin Jacobson suggests that venturing into "wild" spaces calls up a particular character trope and invites associations with a frontier mentality: "Extreme environments evoke mythic heroic frameworks and historically specific national narratives" (2020, 62). In other words, the way humans who are habituated to Western knowledge systems think about and move through nonhuman spaces is partially determined by text.

The authors of *Into the Wild* and *Wild* portray the real-life journeys depicted in these books as having bookish origins: Cheryl Strayed writes that she was inspired to embark on her improbable hike by *The Pacific Crest Trail, Volume 1: California*, a book that she picked up randomly in the checkout line of a sporting goods store (*Wild*, 51), and Jon Krakauer makes much of Chris McCandless's small portable library, which included books by Henry David Thoreau, Leo Tolstoy, and—especially important for Krakauer's narrative—Jack London. From a Western cultural perspective, when mythic heroic frameworks, Jack London, and a backcountry trail guide are brought together, their shared properties become obvious: there are humans and there is wilderness; a human ventures into the wilderness to prove him or herself; and in both the idea of wilderness and the wilderness adventure there is a tacit mastery of self and place. As Jonah Raskin points out in his discussion of London's *Call of the Wild* and Krakauer's *Into the Wild*, "the wild is a story, a fiction if you will, that we tell ourselves in order to make sense of our lives" (2011, 201). Like all stories we tell, "wild" stories help us determine our conceptions of real place, time, other people, and ourselves. Kristina Groover, speaking about the literary lineage of Mark Twain's Huck Finn, identifies this type of story as "not merely an adventure story, but the central paradigm of spiritual experience in the American literary tradition" (1999, 187). The individual established in this tradition is a loner, most often masculine, self-reliant, resourceful, and in control of his space. The environment through which he moves is the "wilderness"—a space in opposition to the human world, a space that the individual maps, is temporarily undone by, and ultimately conquers.

The land story that comes from Jack London and shapes Krakauer's portrait of McCandless is one of self-determination through dominance:

> The only passage from *The Call of the Wild* that McCandless selected for special attention . . . is a description of Buck after he has killed Spitzbergen, the dog who had led the pack. London calls Buck "the dominant primordial beast." McCandless tweaked the phrase and wrote, "All hail the Dominant Primordial Beast!" which makes it sound like a hymn to brute conquest. (Raskin 2011, 199)

Krakauer shapes the bits and pieces of writing left by McCandless, along with interviews with those who knew the somewhat hapless young man, into a heroic character by means of the mythos created by London. Krakauer purports to see himself and McCandless as something like kindred spirits in their defiance of authority, love of being outdoors, and enjoyment of physical challenge. For example, Krakauer describes how his youthful self hungered for risk and mastery through his own attraction to rock and ice climbing in the remote north: "Climbing *mattered*. The danger bathed the world in a halogen glow that caused everything—the sweep of the rock, the orange and yellow lichens, the texture of the clouds—to stand out in brilliant relief. Life thrummed at a higher pitch. The world was made real" (*Into the Wild*, 134). Krakauer depicts McCandless, and in some ways himself, as a character in the tradition of American outdoor iconoclast, attempting the impossible out of a desire to establish his "heroic masculinity" (Jacobson 2020, 13, 40), but also to experience a deep connection between himself and the "real" (as opposed, I assume, to the human-made) world.

Cheryl Strayed breaks with this "cult of masculinity" (Kam 2015, 353) by assuming the traditionally male role of lone adventurer, becoming the "Queen" of the Pacific Crest Trail (*Wild*, 289). However, she adds a dimension to her journey that remains somewhat latent in the more typically masculine stories. She is seeking a physical experience not only to thrill her into "the real" but also to transform her inner reality, which has been damaged by loss and trauma. Her literary frame is twofold: "It was true that *The Pacific Crest Trail, Volume 1: California* was now my bible, but *The Dream of a Common Language* [by Adrienne Rich] was my religion"

(60). Her outer project—the through-hike—is physical; her inner project is liberatory and spiritual. Shelley Sanders has usefully identified the literary project of *Wild* as part of an "athletic aesthetic" of sports writing (2017, 12), one in which writing and reading can be felt as a "transfigurative practice" (14), possibly one that makes readers move with Strayed, as it were, into the wild. (Among readers in online forums such as Goodreads, this transfigurative practice is identified more simply as "inspiring"). Strayed's book is moving, in both senses of the word. And, though *Into the Wild* can't focus much on McCandless's interiority, both it and *Wild* imply that "venturing away from urban spaces into the wilderness can be particularly therapeutic during periods of malaise and alienation" (Kam 2015, 352). In addition to the transformation of physical state through hard, daily exercise and the occasional thrilling confrontation with danger, Strayed identifies the motivation of long-distance hiking as a need "to witness the accumulation of trees and meadows, mountains and deserts, streams and rocks, rivers and grasses, sunrises and sunsets" (*Wild*, 207). Strayed identifies the experience as "powerful and fundamental" and part of a timeless connection: "It seemed to me that it had always felt like this to be a human in the wild, and as long as the wild existed it would always feel this way" (*Wild*, 207). The therapeutic effect seems to come from all of the above: hard exercise induces euphoria and good sleep; facing and overcoming external dangers creates internal strength and resilience; something as mindlessly mindful as walking for hours allows for intense rumination on dark thoughts and an eventual letting go; and intimacy with trees, rocks, and water is wired into our very brain chemistry (see F. Williams 2017).

Through all of this, however, Krakauer and Strayed make little effort to know and acknowledge where they (and McCandless) are in the way that Jolie Varela suggests. I don't write this to disparage Strayed or Krakauer, or any other past wilderness adventure writer. I write it as a settler hiker myself, and as someone working my way towards a different understanding of my relationship to land, of my own responsibility for justice, and of my own conceptions of "nature." There is altogether a scanty acknowledgment of Indigenous Peoples and history in much of North American nature writing produced by non-Indigenous people. This is an absence, so it is hard to point to or address, but it functions as a kind of wound, a gap in the discourse defining human and non-human relations: "Stories are bigger than the texts and bodies that carry them. When absent, they leave gaps that communicate as surely as the presences" (Justice 2018, 184). In her discussion of Indigenous literature of the American southwest, Joni Adamson points out that "the separation of nature and culture into two separate worlds creates blind spots" and "fails to account for the ways in which some human communities have inhabited land in sustainable ways" (2001, 16). These gaps have real, tangible effects in the lives of Indigenous people.

The rare examples of acknowledgement of Indigenous Peoples that do exist in Krakauer's and Strayed's narratives often only serve to underline the gap or further erase Indigenous presences. Krakauer expends considerable energy, money, time, and print space unravelling the seeming mystery of McCandless's death without ever turning to the very people on whose land he died and, as it turns out, on whose knowledge he relied to survive. McCandless's cause of death was identified as starvation, and in an effort to maintain McCandless's heroic masculinity, Krakauer undertakes to establish that this was not just the result of arrogant stupidity or a suicidal death-wish. Instead, he points to another book in McCandless's library, *Tanaina Plantlore* by Priscilla Russel Kari, an ethnobotanist working with and writing about the Dena'ina people on whose territory McCandless died. *Tanaina Plantlore* was McCandless's main source of information on food foraging in the area. Krakauer speculates that, "had McCandless's guidebook to edible plants warned that *H. alpinium* seeds contain a 'highly toxic secondary plant constituent' . . . he probably would have walked out of the wild" (*Into the Wild*, 212). In the acknowledgements to her own book, Kari makes clear the debt of knowledge she owes to the Dena'ina Elders who helped her to understand the plantlore of the area. McCandless himself placed his life, indirectly, in the hands of the Elders Kari talked to, though he never acknowledged (at least in Krakauer's telling) that the information contained in *Tanaina Plantlore* came from millennia-old stories of land-based living. Yet Krakauer does not appear to have spoken to anyone with Indigenous knowledge of the plants and animals McCandless consumed, instead commissioning costly laboratory studies of plant specimens and interviewing many academics. Nowhere in *Into the Wild* is there an admission that the people with the expertise McCandless might have relied on for help, and Krakauer might have turned to in order to solve his mystery, have lived successfully since time immemorial in the same territory where McCandless perished.

In *Wild*, Strayed similarly neglects to acknowledge Indigenous presence, and for the most part does not acknowledge the traditional territories through which she moves on her Pacific Crest Trail hike. She makes one exception near the end of the book, but that naming of traditional territory is framed as a historical artifact. In the chapter called "Mazama," named for the place also known as Crater Lake, to account for the powerful affect she has in response to the landscape, she offers a geological and cultural history in which she conflates an ancient and implicitly prehistorical past with the Klamath, a present-time people, thereby rhetorically disarming their claim to the land (Deur 2002, 33–43). In Mazama, what is now a lake was once a mountain, a volcano that erupted 7,700 years ago: "The Klamath tribe of Native Americans who witnessed the eruption believed it was a fierce battle between Llao, the spirit of the underworld, and Skell, the spirit of the sky" (*Wild*, 261). At the end of the chapter, she acknowledges the continuation of that history by saying that "the Klamath tribe *still consider* the lake a sacred site" (271; my emphasis). Though Strayed admits here the continuity of human-land relationships that extend far beyond her own personal encounter with "wilderness," this moment remains bracketed from the rest of the hike and seems to align Indigenous authority on the land with the ancient geologic past rather than a living present. Strayed elides Indigenous presence in other ways, too. For example, throughout *Wild*, Strayed's history dates the Pacific Crest Trail to before its official designation in 1968, noting that it was used by "hikers and wilderness enthusiasts" as far back as the 1930s (61). But we know, thanks to Jolie Varela and others, that the trail is much older than this. For example, the John Muir Trail (JMT)—part of the Pacific Crest Trail—was not "discovered" by John Muir: "These are our ancestral trade routes. They were there long before John Muir was. So I'm going to do the JMT but I'm going to call it the Nuumu Poyo—which means the Paiute Road or Paiute Trail, but directly translates as the People's Trail" (Varela in Johnson-Groh 2018).

These lacunae in *Into the Wild* and *Wild* reveal the work of the continuous erasure that goes into preserving a particular story about "wilderness." As is typical in the adventure story genre, these two books mostly represent the land as being free of humans; they both imply that by venturing into wild space, the outdoorsperson becomes more self-aware and more human, stronger and more self-reliant. In the process, or perhaps as a result of this understanding of nature as "other," neither Strayed nor Krakauer see the presence of the people whose land the heroes of their stories—themselves or another—cross. As Kylie Crane puts it, "wilderness entails a colonial gesture, placing indigenous presences and practices under erasure" (2012, 2). Thinking critically about the absence of land acknowledgements in wilderness adventure stories leads to an ecocriticism with social justice in mind:

> [T]he ecocritic's default loving attitude toward North American nature . . . is a condescending artifact of colonialist settlement in North America. . . . [I]f our territorial acknowledgements about unceded lands are genuine, as they must be, then the basic conception of "wilderness" is misplaced in any discussion of nature or place here, and destructive of any possibility of building a settler-colonial ecocriticism to be proud of. (Pickard 2018, 321)

Decolonizing wilderness adventure narratives also has pedagogical importance insofar as it may help readers develop an integrated understanding of humans' relationship with the world. Lisa Kortweg and Jan Oakley, discussing the decolonization of similar narratives in film, argue for this point: "We hope that a 'Land education' approach focused on epistemological and cosmological *relations* between all peoples, land, water, and flora and fauna will take *the place* of (Eurocentric) place-based environmental education" (2016, 140–41). Decolonizing narrative thus takes us a step closer to two goals: decolonizing the land itself and shifting human perception of land from object to relation.

WALKING HOME: *MEDICINE WALK*

The ways in which stories are told, and who or what tells them, is central to Wagamese's *Medicine Walk*. The novel tells the story of sixteen-year-old Franklin Starlight, the son of a half-Cree mother (Angie) and half-Ojibwe father (Eldon), who has been raised by a White farmer (Bunky) near a small logging town called Parson's Gap. From its first page, *Medicine Walk* invites readers to draw associations between Frank's story and a wide history of other kinds of storytelling. As he walks his horse out of the barn in preparation for his journey with his father Eldon, for example, Frank sees the horse's hoofprints: "The tracks looked like inkblots in the seeping melt, and he stood for a moment and tried to imagine the scenes they held" (1). This moment suggests a connection with classic adventures texts from the

Anglo-European literary tradition such as the Arthurian quest romances or Miguel de Cervante's satirical *Don Quixote*. In a more popular vein, there are associations with scenes from wilderness adventure stories by writers like Jack London, and from cowboy stories. Importantly, it is the tracks themselves that tell these stories, which also invites comparisons with non-print traditions of storytelling, such as oral storytelling or another type of story told by tracks: the movement of an animal across a landscape. This is a powerful feature that often recurs in Indigenous fiction, for instance in Louise Erdrich's novel *Tracks* (1988), which weaves together the various dark consequences for a people dispossessed by colonialism from their lands. The opening scene in *Medicine Walk* is a signal to consider how a wide variety of journey storytelling shapes the perception of time, space, and self.

In many ways, *Medicine Walk* echoes the traditional Western heroic monomyth. In the middle part of Frank and Eldon's journey, for example, they find refuge from a storm with Becka, a woman living alone in her dead father's cabin, who makes space for Eldon's first story. In line with the quest romance tradition, Wagamese portrays Becka as a spirit guide, almost a witch: Frank thinks with amusement that she looks like a "gnome" (75). When they leave Becka's place, Frank encounters a frightening "monster" on the trail in the form of a large bear. Like a knight of yore, he must challenge the bear in order to continue. Interestingly, versions of this type of scene also appear in the film adaptation of *Into the Wild* (Penn 2007)—when McCandless (played by Emile Hirsch) comes face to face with a bear—and in Strayed's book *Wild* (91). In all three stories, the lesson is about building strength not by killing another creature but by moving forward in spite of obstacles and fear. As Frank says in *Medicine Walk*, "the only way was forward" (108).

While certain resemblances are clear, Wagamese changes the outline of this mythic narrative. As I have argued above, *Into the Wild*, *Wild*, and other popular adventure stories are stories of personal transformation that implicitly equate the individual conquering the land with a conquest over trauma or disaffection. In contrast, *Medicine Walk* is a story about individuals building relationship with land, trauma, and each other. The settler-colonial outdoor adventure narrative usually adopts the out-and-back rubric of the quest structure: the protagonist or writer leaves home, conquers obstacles, learns something new, and returns a hero (or, in the case of Chris McCandless, not returning makes him a tragic hero). In a way, *Medicine Walk* inverts that structure, and redefines the notion of wilderness because Frank and Eldon's journey is not about moving away from home and into the wilderness only to move out of it again, but about moving towards a sacred centre of land as home. In Wagamese's novel, "the wild" is not an antagonist to be conquered but a collaborator, supporting Frank and his father Eldon physically and emotionally. Settler narratives like Krakauer's and Strayed's erase Indigenous presence and history on the land by leaning on the trope of the "wild" as a seemingly human-free space, and thereby tacitly reaffirm the continued colonial occupation and exploitation of that place. In *Medicine Walk*, the relationship forged between humans and the land reclaims Indigenous rights to land. This replacement is deeply affirmative because it demonstrates the necessity for everyone who lives on any land (namely, *everyone*) to see human-land connections as relational and supportive, not as separate and exploitative.

Medicine Walk is set sometime in the early 1970s (although we can only infer this from the fact that Frank's father, Eldon, fought in the Korean War, which ended in 1953, and Frank, who is now sixteen, was born about five years later). Though the town in which Frank was raised, Parson's Gap, seems to be a fictional location, there is a town called "Parson" in the Columbia Valley in interior British Columbia. The landscape of the novel is similar to Kamloops, the traditional territory of the Tk'emlúpsemc, the people of the confluence, now known as the Tk'emlúps te Secwépemc, where Wagamese lived until the end of his life. Frank's adoptive father Bunky, sometimes referred to simply as "the old man," is a somewhat idealized example of a White settler who loves the land he "owns" and who works with it rather than exploiting it. Bunky does his best to honour Frank's Indigenous heritage, in part by taking him into the backwoods to learn to hunt, forage, and survive in a good way. As Wagamese writes of Frank:

> He was Indian. The old man said it was his way and he'd always taken that for truth. His life had become horseback in solitude, lean-tos cut from spruce, fires in the night, mountain air that tasted sweet and pure as spring water, and trails too dim to see that he learned to follow high to places only cougars, marmots, and eagles knew. (5)

Rather than replicating a social ideology of assimilation, Bunky builds a respectful and mutual relationship with the land and with the Indigenous members of his community whom his colonial assumption of land ownership has displaced. Ultimately, Bunky gives back to Frank some, but not all, of what the younger man has lost to centuries of occupation and racism. One central element of Frank's sense of self that Bunky feels unable to give him is the story of Eldon, Frank's biological father.

In narrative's present, Frank has been called by his dying father to perform a service—namely, to bring Eldon to the back country to die and then to bury him. What follows is the alternating storylines of Frank and Eldon's present-time journey into the wilderness and the gradual unfolding, through Eldon's storytelling, of their past relationship, Eldon's own history, and the story of Frank's origins. Stories and land are integral to building a strong self in relationship with the world and all its beings. Moreover, storytelling itself is embodied, and journeys are one of the most elemental narrative forms to express both restoration and transformation. As Warren Cariou suggests, oral storytelling "'keeps and transforms' the meaning through embodied practices that move from one body to another" (2016, 475). Frank's mother Angie, in a flashback to a time before her death, emphasizes that stories can be both comforting and transformative: they can "calm you down" (191), and "when you share stories, you change things" (203). Frank and Eldon's journey demonstrate this. Their physical journey through the land has a restorative effect for both of them, and in their emotional journey, Eldon's storytelling is key to forging a relationship between father and son. Taken together, these elements make Eldon's passage out of life less painful and more meaningful.

The novel makes other strong connections among land, journeys, stories, and Indigenous place. The first stop on Eldon and Frank's "hike" is an ancient rock painting. When they reach these "symbols painted in dull red, black, and a stark greyish white," Eldon wonders what they mean (68). Frank replies that he imagines them to be stories about travelling, but he also notes that sometimes "'you gotta let a mystery be a mystery for it to give you anything'" (68–69). This moment represents the idea that travelling and storytelling are ways for humans to understand their relationship to existence and to each other. Frank and Eldon's journey is, at the outset, not unlike Strayed's or McCandless's: an attempt to get "away" from personal "malaise" and social "alienation." Driven by alcoholism and abandonment, they look for healing in the woods and mountains. However, though Frank returns alone, they undertake the journey *together*, and what Frank achieves is something more like integration than individuation. Like McCandless and Strayed, though with more knowledge and experience, Frank and Eldon seek healing in being on and in the land. While for McCandless and Strayed, their journeys start as recreational, all of these "characters" find space away from others for re-creation. However, for Frank and Eldon the journey across the land is less about moving away from and more about moving towards a home. Though their literal meaning is mysterious to the men, the paintings fill a gap. Left directly on the land itself, they are signs, from past people to the present, of the continuity of land and story. This restored continuity is mirrored in the relationship between Frank and Eldon, with Eldon's story-telling about his life filling a gap in Frank's knowledge of himself. Maybe most importantly, these paintings are statements—acknowledgment, as it were—of connections between people and land since time immemorial. In honouring this statement from the past, in feeling its pull in the present, Frank and Eldon take their place respectfully on this ground. As Eldon says, he wanted to die out in the land because "'[t]his here's the only place I felt like I belonged'" (150). He is not saying that the land belongs to him, but that he belongs to the land.

The final destination in Eldon and Frank's journey, the ridge where Eldon wants to be buried, though very far away from where they began, is revealed to be a spiritual home. The ridge is deep in the wilderness, the farthest distance from either man's house and the highest point in elevation. In another sense, however, it is close to the heart of existence, a place that Frank went, in younger years, "when it got too noisy in my head" (144). It is also a place that Eldon had been when he was just a year younger than Frank: "'I come here when I was fifteen. . . . Stayed here for two days just sitting on the edge of the cliff looking at it all'" (149). This wild spot, the faint trails, the trees, and streams, are all familiar and welcoming to Frank and Eldon. The outermost point of their trek is actually a homecoming, an embeddedness in place that is materially reinforced when, after two final stories from Eldon, Frank buries his father. In doing so, Frank fulfills his promise to Eldon, and Eldon, in a way, brings closure to a promise of his own. One of the layers of trauma Eldon unpacks for Frank is the story of his role in Jimmy Weaseltail's death when they were soldiers together in the Korean War. Eldon recalls that had had promised to bury Jimmy "in the warrior way": "'Ojibs usedta bury their warriors sat upright in the ground, facin' east where the sun rose'" (160). However, Eldon was never able to fulfill that promise to Jimmy. When Frank buries his father, this also allows for Eldon to close the circle with his dead friend.

Along their journey, Eldon's stories serve as confessions or talk therapy, allowing him to pass out of life peacefully. They also fill in historical gaps or wounds for Frank, allowing him to heal, to be a little less alone. When Eldon makes his burial request to Frank at the outset of the novel, he says that stories are "all I got to give ya." Frank replies, "Ain't never gonna be enough" (23). What Frank learns on this journey, however, is that relationships are not conducted in an exchange economy characterized by claim and debt. Instead, Frank "takes it all in" from his father and finds compassion and love for him despite Eldon's dark past. Rather than being heroically powerful, ascendant, and essentially independent, Frank's alternative kind of heroism consists in being expansive, open, and essentially connected with others. At the same time, Frank realizes that some gaps can never be closed: "His father would die and he would never know his mother. . . . She would remain as shadowed as the trees and rocks and bracken that surrounded him. There was a hole in his history and there was nothing that would ever fill it" (223). The comparison between his lost experience of his mother and the forest shadows around him hint that, though tragic, this gap is another one of those "mysteries," the traces of a story, like the images on the rock face. In many ways, even Eldon's stories, the ones that did fill gaps, leave Frank feeling empty. He notes that he had originally thought that knowing his history "might have filled him but all he felt was emptiness and a fear that there would be nothing else that would fill that void" (232). When he returns to the farm, he tells this to Bunky, which leads to the following exchange:

> "Sometimes when things get taken away from you, it feels like there's a hole at your centre where you can feel the wind blow through, that's sure," the old man said.
> "Whattaya do about that?"
> "Me, I always went to where the wind blows. . . . Don't know as I ever got an answer but it always felt better bein' out there." (244)

Some mysteries are as elemental as the land that breathes life into beings and takes it away again. The wind, the shadows in the forest—these are not just metaphors for unknown and uncontrollable emotional forces. In this conversation, Bunky moves from using the wind as a simile to emphasize the emptiness at the heart of grief to finding solace in *real* wind as a comfort rather than an enhancement of loss.

In *Medicine Walk*, humans and "nature" have porous boundaries. As Robert Bringhurst says in "The Mind of the Wild," "Humans are liminal creatures. We exist on the margins of the wild. The idea that we might exist in perfect bliss entirely within the wild is rich, romantic fiction. The idea that we might ever exist entirely outside the wild is equally fatuous" (2018, 32). Expressing a different dimension of this recognition, Robin Wall Kimmerer points out that "[i]t takes a real effort to remember that it's not just in a wigwam that the earth gives us everything we need. The exchange of recognition, gratitude and reciprocity for these gifts is just as important in a Brooklyn flat as under a birchbark roof" (2013, 240). In *Medicine Walk* there are certainly spaces and places that are more wild, like the backcountry where Frank takes Eldon, and less wild, like the sad, industrial town of Parson's Gap that looks like a "bruise" on the landscape (6). The farm where Frank lives with Bunky is nicely in between the two, and its liminal status is continually reinforced. When Frank leaves the farm to start his journey, he crosses a gradual threshold: "The bush started thin where the grass surrendered at the edge of the field" (4).

Just as "nature" and "culture" are a continuity, not an opposition, so is the individual not a bounded fortress, separate from everything around them. Joni Adamson explains Stacy Alaimo's idea of trans-corporeality as "the idea that the bodies of human and nonhuman species are made up of cells and that organic and inorganic matter can move across sites and through bodies in surprising, unpredictable or even unwanted ways that reveal the interconnections of human bodies with the more-than-human world" (2012, 157). In *Medicine Walk*, the characters are connected to, and in relationship with, each other and the land through embodiment. For example, at the start and end of Frank's journey, he has farewell and welcome-back encounters with Bunky in the barn (itself a liminal space). Frank absorbs the relationship with the elements that make up the space he is in: "There was the smell of leather, liniment, the dry dust of feed, the low stink of mould and manure. He heaved a big breath of it into him" (2). When Bunky embraces Frank after he returns from burying Eldon, Frank "could smell the oil and grease and tobacco on him and it was every smell he recalled growing up with and he closed his eyes and pulled it all into him" (244). Frank is not an individual human who stakes his claim on identity with a fictional boundary between in here and out there. Instead, he takes the world in, and by implication, breathes it back out again. He is a permeable barrier. His apprehension of love and belonging is felt not just as words and named emotions but with every sense.

Let's assume that *Medicine Walk* is a teaching story. What does it teach? Frank's heroic quest is a test of physical strength and courage. He achieves greater wisdom and maturity in overcoming the obstacles along his way. So much is typical of the mythically inclined adventure story, of which *Into the Wild* and *Wild* are prime examples. More than all this though, *Medicine Walk* posits that the hero needs to have their boots on the ground to be grounded. They need to breath the air made by trees to stay alive. And to be fully alive, they need to walk their stories. Frank is not just a better individual in his successful quest; he is a more integrated individual or, rather, he has lost some separation and come into greater connection through bringing his father back into the land. Eldon creates a relationship with Frank by confronting him with a responsibility of care even when he is angry, and Eldon's body literally fills a hole in the land left by the legacies of colonial erasure. By travelling over the land, acknowledging its human history, and integrating the more-than-human elements of place, Frank and Eldon shift the adventure genre from one of human mastery over the wilderness to one of relationship with it. For readers who have absorbed colonial tropes of Western wilderness adventure genres, this story potentially opens a new way of thinking about the work of decolonizing the land under our feet.

WORKS CITED

Adamson, Joni. 2001. *American Indian Literature, Environmental Justice, and Ecocriticism: The Middle Place.* Tucson: University of Arizona Press.

Adamson, Joni. 2012. "Indigenous Literatures, Multinaturalism, and *Avatar*: The Emergence of Indigenous Cosmopolitics." *American Literary History* 24 (1): 143–62.

Bringhurst, Robert. 2018. "The Mind of the Wild." In *Learning to Die: Wisdom in the Age of Climate Crisis*, by Robert Bringhurst and Jan Zwicky, 7–39. Regina: University of Regina Press.

Cariou, Warren. 2016. "Who Is the Text in This Class? Story, Archive and Pedagogy in Indigenous Contexts." In *Learn, Teach, Challenge:*

Approaching Indigenous Literatures, edited by Deanna Reder and Linda Morra, 467–76. Waterloo, ON: Wilfrid Laurier University Press.

Crane, Kylie. 2012. *Myths of Wilderness in Contemporary Narratives: Environmental Postcolonialism in Australia and Canada*. New York: Palgrave McMillan.

Deur, Douglas. 2002. "A Most Sacred Place: The Significance of Crater Lake Among the Indians of Southern Oregon." *Oregon Historical Quarterly* 103 (1): 18–49.

Erdrich, Louise. (1988) 2017. *Tracks*. New York: Harper Perennial.

Groover, Kristina. 1999. "Re-visioning the Wilderness: Adventures of Huckleberry Finn and Ellen Foster." *The Southern Quarterly* 37 (3–4): 187–97.

Henzi, Sarah. 2016. "'Betwixt and Between': Alternative Genres, Languages and Indigeneity." In *Learn, Teach, Challenge: Approaching Indigenous Literatures*, edited by Deanna Reder and Linda Morra, 487–92. Waterloo, ON: Wilfrid Laurier University Press.

Jacobson, Kristin. 2020. *The American Adrenaline Narrative*. Athens, GA: University of Georgia Press.

Johnson-Groh, Mara. 2018. "Jolie Varela on Indigenous Women Hike and the John Muir Trail's Real Name." *Backpacker*, June 10, 2018. https://www.backpacker.com/stories/jolie-varela-indigenous-women-hike.

Justice, Daniel Heath. 2018. *Why Indigenous Literatures Matter*. Waterloo, ON: Wilfrid Laurier University Press.

Kam, Tanya Y. 2015. "Forests of the Self: Life Writing and 'Wild' Wanderings." *Life Writing* 13 (3): 351–71.

Kari, Pricilla Russel. 1987. *Tanaina Plantlore/Dena'ina k'et'una*. Anchorage, AK: Alaska Park Service.

Kimmerer, Robin Wall. 2013. *Braiding Sweetgrass: Indigenous Wisdom, Scientific Knowledge, and the Teachings of Plants*. Minneapolis: Milkwood Editions.

Korteweg, Lisa, and Jan Oakley. 2016. "Eco-heroes Out of Place and Relations: Decolonizing the Narratives of *Into the Wild* and *Grizzly Man* through Land Education." In *Land Education: Rethinking Pedagogies of Place from Indigenous, Postcolonial and Decolonizing Perspectives*, edited by Kate McCoy, Eve Tuck, and Marcia McKenzie, 131–43. Abington, UK: Routledge.

Krakauer, Jon. 1996. *Into the Wild*. New York: Anchor Books.

Nixon, Rob. 2011. *Slow Violence and the Environmentalism of the Poor*. Cambridge, MA: Harvard University Press.

Penn, Sean, dir. 2007. *Into the Wild*. Hollywood: Paramount Vantage.

Pickard, Richard. 2018. "Acknowledgment, Disruption, and Settler-Colonial Ecocriticism." *ISLE: Interdisciplinary Studies in Literature and Environment* 25 (2): 317–26.

Rane, Jordan. 2020. "The Tragic Allure of the 'Into the Wild' Bus." *CNN*, July 3, 2020. https://www.cnn.com/travel/article/alaska-into-the-wild-bus-tourist-allure/index.html.

Raskin, Jonah. 2011. "Calls of the Wild on the Page and Screen: From Jack London and Gary Snyder to Jon Krakauer and Sean Penn." *American Literary Realism* 43 (3): 198–203.

Sanders, Shelley. 2017. "'As Certain as the Sky': Appreciating the Fox, Fascinations and Style of Cheryl Strayed's *Wild*." *South Atlantic Review* 82 (1): 9–21.

Strayed, Cheryl. 2012. *Wild: From Lost to Found on the Pacific Crest Trail*. New York: Vintage Books.

Wagamese, Richard. 2015. *Medicine Walk*. Toronto: Emblem Editions.

Williams, Allison. 2015. "The 'Wild' Effect: How Cheryl Strayed's Memoir Inspires Hikers." *CondorNast Traveller*, April 4, 2015. https://www.cntraveler.com/stories/2015-02-04/the-wild-effect-how-cheryl-strayeds-memoir-inspires-hikers.

Williams, Florence. 2017. *The Nature Fix: Why Nature Makes Us Happier, Healthier, and More Creative*. New York: W. W. Norton.

Part III
Gender, Race, and Class

8

Cory Willard

"Maggie's Own Sphere"
Fly Fishing and Ecofeminism in Ethel Wilson's *Swamp Angel*

*Men claim the easiest spots stand knee-deep in calm dark
water where the trout is proven.*

Audre Lorde, "Fishing the White Water"

When I think of a fly fisher, I think of a middle- to upper-class white male
with a tweed jacket or vest covered in pockets—maybe even smoking a cigar
or pipe. He probably has a distinguished-looking beard, or perhaps an old-
timey moustache. In North America, masculine literary figures like Ernest
Hemingway have contributed a great deal to this image. Almost a century
after Hemingway published his classic short story "Big Two-Hearted River,"
and more than forty years after Norman Maclean published the Pulitzer
Prize–nominated *A River Runs Through It*, the white, male fly fisher archetype endures. Statistically, this archetype has some basis in fact. According
to a report from the Recreational Boating & Fishing Foundation and the
Outdoor Foundation, 73.5% of fly fishers in the United States are white
and 70.4% of them are male (2019, 28). Data from Fisheries and Oceans
Canada suggests that trends in Canada are not much different (2019, 5).

While at first glance these numbers paint the picture one might expect,
the same Recreational Boating & Fishing Foundation report also notes
that in 2018, in recreational angling overall, "female participation numbers reached an all-time high at 17.7 million" (2). Female participation in

angling is on the rise and fly fishing is the fastest growing form of angling. Currently, roughly 1.4 million women fly fish in the United States, which makes up 13% of all female anglers (48, 28). The increase in female anglers is part of a larger demographic shift in recreational fishing, and points to a potential watershed moment in how fly fishing—and fly *fishers*—can be culturally understood.

Women are not new to fly fishing. For starters, the first English-language publication on fly fishing was written by Juliana Berners. Little is known about Berners, but she is believed to have been prioress of the Priory of St. Mary of Sopwell, near the cathedral city of St Albans in Hertfordshire, England. Berners's "The Treatyse of Fysshynge wyth an Angle," published in 1496, features a wealth of information on angling, and fly fishing specifically, including technical matters as well as ethical ones. Furthermore, in the nineteenth century, women such as Mary Orvis Marbury (of Orvis Company fame) and Carrie Gertrude Stevens (inventor of the infamous Grey Ghost fly pattern) revolutionized fly tying in America. Marbury, for example, "was put in charge of . . . creating a book that would set the standard for name and pattern according to location. The landmark *Favorite Flies and Their Histories* was published in 1892. By 1896, there had been nine printings" (American Museum of Fly Fishing, n.d.). The success of this book and Marbury's contribution to fly pattern standardization speak to the far-reaching impact of women in the development of North American fly fishing. As Jen Corinne Brown notes, "angling represented a respectable sport for Victorian women, as long as they maintained proper gender boundaries (hence the vast number of early photographs of women in dresses, skirts, and other seemingly inappropriate fishing garb). Women anglers also contributed to sporting periodicals, wrote books, and ran fly-tying businesses, giving them authority within the sport" (2015, 17).

The more recent contributions of women to fly fishing are equally impressive. In the mid-twentieth century, Joan Salvato Wulff was responsible for numerous innovations in the art of fly casting and fly fishing instruction and is personally responsible for much of the terminology and technique used in modern fly casting. In fact, her "demystification of the fly cast" earned her twenty awards as well as places in both the International Game Fish Association's Hall of Fame and the American Casting Association's Hall of Fame (Fogt 2017). Wulff was also a champion competition angler many times over, winning her first state championship in New Jersey at the age of sixteen, and going on to win seventeen national titles by 1960 (Fogt 2017). More recently, teenaged Maxine McCormick, dubbed "The Mozart of Fly Casting" in a 2018 *New York Times* article by Shelby Pope, had captured back-to-back world titles by the age of fourteen, outscoring sixty-one-year-old Steve Rajeff, widely "considered the best fly caster of all time." The simple truth is that, while underacknowledged, the influence of women is all over the history and development of fly fishing.

Like these historical and contemporary examples, Ethel Wilson's novel *Swamp Angel* (1954) provides a valuable illustration of the way the "masculine" sport of fly fishing can be a productive site of personal change and fulfillment for women. The novel, set sometime in the early 1950s, tells the story of Maggie Vardoe (later Maggie Lloyd, after her deceased first husband), a woman looking for a way out of a loveless and oppressive marriage to Edward Vardoe. Fly fishing becomes central to Maggie's escape. After saving up money earned by tying and selling flies, Maggie enlists the help of Joey, a Chinese cab driver, to get out of Vancouver and away from Edward. She ends up in interior British Columbia, at Three Loon Lake (possibly based on Loon Lake in south-central British Columbia), and begins working at a failing fishing lodge owned by the Gunnarsens. The lodge is Haldar Gunnarsen's dream. His wife, Vera, thinks they should abandon it. Maggie, armed with her experience running a fishing lodge back east with her father, saves Three Loon Lake lodge and Haldar's dream along with it. Maggie's success afflicts Vera with immense jealousy—the only major conflict in Maggie's new community. All the while, Maggie continues to exchange letters with her friend Nell Severance back in Vancouver.

Ethel Wilson has stated that she included fly fishing in *Swamp Angel* simply because she loved it. Fly fishing, she says, is "a marvelous thing in life, unique in the deep communion of the senses and rich in contemplation and memory" (1987, 87). Even though the term had yet to be invented, Wilson's view of fly fishing has strong connections to ecofeminist concepts of embodiment and self-actualization. Additionally, Wilson's words call to mind the concept of "flesh," important to understandings of phenomenological embodiment. Jennifer McWeeny argues that "the ontological concept of flesh allows us to affirm the relationality and complexity of lived experience, which does not present beings as either mind or body, active or passive, self or other, oppressed or privileged, but as both of these aspects at the same time" (2014, 277). Considering Wilson's view of fly fishing as something both contemplative and experiential/embodied, as something embedded in both the past and the contemplated future, fly fishing stands out as a rich site for ecofeminist theory.

The overarching concept in ecofeminist theory is that there is a connection between the oppression of women and the destructive treatment of the environment and non-human animals. Catriona Sandilands sums it up thus: "[B]roadly speaking, ecofeminism is a movement and a current of analysis that attempts to link feminist struggles with ecological struggles; the range of possibilities within this general mandate is, therefore, considerable" (1999, xvi). Ecofeminism adds to traditional feminist concerns of gender and equality a concern for the relationship between humans and nature. As Stephanie Lahar says, "ecofeminism sees as destructive not only the perceptual distancing and isolation of different peoples from each other, but also the habits of dualistic thought that separate human society from nature." She adds that "the human/nature dualism is crucial to address and redress, since it is so fundamental, underlying and undermining our relations to the world around us and to that which is embodied and unmediated within ourselves" (1993, 96). The separation of nature from culture and human from animal creates a division that not only allows for exploitation, but also deprives us of the embodied and unmediated richness of the world. "When we set ourselves apart from nature," Lahar argues, "we disembody human experience and sever it from an organic context," which not only has implications on a systems level, but on an individual level as well (96).

In *Swamp Angel*, Maggie seeks to repair her life by connecting to, and embedding herself in, natural processes. She does this, in the first instance, by entering what Canadian literary scholars often term the "pseudo-wilderness." Whereas Canadian settler mythology portrays the "real" wilderness as a dangerous, untamed, and uncivilized place to be conquered, the pseudo-wilderness is a place that is still more or less "wild," but that has markings of civilization—for instance, a fishing lodge, a logging camp, or a forest/mountain/river valley that is accessible from a town or city. In "Women in the Wilderness," Heather Murray argues that "it is the notion of the 'pseudo-wilderness' in both literature and popular belief, and the resultant ways of viewing the land and its values, that have facilitated the acceptance of women authors insofar as their works display themes and scenes seen as distinctly Canadian" (1986, 63). The same is true of the spaces themselves: while the "real" wilderness is, in the Canadian cultural consciousness, masculine-coded in many respects, the pseudo-wilderness, with its various trappings of Canadian character and civility, is a culturally acceptable, if not exactly typical, place for women. In many ways, the pseudo-wilderness has the effect of deconstructing the wilderness-civilization binary and complicating the masculine-feminine one because it allows women to take on masculine-coded activities.

As Murray notes, "pseudo-wilderness may function as a ground for transcendental experience even when a true wilderness is available or accessible" (1986, 64), something that is certainly true in *Swamp Angel*. In this sense, most "wilderness" is pseudo-wilderness and, therefore, matches up well with contemporary views of nature. As Lahar argues,

> there is not a place in the world that does not reveal the touch and bear the consequences of human hands and minds—not Antarctica, not the deepest equatorial jungle, and certainly not Tokyo or New York City. At the same time, there are no people who have not been shaped by the effects of landscape and water, the climate and natural features of the area in which they live. (1993, 91)

Swamp Angel emphasizes the power of place to influence individual consciousness in various ways. When Wilson writes of Joey's visit to Three Loon Lake, for example, she suggests that the area imparts a very different type of energy than that of the city of Vancouver:

> As he sat on the verandah, replete and still, Joey was aware of some enormous difference. This stillness. So it would be like this, would it? His restless eyes ranged the lake, the shores. Joey did not yet know Time that flowed smoothly, as in this place. In all of his life Time had jerked by with a rat-tat-tat, with the beating of a clock, with shrill cries to come to supper, with the starting up of an engine, with the slamming of doors, with the change of radio programme, with the traffic, with the voices, the fire engine, the change of the traffic lights, separately and all together. He did not think of these things, but it was their absence that made the enormous difference. (108)

While Wilson does not necessarily make a moral distinction between the serene beauty of the lake and the bustling, chaotic energy of Vancouver, she does stress the ways in which place becomes part of a person, their energy, and the way they view the world. This stress on the power of place is evident in an often quoted passage about meetings:

> A first meeting. A meeting in the desert, a meeting at sea, meeting in the city, meeting at night, meeting at a grave, meeting in the sunshine beside the forest, beside water. Human beings meet, yet the meetings are not the same. Meeting partakes in its very essence not only of the persons but of the place of meeting. And that essence of place remains, and colours, faintly, the association, perhaps for ever. (75)

The places in which experiences (or meetings) occur are foundational and cannot, it seems, be separated from the developed meaning.

Along these lines, journeys into the pseudo-wilderness are often designed to encounter "the ultimate accessibility of the wilderness state of mind," something the individual takes with them and has continual access to long after the encounter has passed (Murray 1986, 66). Maggie's journey in *Swamp Angel* is certainly of this kind. In seeking to repair her life by a journey into pseudo-wilderness, Maggie repeats a pattern that David Stouck sees throughout Wilson's work:

> The recurrent story in Ethel Wilson's fiction is that of a woman who withdraws from familiar surroundings and sets out on a lonely quest of self-discovery. This woman usually has no mother and, deprived of this intimate bond of family, must establish on her own a link with the larger human community. In isolation she discovers the world is not benign and orderly, but chaotic, ruthlessly shaped by accident and chance; that the larger vision of life's purpose and interconnectedness is not easily achieved and must be actively sought. (1982, 6)

The narrative of *Swamp Angel* brings these notions of the power of wilderness and the interconnections of society and gender together through the main plot: Maggie leaving her husband and the city of Vancouver (a socio-cultural role and an urban space) for the interior of British Columbia where, through working at a fishing lodge (a pseudo-wilderness), she goes through the process of wanting to have no obligations outside of herself to wanting to be a part of a community of her own choosing.

Fly fishing is a key part of Maggie's journey. For starters, it is through the art of tying flies that Maggie is able to save up and hide away the money required to leave her husband in the first place. Living at a time when white, middle-class women were largely homemakers, it is through this angling-related skill that Maggie escapes the economic structures that trapped so many other women. Wilson writes that Maggie "had been most vulnerable and desperate when, more than a year ago, she had taken a small box of fishing flies to the shop known by sportsmen up and down the Pacific coast" (14). When she does so, her flies are scrutinized by the shop owner, Mr. Spencer, who "looked for flaws in the perfection of the body, the hackle, the wings," but found none (14). Despite the eyebrow-raising secrecy with which Maggie wants to come and go and receive feathers for tying, Mr. Spencer sets her up to sell flies through the shop, which ultimately sets her on the course of freedom from her controlling and loveless marriage. Through mastery in a "masculine" discipline, Maggie can escape or transcend her oppressive situation.

When Maggie sneaks off and leaves her husband, all she takes with her is a canvas bag "packed to a weight that she could carry," a "haversack that she could carry on her shoulders," and "her fishing rod" (14–16). Considering this woman is so desperate to leave her husband that she would carry out a meticulous plan to sneak off unannounced with so few possessions, it is telling that her fishing rod would be one of the essentials. Repeatedly throughout the journey, before finally taking her role running the lodge at Three Loon Lake, numerous men and women inquire if she is "going fishing," so much so that we begin to understand they find it surprising for a woman to do so. Yet Maggie always responds pleasantly that indeed she is. In "The Gendered 'Nature' of the Urban Outdoors: Women Negotiating Fear of Violence," Wesely and Gaarder argue that outdoor "sport is an institution through which hegemonic masculinity (Connell 1987) is maintained, and its significance lies in the fact that 'masculinizing and feminizing practices associated with the body are at the heart of the social construction' of gender identity" (2004, 646). They note that "as children, a powerful mechanism through which boys learn to perform masculinity is by using their bodies in skilled, forceful ways, while girls learn to circumscribe their movements and limit their strengths" (646). These are the types of social forces that women fly fishers, including Maggie, struggle against. Engaging with fly fishing can become an embodied form of self-empowerment: a contemplative and embodied outdoor activity that is relatively accessible to women who have been socialized in such ways and that can help them see possibilities beyond these social expectations. In the film *Stepping into the Stream* (Klutinis 2010), Jean Williams ponders the physical side of fly fishing, noting that it is "a very sensual sport. It engages all of your senses as far as taste, touch, smell, hearing, sight, but there's also a part of it that's very much a primitive, instinctive part of your soul." She adds that "you can come to this sport at any time of your life. Part of the aesthetic of the sport is, really, anyone can do it," and perhaps part of the value of fly fishing as an element of personal growth is this promise of rich, embodied sensuality without the need for extensive athleticism.

Fly fishing serves to prepare and purify Maggie for the transformation she is about to undergo in the pseudo-wilderness. During the journey that ultimately ends up at Three Loon Lake, Maggie has the bus driver let her off on the side of the road near the Similkameen River. The first view of the Similkameen River—a real river in south-central British Columbia—provides the opportunity for one of Wilson's evocative landscape descriptions:

> When she first saw the Similkameen River, the dancing river with the dancing name, it was a broad mountain stream of light blue that was silver in the bright morning, and of a silver that was blue. There was a turn in the road, and crowded sombre jackpines hid the Similkameen River. There was another turn, and the river flowed laughing beside the road again. Across the rapid moving river was the forest of lodge-pole pine. Shafts of sunlight smote the first trees and they stood out against the sombreness and denseness of the forests behind them. Maggie looked at, but she could not look into the pine forest, for it was sealed in its density and blackness. The Similkameen River, of fairly uniform breadth, ran blue and silver and alive, level and life-giving past the forests. (37)

The shafts of light and light-giving waters of Wilson's description echo with religious significance. These landscapes become important because, as many Canadian writers at the turn of the twentieth century believed, the Canadian wilderness has the power to shape human character. Different ways of relating to the wilderness shape people in different ways—and perhaps even have the ability to break down oppressive dichotomies that organize their understanding of the world.

It is with Maggie alone, during this encounter with the "dancing river with the dancing name" that is "level and life-giving," that we get the first scene of fly fishing in the novel. Immediately before the stop at the Similkameen, Maggie worries about being overtaken by her husband Edward Vardoe. Up to this point, Edward has loomed over her in the "endured humiliations and almost unbearable resentments" that began soon after their marriage as she lay "humiliated and angry" (13, 16). While it is not explicitly stated that her sexual experiences at the beginning of her marriage with Edward Vardoe were forced or violent, it is abundantly clear that they were not desired or pleasurable. However, "in the pleasure of casting over this lively stream she forgot—as always when she was fishing—her own existence" (38). Once Maggie begins the embodied act of fly fishing, things begin to change for her. As Wesely and Gaarder note, "at the very least, being physically active allows women to be in their bodies in ways that can be qualitatively different from the traditional sexual and reproductive constructs of female physicality" (2004, 647). As Maggie begins to take self-assured control of her own body by stepping into the natural system of the Similkameen River, the language surrounding her experience of the world begins to change. As she fishes, no longer fretting about potential miscalculations in her escape,

> [s]uddenly came a strike, and the line ran out, there was a quick radiance and splashing above the water downstream. At the moment of the strike, Maggie became a co-ordinating creature of wrists and fingers and reel and rod and line and tension and the small trout, leaping, darting, leaping. She landed the fish, took out the hook, slipped in her thumb, broke back the small neck, and the leaping rainbow thing was dead. (38)

Through fly fishing and its attendant embodiment, Maggie is removed from a state of psychological stress to a lively state of sensuous embodiment. Richard Twine argues that "embodiment is of fundamental importance to ecofeminism. Historically, the human body, as a constant reminder of our organic embeddedness, has been the location of the intersection between both the mastery of nature and nature-associated peoples" (2011, 32). This passage emphasizes the bodily nature of fly fishing, but also involves what Alexandra Collins calls a "vengeful moment" where Maggie enacts "rituals of self-purification" (1982, 65–66). In considering the impact of this scene, Murray writes that "to herself and to the narrator she is dead as Maggie Vardoe, and henceforth will be known as 'Maggie Lloyd' or simply 'Maggie'" and refers to what is to come as a "resurrection" into a "new life" (1985, 243). Fly fishing allows Maggie to translate the stress, anxiety, and anger of her marriage (destructive feelings) toward the useful action of obtaining food and exercise (productive feelings) in preparation for starting over.

The value of fly fishing is related to place—the river—in which fly fishing occurs. The river, *Swamp Angel* suggests, is a sacred place: "Maggie walked down to the margin of the river as in an enchantment. The pine-needle earth felt soft. She set down her things, gazed up and down the stream, sat down, and then lay down, looking up at the sky. . . . She gave herself up to the high morning" (37). Purged of her anger and fear through the killing of the trout, and perhaps symbolically killing her past self (or her oppressive husband), Maggie can now enter a state of calm. After catching and killing the first fish, "Maggie drew in her line and made some beautiful casts. The line curved shining through the air backwards forwards backwards forwards, gaining length, and the fly dropped sweetly. Again she cast and cast. Her exhilaration settled down to the matter of fishing" (38). This "matter of fishing," as Wilson dubs it, calls to mind the transcendental or meditative quality writers often give to fly fishing. The repetitive and ritualistic motions, coupled with the necessary attention, seem uniquely capable of putting the practitioner in a Zen-like flow state, in the realm beyond words. Through fly fishing, practitioners experience what Sandilands calls a "web of relations and experiences so complicated and diverse that it defies linguistic appropriation and can only be experienced as strange and wonderful" (1999, 200). Achieving this meditative state where the self seems to melt away is what often inspires writers to put fly fishing in religious terms, and yet it just as easily fits Sandilands' notions of wild nature as beyond human language.

The only other activity that seems to have the same transcendental quality for Maggie is swimming alone in Three Loon Lake. Wilson introduces another spiritual element, writing that Maggie's avatar, a divine presence, "tells her that she is one with her brothers the seal and the porpoise who tumble and tumble in the salt waves" (99). This creates a connection to both embodied animality and to the crisis of meaning in life that Maggie is attempting to solve. Through the swim, Maggie works through her resistance to society, asking, "Who would not be a seal or porpoise? They have a nice life, lived in the cool water with fun and passion, without human relations, Courtesy Week, or a flame thrower" (100). In swimming, Maggie is transformed. It is specifically because she is a strong swimmer that she realizes she can endure. She is resilient. Just like the transcendental moments of fly fishing where crises of both past and future flow away in the current, Maggie swims "strongly out into the lake, forgetting past and future, thrusting the pleasant water with arms and legs" (100). In this forgetting, Maggie realizes "[s]he is not a seal. She is a god floating there with the sun beating down on her face with fatal beneficent warmth, and the air is good" (100). It is in the embodied moment of swimming, taking in the world through the senses and becoming one with the water, that Maggie is able to further recognize her own inner strength—her godliness.

The embodied oneness of the swim is an ecologically important realization. As McWeeny notes, "We are always already immersed in bodily relationships with one another. We are always already affecting and being affected, sensing and being sensed, touching and being touched. . . . However, this relationality is not homogeneity; that one's flesh is the material site of infinite and varied configurations of relation makes it radically particular" (2014, 277). While every living thing may be entangled to some degree, the entanglement of Maggie with Edward Vardoe through the bonds of marriage was stifling. Becoming one with aquatic systems through fly fishing and then through swimming, however, is not. This entanglement allows Maggie to move beyond her trauma into a more productive web of interconnections:

> There was this extra feeling about the swim: Maggie's life had so long seemed stagnant that—now that she had moved forward and found her place with other people again, servicing other people again, humouring other people, doing this herself, alone, as a swimmer swims, this way or that way, self-directed or directed by circumstance—Maggie thought sometimes it's like swimming; it is very good, it's nice, she thought, this new life, servicing other people as I did years ago with Father; but now I am alone and, like a swimmer, I have to make my own way on my own power. Swimming is like living, it is done alone. . . . I will swim past obstacles . . . because I am a strong swimmer. (99)

Fly fishing allows Maggie to banish the horrific feeling that Edward might be pursuing her. Similarly, this swim allows her to gather the resolve necessary to enter and navigate a web of human relationships by choice—an extension of the environmental and ecological themes Wilson introduced previously through Maggie's purification process of fly fishing.

For Wilson, the character, or notion, of the fly fisher is just as uniquely situated within the realm of environmental experience as the act of fly fishing itself. Wilson draws upon the necessity of experience and the power of communing with place to explain the relationship between fly fisher, fly fishing, and the more-than-human world. The second fly fishing scene centres not on Maggie but on a seventy-five-year-old American man named R. B. Cunningham who ventures off alone onto the lake "according to his own private system" (133). Wilson's narrator illustrates this episode through a rumination on fishing and fly fishers:

> There is a mystique in fishing which only the fly-fisherman (a
> dedicated sort of person, or besotted) knows anything about.
> All fly-fishermen are bound closely together by the strong desire
> to be apart, solitary upon the lake, the stream. A fisherman has
> not proceeded far up the lake, not out of sight of the lodge, before
> he becomes one with the aqueous world of the lake, of a sky
> remarkable for change, of wind which (deriving from the change-
> ful sky) rises or falls, disturbing the water, dictating the direction
> of his cast, and doing something favourable or unfavourable to the
> fish. (133)

While this passage is about Cunningham setting out on the lake alone, the language is also general, indicating qualities applying broadly to fly fishers. Maggie's journey is also one that is undertaken alone through private moments fly fishing on the Similkameen River and swimming in solitude on Three Loon Lake. Beyond solitude and personal resoluteness, this language of unity and directed attention is not unlike the episodes of Maggie's fly fishing and swimming earlier in the novel. When Maggie fly fishes, she is so overcome with her "matter of fishing" that she able to put aside deeply held traumas. When she goes swimming, she goes beyond psychological unity or attention and quite literally enters "the aqueous world" and its web of interconnections. Fly fishers, the novel suggests, have this ability to transgress the human-nature boundary and dissolve into interconnection with the environment, an ecological existence.

Wilson furthers this notion in her description of Cunningham's outing:

> He is sometimes aware of the extraordinary beauty, majesty, of
> the clouds, white or angry, which roll up in that weather breeder,
> that sky not far above, which caps the lake and him. . . . He does
> not look too long (for he is fishing) but the green and the greens,
> the blue, the sombre, the white, the deceptive glamour of the lake
> surface enter into this mystique of fishing and enhance it, and they
> enter into him too, because he is part of it. There is no past, no
> future, only the now. (133–34)

Due to the contemplative nature of fly fishing and the attention paid by the fly fisher, it is not long before the boundaries of place and individual begin to erode. While the fly fisher surely enjoys the aesthetic beauty of Three Loon Lake, or any other beloved place for that matter, Wilson suggests that through the act of fly fishing—through the repetition, the solitude, the attention paid—one becomes "part of" the place. The power of the lake does not simply please Cunningham; it enters him and is a part of him. Of particular note is the dissolving of time into a single, embodied moment: "no past, no future, only the now." This description of Cunningham's inner fly fishing experience stresses the power of fly fishing as an embodied practice that values connection. For both Cunningham and Maggie, fly fishing casts a person beyond the aesthetic or the Other. There is a moment of convergence between person and place that renders purely rational conceptions of time, individual, human, and non-human fluid and embodied, likely leaving both person and place changed.

Cunningham is portrayed in the novel as enterprising, masculine, and well-respected. Haldar Gunnarsen says, "that old fella" possesses "fear-lessness," and for the narrator, his trip out on the lake alone represents his indifference to "opposition from man, market, or weather" (133). Despite Cunningham's rugged masculinity—an aspect of the classic fly fisher archetype—it is Maggie who plays the proverbial role of hero to the dam-sel in distress when Cunningham, exhausted and hypothermic, is struggling to row his way back to shore. In this moment, Maggie recognizes him not as "*the* Mr. Cunningham" that everyone at the lodge so reveres, but only as "someone in need" (136). Cunningham, "[a]s independent as a mountain"

(136), is not used to asking for help, but knows that, despite his status, "he had been near the point where Being touched Non-Being, and that if the wharf had been fifty yards farther off, he would no doubt have died—unless, of course, this Mrs. Lloyd," that is, Maggie, "had come for him" (137). In an attempt to repay Maggie for saving his life, Cunningham sends·her some fine china and a lucrative job offer away from Three Loon Lake. Maggie accepts the china but declines the job. She does not need rescuing; she is a "strong swimmer" that can "swim past obstacles" (99), and she has dedicated herself to her chosen place in spite of them.

Ultimately, in *Swamp Angel*, fly fishing functions as a path to female independence and a way to productively interact with place and other people. In the novel, as Heather Murray argues, "the wilderness aids comprehension and mastery of the self, but it also holds out the dangerous and attractive lure of a selfless existence to those who choose to enter the wilderness permanently rather than contact and then leave it" (1985, 244). For Maggie, it is through leaving her unhappy marriage in urban Vancouver and travelling to the pseudo-wilderness of Three Loon Lake in interior British Columbia that she is able to gain independence and self-assurance: the "tormented nights of humiliations between four small walls and in the compass of a double bed" are now gone, "washed away by this air, this freedom, this joy, this singleness and forgetfulness" (96). She does not choose a selfless existence, but instead re-enters a meaningful community of her own choosing. In the liminal space of this pseudo-wilderness, "the camp's simultaneous isolation and community provide the setting and motivation for Maggie's resolution of the responsibility of self to others" (Murray 1985, 244).

The novel also uses fly fishing as a means for Maggie to her assert a mastery of self through coordinated embodiment. What she enacts, effectively, is an escape from a hierarchical version of gender and the body to a more democratic and ecological one. This is further shown in her interactions with Cunningham, another fly fisher, seen by other men as a paragon of masculinity. In saving him, Maggie asserts her value and capability, qualities she has already demonstrated many times. It is through fly tying that Maggie secures the economic means to leave her husband Edward Vardoe. It is through her knowledge of fly fishing and fishing lodges that she establishes herself as indispensable to the Gunnarsens and their guests.

The one conflict that stands in Maggie's way is the jealousy of Vera Gunnarsen, who is envious of Maggie's ability to turn the business around and afraid that Maggie will steal her husband Haldar (even though Maggie has shown absolutely no desire to do so). In reality, it is not only Vera's jealousy, but her inability to see beyond gendered expectations that causes such a rift between her and Maggie. Maggie's friend Nell suggests that Maggie sever ties with the Gunnarsen's over this difficulty and take Cunningham up on his job offer: "Leave these tiresome people. Go to that man Cunningham's. Are they really your affair?" To this question, Maggie simply responds, "Yes" (152). Although she would have been justified in taking the opportunity to run from her troubles at Three Loon Lake, Maggie faces the conflict head-on. As an attempt at reconciliation, she creates a new variation of a Coachman fly, which she dubs the "Little Vera." Unveiling this fly gives Maggie a chance to be vulnerable with the Gunnarsens and share more about her past. In the long run, this makes it possible for Maggie to remain an important member of her community.

Sandilands articulates a big-picture argument that I see as relevant to big-picture thinking about fly fishing and works of fly fishing literature like *Swamp Angel*: "[T]o heal the wounds between nature and culture, between men and women, between mind and body, between reason and emotion, it is necessary to challenge dominant dualistic traditions of Western thought and to replace them with a more integrated or holistic understanding, one that emphasizes the interconnections among various aspects of human and nonhuman life" (1999, 195). Even though fly fishing is historically grounded in a white, predominantly male, leisure class, the literature of fly fishing has the potential to break down these dualistic barriers. By examining fly fishing literature and texts by women, we can see how women have navigated relationships with both masculine spaces and the natural world. In *Swamp Angel*, we watch as fly fishing transforms Maggie Vardoe, allowing her to communicate with her own body and with the world around her in new, meaningful, and less prescriptive ways than were possible in Vancouver, where she begins. This type of communication is what Sandilands might call a "mutant language"—an interaction that fills the "space between human and nonhuman animal sociality" (1999, 184). Fly fishing, I argue, is one such language.

American Museum of Fly Fishing. n.d. "Mary Orvis Marbury (1856–1914)." Accessed March 22, 2023. https://www.amff.org/portfolio/graceful-rise -yesterday/agr-mary-orvis-marbury/.

Brown, Jen Corinne. 2015. *Trout Culture: How Fly Fishing Forever Changed the Rocky Mountain West*. Seattle: University of Washington Press.

Collins, Alexandra. 1982. "Who Shall Inherit the Earth? Ethel Wilson's Kinship with Wharton, Glasgow, Gather, and Ostenso." *The Ethel Wilson Symposium*, edited by Lorraine McMullen, 61–72. Ottawa: University of Ottawa Press.

Fogt, Jan. 2017. "Virtuoso." *Anglers Journal*, May 16, 2017. https://www .anglersjournal.com/freshwater/virtuoso.

Klutinis, Barbara, dir. 2010. *Stepping Into the Stream*. San Francisco, CA: Klufilms.

Lahar, Stephanie. 1993. "Roots: Rejoining Natural and Social History." In *Ecofeminism*, edited by Greta Gaard, 91–117. Philadelphia: Temple University Press. http://www.jstor.com/stable/j.ctt14bt5pf.7.

McWeeny, Jennifer. 2014. "Topographies of Flesh: Women, Nonhuman Animals, and the Embodiment of Connection and Difference." *Hypatia* 29 (2): 269–86. https://doi.org/10.1111/hypa.12087.

Murray, Heather. 1985. "Metaphor and Metonymy, Language and Land in Ethel Wilson's *Swamp Angel*." *Journal of Postcolonial Writing* 25 (2): 241–52. https://doi.org/10.1080/17449858508588945.

Murray, Heather. 2013. "Women in the Wilderness (1986)." In *Greening the Maple: Canadian Ecocriticism in Context*, edited by Ella Soper and Nicholas Bradley, 61–81. Calgary: University of Calgary Press.

Pope, Shelby. 2018. "The Mozart of Fly Casting." *New York Times*, August 19, 2018. https://www.nytimes.com/2018/08/19/sports/maxine -mccormick.html.

Recreational Boating & Fishing Foundation and The Outdoor Foundation. 2019. *2019 Special Report on Fishing*. Alexandria, VA: Recreational Boating & Fishing Foundation; Boulder, CO: The Outdoor Foundation. https://asafishing.org/wp-content/uploads/2019/07/2019-Special-Report-on -Fishing_RBFF_FINAL.pdf.

Sandilands, Catriona. 1999. *The Good-Natured Feminist: Ecofeminism and the Quest for Democracy*. Minneapolis: University of Minnesota Press.

Stouck, David. 1982. "Introduction." In *Swamp Angel*, by Ethel Wilson. New Canadian Library Classic edition. Toronto: McClelland & Stewart.

Twine, Richard T. 2001. "Ma(r)king Essence: Ecofeminsim and Embodiment." *Ethics & The Environment* 6 (2): 31–58. https://www.jstor.org/stable/40339012.

Wesely, Jennifer K., and Emily Gaarder. 2004. "The Gendered 'Nature' of the Urban Outdoors: Women Negotiating Fear of Violence." *Gender and Society* 18 (5): 645–63. https://www.jstor.org/stable/4149423.

Wilson, Ethel. (1954) 1982. *Swamp Angel*. Toronto: Macmillan. New Canadian Library Classic edition, Toronto: McLelland & Stewart.

Wilson, Ethel. 1987. "Somewhere Near the Truth." In *Ethel Wilson: Stories, Essays, and Letters*, edited by David Stouck, 81–90. Vancouver: University of British Columbia Press.

9

Veronika Schuchter

"Don't Expect Rodeo to Be a Sweet Sport"

Ambiguity, Spectacle, and Cowgirls in Aritha van Herk's *Stampede and the Westness of West*

"This west, the story goes, is a real place," opens the last piece in Aritha van Herk's prose poetry collection *Stampede and the Westness of West* (2016, 92). The quotation encapsulates the mythical qualities "the West" occupies within the Canadian imagination. Writing the stories of this "real place" has been a central occupation of much of van Herk's oeuvre (see Roberts 2010; Polić 2016). For example, van Herk's earliest novels, *Judith* (1978), *The Tent Peg* (1981), and *No Fixed Address* (1986), were feminist literary undertakings that opened western Canada to women's stories by challenging the male-dominated concept of the rogue. Since 2000, van Herk has increasingly focused her literary efforts on localized explorations of history, especially of her home province, Alberta. Her *Mavericks: An Incorrigible History of Alberta* (2001) has become a staple reference book for the history of the western Canadian province and has inspired a permanent exhibition at the Glenbow Museum in Calgary. In her collaborative projects with photographer George Webber, *In This Place: Calgary 2004–2011* (2011) and *Prairie Gothic* (2013), van Herk explores the urban and rural configurations of Alberta as well as the tensions and hesitations between place and settler.

Stampede and the Westness of West continues van Herk's exploration of the "real place" of the west with an imaginative response to the urban spectacle of the Calgary Stampede. Through fifty-six prose poems, the products of van Herk's artistic residence at the Stampede in 2012, the author considers the embodied performance of urban and rural rituals during the annual ten-day event traditionally held in July. During her artistic residency, van Herk took on the role of the observer, witnessing the spectacle where she would "inhale the flavour, pay attention, look behind the bleachers and behind closed doors" as she filled her notebooks. She describes the resulting collection as offering neither "critique" nor "total praise" of the Stampede, but rather an exploration of the event's cultural and historical significance, especially for those who call Calgary home. The book's title reflects van Herk's resistance to essentializing "the west or the westness of the Stampede celebration." For her, the Stampede ultimately "distills how we try to understand our connection to the land, our place within it, our connection to the sky, the weather, and all the other generous and renegade parts of our city" (van Herk 2016b). But this distillation is ambiguous: it positions the Stampede between historical authenticity and hedonic spectacle, between cultural preservation and cultural creation, between beloved festival and despised inconvenience. Van Herk draws out the many tensions at the heart of Stampede without taking sides, revealing the complex ways in which Calgarians relate to and find meaning in the event. In this chapter, I follow the prose poetry collection's mode of ambiguity. I analyze this mode as a generative way to allow space for multiplicity and double meaning, but I also view this ambiguity critically as a way of not taking a position in the face of systemic oppression and exclusion. The chapter's first two sections interrogate *Stampede*'s playful engagement with the Calgary Stampede, specifically in terms of its complex relationship with authenticity and the ways in which its main sporting event, rodeo, includes as much as it excludes. In the final section, I turn to the fascinating stories of several female rodeo athletes as well as rodeo's history of both reproducing and defying traditional gender roles. Ultimately, *Stampede and the Westness of West* offers a multi-faceted and somewhat ambiguous portrait of rodeo that, like the book's larger portrait of the Stampede, casts important light on the culture and history of western Canada.

The collection's first piece, "The dreaming," charts the Stampede as an inevitable event that has become a fixture in Calgarian life: "Stampede coming. A certain anniversary that will arrive despite resistance / or annoyance, despite the strange thrum of 'until.' Not tomorrow, but / always in the seventh month, the off-centre pivot of the year turning on its axis, saturnalia biding its time" (11). Here, the event is presented as an unavoidable part of the Calgarian social calendar that occurs every year, whether it is loved or loathed by locals. The piece humorously suggests that no matter how locals feel about the Stampede, it is central to their identity: "Some say / you're not a true Calgarian until you leave town to avoid the Stampede" (11). The importance of the Stampede to Calgarians' self-concept, whether in terms of attending or avoiding the event, is in fact not a recent development but has accompanied the event since its inception in 1912.

Questions of identity, self-transformation, and authenticity were front of mind for Guy Weadick, the Stampede's founder, when he first held the event in Calgary. Weadick himself was born on the east coast of the United States and although he organized the first Calgary Stampede in 1912, he didn't permanently settle in Calgary until 1920. There, he became a passionate advocate for the history, traditions, and stories of western Canada. Ellen Kelm argues that Weadick envisioned the Stampede as a multi-day, community-oriented event that would allow Albertans to connect with their collective, western history and, more than this, "eventually contribute to their distinctive identity within Canada" (2009, 715). In this endeavour, the concept of authenticity became a key element: Weadick rejected the supposed inauthenticity of American Wild West shows, which he perceived to be "staged exaggerations" (Foran 2009, 254), and aimed to depict cowboy lifestyles "more accurately" through his curation of the Stampede. One might question Weadick's claims about the authenticity of the Stampede considering his practice of hiring predominantly American cowboys and his own origins in the States, but for Weadick, a key aspect of western authenticity was adaptation, the ability to transform oneself in order to survive what was, at least for recent settlers to the area, a new environment, a new climate, a new way of living (Kelm 2009, 717). Weadick "personified the promise of the West as a place of transformation" (715) and was a "genuine Westerner" according to his own definition: "If you live in Calgary—you are a Westerner—it does not matter how long you have been here" (in Kelm 2009, 729). Through the Stampede, Weadick was, in effect, "making himself over into a local" (728) while at the same time offering "authenticity to all who, like himself, had been transformed by the West" (729).

Several of van Herk's pieces in *Stampede* pick up on the ambiguity of the Stampede's relationship to authenticity, transformation, and identity, in particular by exploring the purpose of the event. For example, she dedicates a three-page piece to Weadick in which she explores his aspirations as a writer and his keen interest in preserving the stories of the Canadian west and its ranching and rodeo traditions. The piece explores how he came to Alberta by chance and how the place piqued his interest, highlighting the perceived western authenticity that would ultimately tempt him to stay and transform local events. Van Herk writes in her poem "Weadick" that, before Weadick's arrival in Alberta, "[t]here were plenty of counterfeit wild west shows, disputable and fraudulent, pretending to be authentic. Plenty of circus tricks and bluffers. And what does authenticity measure except its own imitation? The vanishing west, gone to fence, memorialized" (58). It was Weadick's mission to transform these fraudulent events and memorialize a western lifestyle. As Max Foran points out, "Weadick had . . . a keen interest in the stories of the old-timers. He was acquainted with hundreds of cowboys and ranchers and was interested in preserving their stories." Foran adds that "it is unfortunate that his role as a chronicler has gone largely unnoticed" (2009, 254). Van Herk highlights the side of the Stampede that is meant to preserve history through her depiction of Weadick as a passionate promoter of rural western traditions, writing "letters until his hand was sore" and "hammer[ing] out his pleas and persuasions" on the typewriter he travelled with (*Stampede*, 58–9). By including these details of Weadick's life, van Herk insists on the history-preserving aspects of the Stampede's beginnings, suggesting that these aspects are woven into the fabric of the event. Other pieces explore the Stampede in a different, less historical register, giving voice to both those who are annoyed that the event takes over the city every year, and those who wait for it with anticipation. "The dreaming," for instance, considers the criticism the Stampede faces from locals who see it as a primitive and excessive event for the masses—a criticism that, in van Herk's words, treats "popular jubilation" as "suspect" and gives joy "no respect" (11). The poem "Anticipation," meanwhile, focuses on the joy itself, and the excitement the event brings to both locals and visitors: "Stampede on its way. A rush, a flight, a charge, headlong" (14). This line encapsulates the overall spirit of the collection, which, though critical of some aspects, also translates an enthusiastic viewpoint to its readers.

By placing the dimensions and intentions of historical preservation that Weadick brings to the Stampede's origin story alongside depictions of the event as an extravagant affair that attracts opposing viewpoints, van Herk insists on the ambiguous identity of the Stampede itself, somewhere between popular spectacle and display of authentic, traditional western lifestyles. She makes this ambiguity even more visible in the questions she raises about the purpose of the event in the poem "History": "Where does Stampede come from, history and its bones rattling down the / road? It's the old pretending to be new and the new pretending to be old" (42). "History" gestures to important issues of authenticity—in particular, the intersections of authenticity with myth, contradiction, and performance—that are further elaborated in "Apology":

> The city loves Stampede, embraces it, enjoys it.
> Reviles it, excoriates it, repudiates it.
>
> What's the myth? . . .
>
> The myths of Stampede:
>   real action
>   real cowboys
>   real horses
>   roping, riding, rooting
>
> More than a backdrop, a practised set of performers? (80)

What "History" and "Apology" have in common is a kind of self-conscious negotiation of the Stampede as an event caught between paying homage to its origins in a western tradition of farming and horse culture and its modern-day, circus-like spectacle that is embraced and enjoyed as much as it is criticized and rejected. This ambiguity is encapsulated by the last line of "Apology," quoted above. A statement more than a question, it nonetheless ends in a question mark, leaving these last words open to interpretation and giving readers space to come to their own conclusion. The piece "Surprise" articulates some of the questions readers may ask themselves: "What is the attraction? / Nostalgia for the past . . . ? / Mourning the recent past? / Claiming the future?" (76). What constitutes an authentic West is ambiguous when it comes to the Stampede and has been since the beginning. The event itself is neither authentic nor inauthentic. Its many meanings solidify only at the individual level.

"EIGHT SECONDS IS A LONG, LONG TIME": PERFORMING RODEO AT THE STAMPEDE

The various rodeo competitions featuring well-known cowboys (and cowgirls, whom I discuss in the final section) have been integral to the Stampede since it began. Van Herk examines rodeo like she does the Stampede: with a measure of ambivalence, positioning it between a sporting event and a theatrical performance, and observing the tensions and apparent contradictions at its heart. Rodeo occupies several unique places in the world of sports. Because of its roots in ranching and farming culture, it is considered a work-based sport that also keeps close ties with the animals, communities, and traditions of specific geographical locations in western North American.

Many different kinds of competitions take place under the umbrella term of *rodeo*, but I will use it to refer to perhaps the best known of these competitions: the event in which a cowboy or cowgirl tries to remain on a horse (referred to as a "bronc") or a bull while it "bucks," trying to shake off its rider. The earliest rodeos at the Stampede did not have a time limit for this event, which would usually go on until the rider fell or the animal came to standstill. Now eight seconds, an interval "unique to rodeo in sport," is "synonymous with rodeo, even if its origins are hazy" (Canadian Press 2018). One of the most successful bronc riders explains that when "you get on a horse that's bucking really hard, they're exerting as much energy as they possibly can. . . . Six seconds I don't believe would be long enough to showcase to the best of your ability or the livestock's. Ten might be a little bit too long" (Canadian Press 2018). This short but intense timeframe showcases rodeo competitors' abilities and forms the climax of van Herk's prose poem "The infield," which refers to the eight seconds as both "impossibly short and impossibly long" (12). "The infield" highlights the performativity, danger, and joy of rodeo and, interestingly, does so without ever referring to the sport by name. The second half of the piece consists of two lists of six lines each. The first list reflects on instances in which eight seconds might seem like an eternity, such as the audience eagerly waiting in anticipation or the eight long seconds after a rider enters the arena. In a mode that highlights the stylized nature of rodeo as a complex sporting competition, van Herk juxtaposes these experiences with the second list, which reflects on brief, everyday activities that make eight seconds pass in an instant, such as answering a phone or falling in love at first sight.

This same piece takes up themes of anticipation, theatricality, and authenticity in the sport of rodeo, which, as we have seen, are also central to the evolution and character of the Stampede as a specific event. The "[s]howdown hovers at the fringe of the arena" (*Stampede*, 12) as the rider and audience collectively wait for the next eight-second eternity to begin. Once in the arena,

> [i]n the combed dirt of the ring, cowboys and horses pretend this tournament is not theatrical, a choreographed dance with fortune, and possibility roster of rules, a wager of prediction, a struggle between balance and bruises. Hazard the probability. A chance to slip the blood, a chance to claim injury, a chance to bite the dust. Gambling the true sport for those who would court thoracic compression, strained biceps, torn posterior cruciate ligaments, C2 fractures, and sheer terror. (12)

In this extract, one can trace an almost comical engagement with the work-based sports competition. Once again, van Herk brings to bear the question of authenticity. Can a sporting performance that seeks to imitate an authentic ranching lifestyle ever be more than just an imitation? She draws attention to how the sport needs this act of pretence to uphold its claim of authenticity, but this same pretence simultaneously feeds into the sport's performativity. Rodeo is a spectacle that draws large crowds who must be entertained. The extract further highlights the deep physicality of rodeo, an aspect that is integral to most sports. More than this, though, it emphasizes the risks cowboys and cowgirls are willing to take by engaging in rodeo in order to satisfy both themselves and their audiences.

It is in poems that centre the performativity of rodeo and Stampede in *Stampede*'s dominant mode of ambiguity that the relative privilege of van Herk's narrator becomes most palpable. While individual pieces reference larger systemic modes of marginalization and oppression at the Stampede, they do so only peripherally without asking bigger questions about who the spectators and benefactors of the rodeo events are and how the events perpetuate colonial violence, not to mention patriarchal and heterosexist gender binaries. There are sparse traces of the presence of Indigenous Peoples in *Stampede*, and their stories in connection with the Stampede are largely elided. The reader learns that "[t]he First Peoples called Calgary 'horse town' because the settlement was a social hub for horses" (22), but van Herk's narrator gives no further specification about who these generalized First Peoples are. The closest van Herk comes to the treatment of Indigenous Peoples at the Stampede is in the piece "Treaty Seven," which asks, "The participation of First Nations people: celebration or exploitation?" (65), but again provides no context and doesn't go into detail. The narrator's ambiguity in these instances serves as a tool to avoid scrutiny of their own privilege and entanglement with the Stampede's problematic enactment of the frontier myth and settler colonialism while also providing a similar tool to readers by not explicitly inviting them to reflect critically on their own positionality and relationship to the Stampede. Ambiguity in the face of inequality and oppression is anything but a neutral stance. As a result, pressing questions about who is entertained by these performances, by whom, and at whose expense are never fully answered.

The theatrical performances at the Stampede are venues for the reproduction of sexist, racist, and classist exclusionary mechanisms that must be deconstructed. Kimberly A. Williams's excellent book *Stampede: Misogyny, White Supremacy, and Settler Colonialism* (2021) outlines how exclusion and discrimination based not only on race, but also on gender, class, and other factors, are significant components of the history of rodeo in Canada, and more specifically the history of the Stampede. Curiously, as Williams points out in her introduction, her book is the first comprehensive critical study of the Stampede in its century-long history. Synthesizing a decade of research and reading, Williams's overarching argument is that "the Stampede is, at its core, a misogynistic, white supremacist institution that is both product and active purveyor of Canada's ongoing settler colonial project" (2). Chapter three, "Who's Greatest Together?", and chapter 4, "Colonial Redux: The Calgary Stampede's 'Imaginary Indians'," provide detailed analyses of how Indigenous Peoples, in particular, have and continue to be part of the Stampede in complex ways. Interestingly, despite Williams's strong, critical point of view, she, like van Herk, also states that her "intention in writing this book is neither to dismiss nor vilify the Calgary Stampede" (17).

Overall, however, compared with *Stampede and the Westness of West*, Williams leaves a lot less room for ambiguity around what this statement means. Her goal, explicitly stated, is not simply to let the ambiguity stand, but "to encourage a more complex understanding" of the ways in which the Stampede's "constructed narrative(s) both helped to create and continue to perpetuate systems and structures that cause many of us to be vulnerable to gender- and race-based violence and exploitation" (17).

While Williams's critique highlights current issues of gender and race at the Stampede and argues for their basis in the event's history, it is almost impossible to reconstruct discrimination at the intersection of gender and race in the early years of the event. There exist few records that document the participation of Indigenous women and women of colour in rodeo, a lacuna that is emblematic of a wider lack of sources that trace the presence of non-white women in sport (Young and White 2007, 143). As the final section details, the ample records that we do have today extensively document the lives of predominantly white women's participation in rodeo, and it is these women's experiences that we most often encounter in van Herk's *Stampede*.

"AND THEY ALL WON AGAINST COWBOYS": THE GENDERED POLITICS OF RODEO IN *STAMPEDE AND THE WESTNESS OF WEST*

Many sports have historically relied on masculinist traditions of participation, and rodeo is no exception. Tensions between masculinity and femininity, and the limitations that come with such binary constructions of gender, can be observed throughout rodeo history, including at the Stampede (on the performance of masculinity in particular, see Stoeltje 1988; Seiler and Seiler 1998; Pearson and Haney 1999; Joudrey 2016). Originally, cowboys entered into the sport by asserting their physical strength and skilled handling of farm animals. Many women, particularly those who were expected to fulfill more traditional roles of femininity aligned with Victorian ideals, did not participate. However, through its unique configuration as a "work-based competition" (Kossuth 2021, 158), rodeo did not outright exclude women. If they had sufficient skill, women were allowed to participate—but many aspects of femininity were not.

At the turn of the twentieth century, "the public image of rodeo cowgirls was as 'loose women' because they participated in a tough, dangerous men's occupation; traveled around the country with men, and often wore men's clothing" (Thomas 2014, 3). The development of rodeo as a professional sport at the intersection of women's athleticism and viewed through a gendered and (proto)-feminist lens is especially compelling. Women's sports in the early 1900s were generally perceived as incompatible with femininity and heterosexuality, and even considered unnatural. It was believed that sport would make women too masculine. Concerns about women's roles in rodeo reveal a hyperfocus on the apparent detrimental effect of the sport on women's reproductive capabilities and a more general concern for how physical exercise would render women unfeminine and therefore undesirable to men. In short, women's sport defied the narrow gender stereotypes of the time (16–17). While the conduct of many professional cowgirls in the nineteenth and early twentieth centuries can be viewed as subversive and proto-feminist as a consequence of their defiance of traditional gender roles and ideas of femininity, it is important to note that most grew up on ranches in rural parts of the United States and Canada where riding and roping were normal parts of their everyday lives. As Mary Lou LeCompte details, many cowgirls were much less influenced by urban Victorian middle-class notions of female fragility than their urban counterparts, and rodeo allowed some of these women to win "several hundred thousand dollars through sport without having to be exceptionally beautiful or deemed 'sex symbols' by the press." Therefore, LeCompte argues, "though few if any cowgirls were feminists, and several insisted they were certainly not, they still helped to change the public image of women and advance the feminist cause" (2000, 3–4).

The lives of successful cowgirls like Lucille Mulhall, Margie Greenough Henson, and Fannie Sperry Stelle feature in pieces in van Herk's *Stampede*, especially in "Horse women." This poem opens with a statement from Stampede organizer Guy Weadick in 1912, saying that the event would be "allowing in the ladies contest, the contestants to hobble their stirrups if they so wished." Speaking of wild horse racing, however, he notes that he would "not advise any lady to participate in this particular event as it is rough enough for the men let alone for the Ladies." The poem's narrator counters, asking, "Who the hell ever told you I was a lady?" (44). The piece then introduces six notable cowgirls who had highly successful rodeo careers. The reader learns about Tilly Baldwin who was a trick and relay racer, the first woman bulldogger, a champion of the Roman standing race, and a rider who rode No Sir, a particularly lively bronc, to a standstill; Bertha Kaepernik Blancett, the first woman to ride broncs at Cheyenne and the only woman to enter all women's events at the Stampede in 1912, placing in several of them; Fannie Sperry, who rode to a standstill a horse that had stomped a man to death a few days earlier, and who could "shoot cigars out of her husband's mouth from the back of a galloping horse"; Lucille Mulhall, the first woman to compete against men in roping and riding—a "cow woman," not a "cowgirl" who was "bossy" and "brusque" paving the way for other women; Goldie St. Clair, who came second in the first Stampede in 1912; Flores LaDue, who could "hang from her horse upside down and rope anything moving or motionless," and who was married to Weadick—as van Herk writes, "Enough said"; and Linda One Spot, who disguised herself as a man for a riding competition in 1952 (45). The piece culminates in a simple, "They all won against cowboys" (45), underpinning the recurring pattern of discriminatory exclusion of women from rodeo competitions, and other sports, despite their superior athletic abilities.

Over the course of the twentieth century, women pushed back against some of the sexist standards in rodeo that initially viewed femininity, both its lack and its excess, as a detractor from cowgirls' actual rodeo skills. As the sport became more popular and rodeo organizations began to pop up, women remained welcome to participate in rodeo events, but their "involvement became increasingly marginalized" (Kossuth 2021, 161). To counteract this development, the Women's Professional Rodeo Association (WPRA) was founded in 1948. Known as the Girls' Rodeo Association until 1981, the WPRA is the oldest organization of female professional athletes in North America but is nevertheless a blind spot in the literature on women's sport history (LeCompte 2000, 4–5). The association "provides opportunities for women across the United States and Canada to compete in the timed events of barrel racing, team roping, breakaway roping, and tie-down roping" (Bleiker 2023), affirming women's longstanding place in rodeo competitions. As of 2023, the WPRA has more than 3000 members. This kind of institutional grounding is important to note as it demonstrates how women were able to successfully cement their presence as amateurs and professionals within rodeo sporting culture and the Stampede.

Today, ideas around women in sport have changed, and femininity is no longer considered antithetical to rodeo. However, at the Stampede, this fact is highlighted through stereotypical and outdated traditions in its daily programme. Each year, "Stampede royalty" are elected, with a long list of requirements that women must fulfil to be eligible. Van Herk tackles the sexist and ageist undertones of these contests in her piece "Queens and princesses." In it, the reader learns that to become Stampede Queen, a woman must adhere to the following rules:

> no husbands
> no children
> no sawhorses
> no hip flasks
> no dropouts
> no arrests or accusation

> Not younger than 19 and not older than 24.
> Never divorced, separated or married.
> Not allowed to marry while in office. (36)

These requirements reveal a classist, heteropatriarchal world order reproduced at the Stampede. In the Stampede royalty contest, a woman is measured by her age, her familial status, and her public record. It is assumed that she is heterosexual and in need of a husband and children, and that after the short, five-year window of eligibility she is "too old." The other requirements exclude those whose lives have taken different turns, including children, ex- or current spouses, leaving school, or being arrested. These rules further construct an implied image of women's desirability viewed through a patriarchal lens where a woman loses value once she is "claimed" by a man through marriage. "Queens and princesses" juxtaposes these rules with questions and commentary that destabilize the patriarchal order. By asking, "Does a married woman ride less well? / Does a married woman refuse to be a queen, give up all rights to royalty?" (36), van Herk's narrator exposes the dated and heteronormative values that centre women's qualifications in relation to men and their reproductive qualities instead of centring their riding ability as one of the core selection criteria.

Along similar lines, given this historical pre-eminence of men in rodeo and the Stampede, the prose poetry collection makes a concerted effort to highlight women's stories alongside those of their spouses or fellow rodeo competitors. One such example is the piece "Turning trick," which continues the story of the founder of the Stampede, Guy Weadick, uncovering the name and life of one of his wives:

> Dolly Mullens, a figure in the shadows, married Weadick after Flores died. There has to be a story there, a sleight of hand. Difficult to cut that knot.

> In the archives a cursive note from Dolly, dated May 11, 1953. She gives him a scolding, tells him, "I am very sick and tired of putting up with and is [sic] one of the reasons which I have definitely decided to dissolve this unpleasant partnership and there is nothing you can say or do which will make me change my mind. I want to forget the whole affair. . . . Please don't make yourself a nuisance by knocking on my door at all hours of the night." (63)

Here, van Herk gives Mullens agency and presents her as a whole person with a voice and trajectory of her own, rather than casting her in the passive role of female companion.

Another instance of women's presence in *Stampede* is the story of the inventor of barbed wire, Joseph Glidden, who "[s]tole his wife's hairpins to fashion into spikes," making him rich and her mad (57). The poem that tells this story, "Fence/lines reprise," is an open-ended piece that gestures to the fragmented recording of women's history and invites the reader to do their own research into the fate of Glidden's wife.

While these pieces render visible some of the exclusion and objectification of women in Stampede and rodeo history, other poems seem to revel in the traditional displays of masculinity in cowboys. The poem "Lust" is one such example. In it, the narrator reports:

> I kissed a cowboy.

> Enough already, I finally kissed a cowboy.
> . . .
> Cowboys concretize the dynamic centre of rodeo. . . .
> . . .
> Although he embodied the form well, the squared shoulders, the camouflaging hat, the rolling walk. . . .

. . .

We are the watchers, sideline excursionists, voyeurs and cowards.
(50–53)

In this piece, the reader can observe a playful inversion of the heteropatriarchal gaze of "Queens and princesses." The narrator is infatuated with the figure of the masculine cowboy whose appeal is also connected to his central role in rodeo sports. The first half of the prose poem indicates an objectification of the cowboy's body through a female gaze in which his traditionally masculine attributes are at the centre of desirability. However, as more personifying features are revealed, the focus shifts and the greedy consumption of the cowboy is turned back onto the spectators who are chided for their voyeuristic fascination.

"Lust" hints at the intersectional entanglements of masculine identities at the Stampede. These entanglements are scrutinized by Mary-Ellen Kelm, who observes that there was "no unified masculinity crafted in this era [the early twentieth century]; rather, it was always inflected with racialization and sexuality, the interest of class, and the contingencies of place." Kelm concludes that, "[g]iven the pervasiveness of the ongoing (and seemingly never-ending) struggle over masculinity, it is not surprising . . . that the Calgary Stampede should have been yet another arena in which masculinities were articulated and contested" (2009, 714). The question of masculinity and its projections onto a "new kind of man . . . the rodeo cowboy" (715) are especially compelling in the context of Guy Weadick's creation of the Stampede, which was conceptualized as an authentic event breaking with what were then stereotypical images of the Wild West to allow for a new kind of identity for Calgarians. Most interesting in terms of gendered rodeo identities is that Weadick was welcoming of women riders from the beginning and, in fact, "[l]ocal journalists praised women riders as 'real cowboys' who demonstrated 'skill and pluck'" (Kelm 2009, 721). The concept of the cowboy in the context of the Stampede has been rather flexible and inclusive, if not unproblematic, from the beginning.

* * *

"It is easier to shoot a saskatoon than to name this awesomely confounding, / unlimited and undefinable space, the westness of west" (*Stampede*, 97). This is the last line of van Herk's *Stampede and the Westness of West*, underlining the slippery nature of the collection's main tropes: Stampede, rodeo, cowboys and cowgirls. Instead of offering tight definitions of these tropes, van Herk presents a mosaic of anecdotes, historical facts, and observations. The playfulness of the prose poetic form allows for a versatile, humorous yet subversive engagement with the Stampede through a contemporary lens. The collection traces the unique history of the rodeo event while staying true to van Herk's claim that she understands her work to be neither a critique nor total praise of the event. She leaves space for ambiguity, enabling readers to reflect on the fine line between orchestrated spectacle and necessary preservation of a historical western lifestyle, or whether such distinctions matter at all today, more than a century after the Stampede first took place in Calgary.

WORKS CITED

Bleiker, Ann. 2023. "Celebrating 75 Years of Women in Rodeo." *Women's Professional Rodeo Association* (blog), April 16, 2023. https://www.wpra.com/womens-professional-rodeo-association-celebrating-75-years-of-women-in-rodeo/.

Canadian Press. 2018. "Calgary Stampede's Bull and Bronc Riders Say 8 Seconds Is Enough." *CBC*, July 5, 2018. www.cbc.ca/sports/calgarystampede/calgary-stampede-8-seconds-1.4734652.

Foran, Max. 2009. "A Lapse in Historical Memory: Guy Weadick and the Calgary Stampede." *American Review of Canadian Studies* 39 (3): 254–70.

Joudrey, Susan L. 2016. "What a Man: Portrayals of Masculinity and Race in Calgary Stampede Ephemera." *Cultural Studies, Critical Methodologies* 16 (1): 28–39.

Kelm, Mary-Ellen. 2009. "Manly Contests: Rodeo Masculinities at the Calgary Stampede." *The Canadian Historical Review* 90 (4): 711–51.

Kossuth, Robert. 2021. "The Development and Organization of Professional Sport." In *Sport and Recreation in Canadian History*, edited by Carly Adams, 149–72. Champaign, IL: Human Kinetics.

LeCompte, Mary Lou. 2000. *Cowgirls of the Rodeo: Pioneer, Professional Athletes*. Champaign, IL: University of Illinois Press.

Pearson, Demetrius W., and C. Allen Haney. 1999. "The Rodeo Cowboy: Cultural Icon, Athlete, or Entrepreneur?" *Journal of Sport and Social Issues* 23 (3): 308–27.

Polić, Vanja. 2016. "Performing the Canadian West: Chuckwagons, Cowgirls, and New Westerns." *Cultural Studies, Critical Methodologies* 16 (1): 40–47.

Roberts, Katherine Ann. 2010. "Sundance Style: Dancing with Cowboys in Aritha van Herk's (New) West." *Journal of Canadian Studies* 44 (3): 26–52.

Seiler, Robert, and Tamara Seiler. 1998. "The Social Construction of the Canadian Cowboy: Calgary Exhibition and Stampede Posters, 1952–1972." *Journal of Canadian Studies/Revue d'études Canadiennes* 33 (3): 51.

Stoeltje, Beverly J. 1988. "Gender Representations in Performance: The Cowgirl and the Hostess." *Journal of Folklore Research* 25 (3): 219–41.

Thomas, Heidi. 2014. *Cowgirl Up: A History of Rodeoing Women*. Guilford, CT: TwoDot.

van Herk, Aritha. 2016a. *Stampede and the Westness of West*. Calgary: Frontenac House.

van Herk, Aritha. 2016b. "What Does the Stampede Mean to Us Calgarians? Author Aritha van Herk Explores These Questions and More in Her New Book." Interview with the Calgary Stampede. *Calgary Stampede* (blog), June 23, 2016. https://web.archive.org/web/20221007102652/www.calgarystampede.com/blog/2016/06/23/what-does-the-stampede-mean-to-us-as-calgarians/.

Williams, Kimberly A. 2021. *Stampede: Misogyny, White Supremacy, and Settler Colonialism*. Halifax: Fernwood Publishing.

Young, Kevin, and Philip White. 2007. *Sport and Gender in Canada*. 2nd ed. Don Mills, ON: Oxford University Press.

Contention, On Rodeo

Aritha van Herk on Rodeo and Writing

One Sunday morning in a pasture by the Battle River some
of us kids were playing rodeo and I got onto a young bull
that bucked—and then I got off. I got off abruptly and vio-
lently. Getting off hurt. It hurt a lot. There are two varieties
of cactus that grow in the coulee hills of the Battle River.
Pincushion and prickly pear. And hardpan is hard. I thought
I might be dying and said so. Someone told me to get up off
my ass and get back onto the bull. In a rebellious moment I
said I was not going to get back onto the bull, I was going to
be a writer.

Robert Kroetsch, "Lonesome Writer Diptych"

So much for playing rodeo. Dismount and recalibrate.

These are the choices: become a bull rider instead of a writer; become a
writer instead of a bull rider. I knew better than to climb onto the back of
a young bull. I did not have to be bucked off to decide that I would need
to become a writer.

The rider/writer distinction. In linguistics, "this phenomenon is one of a
family of phenomena known as **Canadian Raising**. 'Traditional' Canadian
raising involves the systematic vowel quality distinction made for the diph-
thongs /aɪ/ and /aʊ/ when they are followed by a voiced vs. a voiceless

consonant. Generally, they are realized as [ʌɪ] and [ʌʊ], respectively (or some similar variants), before a voiceless consonant" (Musicallinguist 2013).

What the holy hell have I gotten into? A neutralization? A dropped jaw? A de-voicing?

I think I might be dying, confronted now with the sameness of the words and the difference of the actions. On a cold day, which would be preferable? A diphthong or a voiceless consonant?

It is not possible to "play rodeo." It is possible to play hockey, or to play tennis, but rodeo reaches beyond the usual arena of sport.

The temptation haunts us though, built by every child-sized cowboy hat and holster donned for dress-up, every cheesy movie featuring a hero on a saddle riding toward a rosy sunset.

There was a dirt ring beside the Battle River, loftily calling itself the "Edberg Rodeo Grounds." Not much more than a few bleachers and a barbed-wire fence, the announcer's booth ramshackle on its stilts while the ledge of the valley shadowed the horizon. Under the pocked snow silent in its waiting for summer, those yearning boys who wanted to be heroes, riders and not writers, left traces of skin and sweat. "They weren't the kind to turn into husbands" (*Stampede*, 75).

I was an unsporty child, awkward and graceless, shy to a degree of introversion. I had no game plan in those planning stages, never believed that I would write a word about rodeos or chuckwagons or stampedes. Predictions cannot predict, although the idea of rodeo does offer a realm for heroic fantasies shattered by hard pan and cactus and hurt.

Rodeo has developed as a complex intermeshing of practice and homage to the history of a particular field of work. It measures an evolution of skill, a test of nerve, a resolve to fail, a communion of livestock and human. In a circumscribed contest of will or achievement, it tracks the independence of the two—animal and human—in concert and opposition.

If all sport is "a collision of pragmatism and mythology" (Wall 2012, 5), then where does rodeo fall on that spectrum? An outcome of the ranching and agricultural past when roundups and their gatherings involved the harsh burn of branding, castration, dehorning, butchering, it began as grueling work, far removed from the joyous rough and scramble of faux sport.

Rodeo now avoids those requirements, the chores of ranching separated from competition, and yet, its ever-present echoes do draw on mythology. Is this how that transformation happens, how work evolves into play and competition? Or is work enough in and of itself, and the sport of rodeo heralds an alternate version of jouissance and restraint?

Okay then, who has a stake in these competitions? The bronc? The steer? The bull? Being ridden isn't part of his job description. A thorn on his back that he seeks to dislodge.

The audience, spectators slaking some yearning to witness a close-up of sweat transformed into contest?

The cowboy? Only if there's money involved, or pride is at issue. Always more at stake than logic. This is a sport for risk and its redistribution, violence and spectacle, the potential of injury and gore, a contemporary demonstration of machismo.

Which can only insist on a detour into marianismo, not passivity and sexual purity either, but women in rodeo, their recent exclusion outrageously limited to barrel racing, the one event that is sheer skill.

"Beautiful Daring Western Girls and Mexican Señoritas in a Contest of Equine Skill," says a poster from Pawnee Bill's Historic Wild West (Jordan 1992, 189). They competed in racing, roping, trick riding, saddle bronc busting, from "1896, when Annie Shaffer rode a wild one" (189). Rodeos from the 1920s onward featured "ladies' bronc riding, trick riding, and . . . cowgirls' relay race" (191). Talk all you want of strength, agility, speed, the masculine realm of the unmeasurable, but those competitors were full-on rodeo.

The story is that ladies' bronc riding was dropped in 1941 because the war in Europe limited rodeo stock and transportation resources. And the "ladies" were out.

Cowgirl is ridiculous. Horsewoman is closer, and in the working history of equine care, women did everything men did. Horses gave women liberty to move, to run, to feel wind in their hair.

So, rodeo has come to believe its own masculine myth. It subscribes to an idea of purity that infests its rituals, some trial of contention that moves from a task where the human is roped by time and the livestock has all the time in the world.

There are two dimensions to this sport: timed events or rough stock domination. Timed events include steer wrestling, barrel racing, and calf roping; rough stock events include bull, bareback, and saddle bronc riding. Although time judges every outcome.

How long does eight seconds stretch on a bucking horse or a bull? How long is too long when a barrel racer performs her cloverleaf pattern and dashes toward the red line? How long does it take to tie down a horned steer?

The rider: balanced and agile.

The horse: agile, intelligent, reading the human through pressured knees or a turn of wrist.

But there hums an answer. Aside from theatricality and product sponsorship, rodeo seals "sacred, ritual, and everyday practices" (Wall 2012, 9) in blood, chaps and desperate prayers. In a lacrosse of failure and capture, rodeo bakes yearning and horror, desire and repulsion into its contest. It is a sport balanced on a thin wire between adrenaline and terror.

We search for design now, a system that is not a voiceless consonant. Narratology be damned, we cherish our raw desire for structure, for rules.

Rodeo's constraints are story, time, and sequence, although no predictability can capture the turn and twist of the calf, the spinning of the bull, "ritualized mayhem" (Wall 2012, 269) inevitable as bruising.

This rodeo presumes to be an exhibition of skill, different skills in every category, but a mirroring roustabout. This is an envelope sport, folded within itself, the competition of human and animal, human against animal, human against dust, human with dust, human and horse, or human with human. Rodeo rides as a hybrid of sport and spectacle. In Spanish, the preamble to slaughter, a sorting. Round-up and tie-down.

And the lingo of the competition complex, shorthand more than shorthand, the long hand and the ranch hand and the top hand and the cow hand, all using the tools at hand, gloved and knuckled and handy and hand-bagged and hand-picked and handled. Give the game a hand.

The language around rodeo is embedded in myth: agriculture, iconic, symbolism, rural roots. As for its status as official "sport," rodeo sparks confusion and diffusion, not one specific competition but a mélange of events, riding, roping, wrestling, and not to be forgotten sideline sports, drinking and fighting and eating. Cowpunchers and ne'er-do-wells appear to go together, which leads to shooting and wrangling and wrestling, fueled by subsidiary hot sauce and passion.

Every male has at one time or another thought of himself as a cowboy. Self-delusion. Whereas "Cowboy Up!" is not always advice.

Rodeo requires not only human participants but animals, so it arises not from some pure "sport," but from an agricultural conjunction of human and animal, then transformed into a spectator sport of how animals are mastered, which becomes a metaphor for human relationship to land and livestock.

How to frame that? Is rodeo an expression of nostalgia? Or is the "sport" of rodeo a much-maligned translation of some gladiatorial contest, bread and circuses corrupted to blood and subjugation? Augmenting the opinion that rodeos are nothing more than cruelty to animals, agriculture perverted into a spectacle of abuse.

Pain is not skill, but endurance. Let's go for skill, despite rodeo being a sport lockstep with physical pain. Researchers are fond of comparing injury rates in sports: bull-riding has an injury rate ten times greater than football. Take that, pigskin.

Evaluate pain. Rodeo competitors hurt everywhere, in places unimaginable to most, injuries specific to the sport. Chronic results. Increased potential for pain because the factors of high speed and large bodies of mass in motion combine to create kinetic energy with a definite potential for serious injury.

Gory fascination.

Head, face, knee, and shoulder are the most common parts of the body to take the brunt. Hand and wrist fractures, joint instability, elbow degenerative disease, severe ligamentous injury, public diastasis, dislocation, rope burn, concussion, whiplash, inadvertent digit amputation. That would be losing a finger. I think I might be dying.

The reconstructive surgeons rub their hands.

Statistics declare that 100% of bull-riders get injured.

One repeated chant: "The rodeo cowboy is grateful for medical assistance."

Stop. Avert your eyes. Is this a sport or masochism? Masochism and machismo, definite cousins. The rugged individual, but not individual, accompanied by animal. Domination and its outcome. Competition and its performance. The blue ribbon ride. The big cheque win.

Or a more complex deduction: "[R]anching culture has been appropriated as entertainment in the form of rodeos" (Herbert 2017, 113). Ranching culture. Not an oxymoron. Leave that phrase there.

While rodeo performs as a reference joke to measure experience, an idiom indicating that someone is not naive or inexperienced. Note the double negative: "not inexperienced."

But it came out of the mouth of a woman, that phrase, meant to underline Joan Crawford's adamant toughness in *Mommie Dearest*. Faye Dunaway, playing Crawford in Frank Perry's 1981 adaptation, says, "Don't FUCK with me fellas! This ain't my first time at the rodeo!" And there it lands, in common culture, experience narrowing its eyes against a greenhorn, or a deceiver, colloquial calling out of bullshit. In Hollywood no less, capital of bullshit.

Fugitive. This is not my first rodeo. It will not be my last.

I always wanted to be a tough girl/woman. I was a tough girl, with practice as a cow hand, a tractor hand, a hand meant to put my hands to use stacking haybales, stone-picking, and driving a tractor so old that it hardly qualified as functional.

And I am a tougher woman, having had the equivalent of quite a few dustups, been kicked, beaten, and bruised, emotionally and psychologically. Physically, I've bitten the dust, wrenched my shoulder, torn a ligament or two, and landed ignominiously. All without the applause of an eight second ride or a perfect tie-down, but those are male grails. Although I was never bucked off, that dread summary, B.O., never that impetuous or grounded. Was not summarily forced to dismount.

Sam Steele, training would-be NWMP recruits who were bucked off, shouting at them as they lay in the dust: "Who gave you permission to dismount?"

Dismount? I thought I was dying.

So as a settler-colonist feminist, bookworm, text nerd, page addict, grammar queen, what is it with me and rodeo? I try to trace this fascination, my own debate with its masculine slant and violent abruptness, its contest between human and animal, nostalgia and carnival. The tempting costume, a chance to wear jeans and boots, to cross lines, and yes, to celebrate.

I never won a race. Never been bucked off. But I've been hooked on the horn of language, and there I hang, waiting for a rodeo clown to rescue me. So I can keep writing.

WORKS CITED

Herbert, Rachel. 2017. *Ranching Women in Southern Alberta*. Calgary: University of Calgary Press.

Jordan, Teresa. 1992. *Cowgirls: Women of the American West*. Lincoln: University of Nebraska Press.

Musicallinguist. 2013. Reply to "The 'writer / rider' distinction." StackExchange, August 2, 2013. https://linguistics.stackexchange.com/questions/4103/the-writer-rider-distinction.

Perry, Frank, dir. 1981. *Mommie Dearest*. Hollywood: Paramount Pictures.

van Herk, Aritha. 2016. *Stampede and the Westness of West*. Calgary: Frontenac Press.

Wall, Karen. 2012. *Game Plan: A Social History of Sport in Alberta*. Edmonton: University of Alberta Press.

10

Jason Blake

Immigration, Masculinity, and Olympic-Style Weightlifting in David Bezmozgis's "The Second Strongest Man"

High-level athletic careers and immigration have rupture in common. For the immigrant and the former professional athlete alike, life is divided into a clear before and after. Rick Mercer's witty and catchy "Ken Dryden Song" (2005) sums up this split perfectly, keying in on life after hockey: "He was a hockey legend, a master goaltender / now he's moving up the ice as a member [of Parliament] for York Centre." The refrain of this one-minute ditty runs, "Ken Dryden, Ken Dryden, that guy used to be Ken Dryden." The song's humour lies in its absurd yet accurate self-contradiction. Ken Dryden of course remains Ken Dryden, even if he is no longer wearing the Canadiens jersey. But at the same time, the Ken Dryden of political and public intellectual fame is no longer a man of action. The song praises the erstwhile puck-stopper because in Parliament, "he hardly ever fidgets, sits quiet on his ass." In other words, despite his (then) prominent position as a politician, Dryden was a static shadow of his former athletic self.

Sarajevo-born American author Aleksandar Hemon describes a similar rupture in his essay "In Search of Lost Space," this time in the context of immigrant experience. Describing his parents' 1993 move to Hamilton,

I would like to thank those who provided feedback on this chapter: Angie Abdou, Michael Devine, Andrew C. Holman, Don Sparling, and superb copyeditor Kay Rollans. Thanks also to my students.

Ontario, Hemon writes: "This displacement is the central event of their life, what split it into the before and the after. Everything after the rupture took place in a damaged, incomplete time—some of it was forever lost and forever it shall so remain" (2015, 36). For Hemon's parents, the time after the "displacement" from war-torn Bosnia to Canada "is damaged, incomplete" because it is not a smooth continuation of the life story they would have had back in Europe. This new start is made more difficult because they have to learn and communicate in a new language and deal with the cold Canadians who "didn't eat things we ate, and were fat and incapable of truly enjoying life because they worried about getting fat all the time" (38).

The rupture of immigration, mixed deftly with the deep continuity of the world of sport, is a key theme in David Bezmozgis's "The Second Strongest Man." The story is the third in his 2004 collection *Natasha and Other Stories*, about the Bermans, a Russian Jewish family who emigrated to Toronto from Riga, Latvia, in the former Soviet Union. Told from the perspective of ten-year-old Mark Berman, "The Second Strongest Man" centres on weightlifting—specifically, on what happens when a team of Soviet lifters, some of whom Mark's father, Roman, knows from his time as a trainer back in Riga, come to Toronto for a competition. Indeed, Bezmozgis points to the finality of Soviet emigration when a KGB agent accompanying the team to Toronto says to the narrator's father, "remember, you always have a friend in Moscow. Visit anytime" (51). The agent then laughs at his own joke. Even the KGB insider wonders who would ever return to the Soviet Union, turning a social platitude (*Visit anytime . . .*) into a societal criticism.

During the Cold War, sports were a replacement battlefield, a playground for proving that the Western system, the Western way of life, was better than that of the other side. (Think of the 1972 Summit Series that remains at the core of Canada's primary hockey myth.) Olympic medal counts were followed religiously even by people who gave not one hoot about sports. Bezmozgis's fine variation on the sport literature theme is this: he brings East and West, family and old friends together, and uses sport to examine the you-can't-go-home-again theme. As Bezmozgis writes in a short biography of weightlifter (and circus performer) extraordinaire Grigory Novak (1919–1980), behind the Iron Curtain sports were supposed "to show the world the superiority of the Soviet man" (2012b, 91). "The Second Strongest Man" takes a path less travelled in sport literature. It does not worry about whether or how one regime will win the big game; rather, it focuses on a less popular sport that primarily interested and was dominated by "the Eastern bloc countries" (Young 1999, 441).

Weightlifting is an ideal sporting vehicle for examining the analogous ruptures of professional sports and emigration, specifically Soviet emigration. Bezmozgis tells the story of a champion Soviet weightlifter's move from the realm of glory to relative failure after a loss at an international competition in Canada. Through a series of doublings, "The Second Strongest Man" parallels this athletic fall from grace with the trials of immigration experienced by Roman Berman and his family, each being defined by feelings of powerlessness in a new life situation. Through weightlifting, Bezmozgis examines the inescapable in-betweenness of immigrant experience, tying it to explorations of masculinity and the fleeting nature of athletic fame.

"The Second Strongest Man" begins with a snapshot of struggle: "In the winter of 1984, as my mother was recovering from a nervous breakdown and my father's business hovered precipitously between failure and near failure, the international weightlifting championships were held at the Toronto Convention Centre" (39). A former weightlifting coach and functionary in the Soviet Union, Mark's father is now, in Mark's words, a "massage therapist and schlepper of chocolate bars" (39). Mark uses the derogatory Yiddish term for a lowly, incapable labourer to describe Roman Berman's toils at a local chocolate bar factory. Roman is a nobody, but when he is invited to judge the weightlifting competition, he is taken back to a world when he was not anonymous, back to a world when he administered the Riga Dynamo sports club, hobnobbed with legendary hockey coach Viktor Tikhonov, and ran an illegal after-hours weightlifting class out of the back of the club.

Back then, Roman Berman encountered a problem with his gym: many of his Jewish clients were requesting permission to leave the Soviet Union for Israel. "It was pointed out to one of my father's directors that there was a disturbing correlation between my father's bodybuilders and Jews asking for exit visas" (41).[1] The narrative clock begins to tick faster; unless the

---

1 Jews could be allowed to leave the Soviet Union for Israel, but the application process was a perilous one: "Jews who applied to emigrate in the 1970s from the USSR lost their jobs, were stripped of citizenship and were labelled traitors by their neighbours—this happened not only to those who applied, but to their relatives as well" (Stoffman 2011).

schemers can justify the class's "existence in an official capacity" (41)—that is, by discovering a world-beater athlete—the club would be shuttered. At the last moment, as Mark tells us, Roman comes across a weightlifting miracle: "[M]y father discovered Sergei Federenko" (43). The discovery scene is a wry twist on finding athletic greatness far from the madding crowd. Roman does not discover his born athlete springing through the jungle (as in the 1973 film *The World's Greatest Athlete*), or his chess genius in an orphanage (as in the 2020 series *The Queen's Gambit*); he finds his strongman "pissing against the wall" outside the gym (42).

Roman takes Sergei Federenko under his wing and soon the young athlete is on his way to fame and fortune as a full-time weightlifter, a professional in everything but name thanks to the Soviet system of "shamateurism" whereby Soviet athletes were officially employed by the military, but in fact trained for a living (Dunning 1999, 115). Literature loves orphans, and Sergei is essentially parentless because "[h]is father was an alcoholic and his mother had died in an accident when he was three" (45). Like Harry Potter and Anne of Green Gables, Sergei has unbounded potential for growth. Rescued from the army and a life of drudgery on a *kolkhoz* or collective farm, within a few years Sergei is a champion lifter who "could no longer walk down the street without being approached by strangers. In Latvia, he was as recognizable as any movie star" (45). The form of the discovery and rise-to-greatness story is familiar, but Bezmozgis's focus on weightlifting is not. In North America, football, basketball, and baseball compete for the popularity podium, leaving ice hockey—despite its enormous status in Canada—battling tennis and golf in a fight for fourth. Unless (and sometimes even if) they win Olympic gold, other pro athletes can walk unbothered down the streets of Toronto or New York. Even track and field stars Perdita Felicien, Andre De Grasse, and former world record holder Donovan Bailey are less recognized than most NBA or NHL stars. This is Bezmozgis's literary tweak to the typical Canadian sport literature tale: beyond immigrant communities, no weightlifter would approach the fame of a movie star in Canada.

The weightlifting championships are important for young Mark because he will get to see his hero: the 52-kilogram weightlifting phenomenon Sergei Federenko, whom he knew as a "four-, five-, and six-year-old" (45) back in Riga, whose records he had "memorized . . . the way American kids memorized box scores" (48), and whose exploits he knew from "memories, largely indistinct from my parents' stories" (45). Memory and artful stories clearly mingle with and muddle each other. In another blurring of clear lines, though Sergei is a legend in Riga, he is little known in Toronto beyond the Bermans and a niche clique of weightlifting fans. On hearing that the star athlete might be coming to visit, Mark recalls, "I pranced around the apartment singing, Seryozha, Seryozha, Seryozha. Seryozha is coming!" (40). The Russian diminutive form of "Sergei" is estranging to the eye trained in English. This minor bewilderment is standard, since Bezmozgis often imports realia—untranslated, culturally specific terms and touchstones—into the Toronto suburb where the Bermans live.[2] *Natasha and Other Stories* takes place in Canada, but it is an in-between world of "assorted Russian bonbons: Karakum, Brown Squirrel, Clumsy Bear" (53) in which characters smile "the familiar Soviet smile" (63). How many Canadian readers know those candies? What does that so-called familiar smile look like? Is a Soviet smile somehow different from a Canadian smile? Bezmozgis's realia give readers a sense of authenticity, and of the slippery space between the local and the global, craftily excluding many with the adjective *familiar*.

WEIGHTLIFTING AND MANLINESS

As its title suggests, "The Second Strongest Man" brims with the expectations that hegemonic masculinity or hypermasculinity in the age of the Cold War implied. If physical strength is a marker of manliness, then weightlifting is the marker par excellence. In a work of nonfiction about weightlifting in the Soviet Union, Bezmozgis writes that his "earliest conceptions of manhood stemmed from this world" and also from the stories his father "told and retold, often at my bidding" (2012b, 90–91). Boxers can at least bob and weave to avoid blows. Though technique is crucial to Olympic weightlifting, lifting heavy weights involves no trickery—aside from steroids, which in this sporting world are assumed to be taken by all,

---

2 Realia have various uses: they can bridge a lexical gap between languages, provide a touch of the real, and impart local colour (such as when travel writers mention a delicacy that can't be translated). In Bezmozgis's experience as a reader, when authors use realia, it "feels authentic," not like "I've been talked down to [by the author]" (in Baer 2004). On how Bezmozgis uses English-Russian code-switching to present complexity in his own writing, see Kaloh Vid (2019, 168).

thus levelling the playing field. With utter coolness, Mark states, "In his capacity as Dynamo administrator it had been my father's responsibility to ensure that all the weightlifters were taking their steroids" ("Second Strongest," 48).

The world of hypermasculinity is a world of competition, preening, braggadocio, and skating on the edge of violence. When the primarily "Jewish university students and young professionals who wanted to look good on the beaches of Jurmala" (41) exit the gym on the night Sergei is discovered, they pick a fight with a trio of drunken soldiers. The scene may be in faraway Riga, but we can recognize the pattern from just about any night club or bar. The space outside this Riga gym differs little from the puerile, boozy space catalogued, parodied, and immortalized in Elton John's "Saturday Night's Alright for Fighting." The insults hurled range from the anti-Semitic to the homophobic slurs so frequently employed "to diminish or mock," since "heterosexuality is the main component of hegemonic masculinity" (MacDonald 2018, 348).

The cause of the feud is petty: one hobbyist bodybuilder "decided to flex his new muscles," calling the smallest soldier "a dog" and saying "unflattering things about his mother"; "the two bigger soldiers got ready to crack skulls" (42). Escalation is immediate, despite Roman's attempt to curtail violence through humour: "Doctors had proven that as muscles grow the brain shrinks." There is a flurry of generic insults ("cocksucker," "Chaim," and "faggot"), but no punches are thrown (43).

They decide to settle the matter like men, albeit with a twist, as Bezmozgis yet again masterfully retreats from fulfilling the expectations of violence he has set up. "Listen, faggot," gripes a soldier, "if one of your boys can lift the Moskvich [a small car] we'll forget the whole thing" (43). Suddenly the scene seems staged, as if the two soldiers were not out to escalate aggression but to exploit the opportunity to show off their little gem, to bask in the reflected glory of their petit comrade: the smallest soldier, Sergei. Next to the hobbyists, Sergei's muscles don't look like anything to write home about—but Sergei is more of a lifter than a looker.

Bezmozgis carefully differentiates between bodybuilders and weightlifters. The hobby boys at the semi-legal club are not sportsmen like Sergei is, since as Colin McGinn writes, bodybuilding "*isn't sport*. It's exercise." Why? Because "[b]eyond minimal coordination it requires no real skill, just the necessary will power and some enlightened masochism" (2008,

46). So after the hobbyists agree to the pact, they predictably fail to lift the vehicle. In accordance with the logic of ritual street fights, the soldiers now have a legitimate basis for smearing the walls with their foes. Instead, one of the bigger soldiers turns to Sergei and says, "show Chaim what's impossible" (44). Sergei, putting down his drink, springs into action, transforming the hypermasculine world of soldiery, late-night drinking, and potential fisticuffs into a more ordered but still masculine world where "men lift heavy things in preparation for lifting very heavy things" in search of glory (57).

PLACELESS REALMS AND SPORTS

Sports fans ceaselessly complain that new stadiums have no character, arguing that the new edifices lack the aura of, say, Maple Leaf Gardens or the Montreal Forum. Such complaints are often misguided. The point of modern sport is to have a playing space that replicates the playing space in any other town, in any other country. Gone are the days when sport was relatively unstructured. Athletic contests are bound by carefully constructed and formal rules and almost-as-rigid "codes" of expected behaviour. Even a contest as seemingly simple as the Olympic clean and jerk is utterly standardized. From the perspective of the spectator, sport becomes essentially placeless: whether in Toronto or Riga, it is roped off by the same equipment, the same rules, the same routines. "By becoming sequestered," writes Steven Connor, "sport has been able to approach ubiquity" (2011, 49). In this sense, the COVID-induced 2020 NBA Bubble at Walt Disney World was a mere continuation of what Connor dubs the "coalescence of the local and the global" (49). Olympic-style weightlifting is especially well suited to a sense of placelessness because, unlike Major League Baseball with its different distances to left field in Fenway Park (310 feet) and Wrigley Field (355 feet), lifting 150 kilograms in Boston is the same as lifting 150 kilograms in Chicago. It is therefore symbolically apt that the competition in "The Second Strongest Man" is at the Toronto Convention Centre, a venue so characterless it makes even the dullest corporate football stadium seem indelibly linked to its suburban surroundings. Once the weightlifting competition is over, the Convention Centre can clean itself up and let the dogs in for a canine convention, and perhaps follow up with an international soap show.

This placelessness contrasts with the ways in which sport easily plays into national identity: when players from "our" team compete against "their" team, for once we can, for example, see exactly where "we" stop and "they" begin—by looking at the colours of and patterns on the uniforms. To quote Eric Hobsbawm, an "imagined community of millions seems more real as a team of eleven named people" (1990, 143). Bezmozgis gives this trope a twirl, downplaying the concerns of national identity and individualism so common in sports discourse. When Mark is allowed into the warm-up area at the convention centre, he gets lost in a sea of different coaches, trainers, and athletes from different nations. "Teams could be distinguished from one another by the colors of their Adidas training suits" (56), but otherwise these ideologically opposed individuals and nations have much in common. Unless you were already familiar with the colours of a Russian uniform or a Turkish uniform, you would not be able to discern Cold War tensions.

Within this neutral territory, Mark's father recedes into his previous self, into his old picture. Mark has often perused a "photo of him [Roman] taken years before the trials of immigration," when his father's "face carried the detached confidence of the highly placed Soviet functionary." Mark reflects, "It was comforting to think that the man in the picture and my father were once the same person" (39). Immigration has taken its toll on Roman Berman, but in the neutral space of the competition, among the other judges, "he looked very much like his old picture in the IWF [International Weightlifting Federation] passport" (57). In a past world of exit visas, anti-Semitism, and decaying empires, the IWF passport obtains a comfortable solidity. Yet it will not last. Roman may look like a lofty functionary of yore in this placeless realm, but after the competition he will exit into the streets of Toronto and return to his new life as an immigrant.

DOUBLINGS

In a piece on Leonard Michaels, Bezmozgis praises the writer's "humor, pathos, and . . . appreciation for the absurdity to be found in everyday life" (2012a). For much of "The Second Strongest Man," humor, pathos, and absurdity straddle the East and West, hinting that universal experience transcends politics. In one such humorous moment, Bezmozgis lets us know that the Soviet team's accompanying KGB agent does not initially realize that Roman had emigrated. Early in the story, the agent says, "Roman

Abramovich, you're here? I didn't see you on the plane" (46). The comment points to Roman's existence between his Soviet past and Canadian present, an in-betweenness that the author neatly captures through a series of doublings or parallels that at times make one question whether life in the Free World is in fact all that different from life behind the Iron Curtain. Bezmozgis sees similarities as well as ideological divides.

In Latvia, Roman "had operated a very successful side venture out of the gym at Riga Dynamo" (40), which required paying "kickbacks to the Dynamo directors" (41). This grey market activity has a counterpart in Toronto, where a capable dentist's Soviet credentials go unnoticed. Now the Berman family's dentist in Toronto, Dusa had been "a top professional in Moscow" (47) who now "worked nights as a maid for a Canadian dentist" because she was not yet qualified to practice in her new country (47). She was, however, allowed to "see her own patients, for cash, under the table," as long as she gave her boss half of her profits—though, "in the event of trouble, he would deny everything and it would be Dusa's ass on the line" (47). On the surface, the social distance between Canada and the Soviet Union seems miniscule: minor rule-bending and rule-breaking exist as Russians in both the Soviet Union and in Canada attempt to get by.

But we should not push this parallel too far. In "Roman Berman, Massage Therapist," the story that precedes "The Second Strongest Man" in *Natasha and Other Stories*, Roman has an iffy side-job "at the Italian Community Center, where he massaged mobsters and manufacturers and trained seven amateur weightlifters" (21). *Plus ça change*, the narrator seems to suggest. But by the early 1980s, "Russia was becoming a colossal piece of shit" (60)—a key, if over-stated line—and the prevalence of anti-Semitism within the Soviet Union clearly made Canada an attractive destination. As the seven linked stories forming the arc of *Natasha and Other Stories* progress, the Bermans achieve upward mobility and declare Canada the better option. In other words, the double structure of struggling in Russia and struggling in Canada is not a perfect parallel. Laura Phillips astutely and eloquently observes that, for Mark, Sergei's visit "is an object lesson in disillusionment, rather like the feeling one has on revisiting a favourite childhood haunt only to find it smaller, meaner and shabbier than one remembers" (2005).

The most significant of the doublings has to do with the life of the professional weightlifter. Like other professional athletes, the life of a weightlifter reflects the life cycle we all have, but theirs is more compact and on display. Because athletes retire young, we are tempted to look at their careers as a symbolic representation of life. Eventually a hockey player can no longer keep up with younger, faster players, the aches and pains take a little longer to heal—but isn't this just like the slowing-down we all face as we age? As Michael Oriard reminds us, "[t]he retired player faces the predicament of every human growing old, but at a much earlier period in his life" (1982, 152).

It would, however, be more accurate to describe the athlete's life as a distorted reflection of the usual life cycle. In his 1983 book *The Game*, Ken Dryden notes, "If it is true that a sports career prolongs adolescence, it is also true that when that career ends, it deposits a player into premature middle age" (14). Unlike Dryden the lawyer-goalie, many athletes have few other career options, meaning that they have to survive for decades on low skills and often broken bodies, given the physical strains a sports career entails. In "The Second Strongest Man" we are told that "[a] weightlifter's career was five, maybe seven years," and even though the Soviet system took care of its retired athletes through sinecures—"[a] lucrative job with customs. Maybe a coaching placement, or moving papers from one corner of the desk to the other" (60)—they faced a similar fading into obscurity.

Inevitably, at some point Sergei Federenko—the strongest man in the world—must lose—and he does, in Toronto, to Krutov, "a new young lifter . . . who showed considerable promise" (55). This public loss merely mirrors the natural order. Father Time comes for us all. Young defeats old, eventually—even when the young contender is an earlier version of ourselves. In another instance of doubling, when Krutov and Sergei compete in the clean and jerk, the clock becomes a symbol of cruel truth: "I watched the seconds on the huge clock behind him tick away. Just to stay in the competition, he had to match his own world record" (58). To stay in the game, Sergei must defeat his younger self. When he fails to lift a weight he used to be able to lift, he loses the competition to the younger Krutov (whose name evokes the Russian word for "cruel"). This doubling is reflected in the story's hyphenless title: not "The *Second-Strongest* Man" but "The *Second* Strongest Man." By beating Sergei, the original strongest man, Krutov becomes the new strongest man: the second one. At the same time, Sergei also becomes the second strongest man: a has-been in terms of absolute rankings.

Initially, Sergei does not appear to lament his defeat and relegation. He lets Mark hold his medal and says, redundantly, "A silver medal. It's not gold, but I guess you don't find them lying in the street" (58). Because Bezmozgis is such a subtle, sparse writer, this statement invites us to look more closely. Sergei's obvious listener is the boy, but at the same time he is speaking to himself, talking himself into a truth and consolation that he, a former king of the weightlifting world, does not truly feel. Like the many athletes who refer to themselves in the third person or consider their bodies to be machines, Sergei objectifies himself and considers himself not as an individual but as part of a team, a cog in the wheel. "Don't forget to congratulate Comrade Ziskin on another great day for Dynamo," he tells Mark blandly, sliding in the epithet "Comrade" (otherwise used only by the KGB agent), and following up with, "Another one-two finish. What difference does it make to him [the coach] if all of a sudden one is two and two is one?" (58). Sergei realizes his glory days have passed. Though he is as revered as a movie star, he is ultimately a placeholder who, in the Soviet sports system, is replaceable.

Bezmozgis highlights the accelerated aging process we know from professional sports. We read that Sergei looked "as though he hadn't changed at all in the last five years" (50), but what is praise for most of us—"You haven't aged a day!"—contains a jagged truth: five years is a lifetime for athletes. At the competition, we see Sergei age on the spot. "[S]training under the bar," he looks old compared to the younger "blond weightlifter" (57). After the competition Sergei visits Mark's home, consumes a great deal of vodka, and staggers off to the boy's bed. The symbolism is overt: Sergei is simultaneously the old, drunken athlete and a child being sent to bed. When Mark enters the room, Sergei challenges him: "Let's go. You and me. Fifty push-ups" (61). Machos use similar phrasing when challenging others to a fight. He then tells Mark, somewhat creepily, to get into the bed: "His tone left no room for negotiation. I kicked off my shoes and lifted the covers" (62). Years after he blithely and drunkenly "lifted the car a meter off the ground" (44), Sergei proceeds to lift the entire bed, with Mark in it, his face straining just as it had when he was at the Convention Centre.

Becoming young again is the realm of fantasy and hope in the sporting world and in life alike. In the sports world, maturity often is a means of hanging on, not winning. Instead, commentators speak of athletes being "back to their old self"—that is, young. Literature, too, makes use of this trope. In Ernest Hemingway's baseball-happy *The Old Man and the Sea*, first published in 1952, Santiago finds faith and solace in the New York Yankees—"Have faith in the Yankees my son. Think of the great DiMaggio" (18)—and is relieved when "The great DiMaggio is himself again" (22). The disturbed narrator in Frederick Exley's sublime 1968 novel *A Fan's Notes* hitches his life and existence to football player Frank Gifford and suffers psychologically as Gifford's skills decline. In one passage, the narrator hopes for a time machine, wishing that New York Giants quarterback George Shaw could choose to throw to one of two different versions of wide receiver Frank Giffords: the current over-the-hill Gifford and the young Gifford in his prime: "Shaw would not, of course, pass to the Gifford who was even now flanked wide to the left side of the field but to some memory of the ball player he once had been" (346).

By the end of "The Second Strongest Man," Sergei's return to a younger self is marked by sadness. He has reverted to the alcoholic state in which Roman Berman first found him back in Riga, when Sergei remained "completely unperturbed," hovering on the edge of conversation drinking vodka while the amateur bodybuilders and Soviet soldiers trash-talked each other outside the Dynamo gym (43). A near-identical event happens at the Bermans' Toronto apartment. While the old friends enjoy a meal together, discussing old times and bringing East and West together, Sergei silently "listened to all the conversations and drank," and "continued to address the bottle of vodka . . . after the requisite toasts" (59).

When Sergei finally does speak up at the dinner table, he praises Roman for getting "the hell out" of the Soviet "cemetery" because now he can "look forward to a real life" (59). Sergei then turns on Gregory, his coach, and thus also on the sporting system that helped turn him into a star: "And what do we look forward to? What kind of life, Gregory Davidovich, you KGB cocksucker!" (59). The slur, too, takes us back to the beginning of the story: one of the hobbyist bodybuilders used it against Sergei's soldier friend while claiming that nobody could lift a Moskvich ("Impossible even for a stupid cocksucker like you" [43]), and the soldier repeated it in his build-up to Sergei's performance ("you watch the stupid cocksucker" [44]). Now, Sergei uses it. And just as Sergei once put the hobbyists in their place, now Gregory does the same, admitting that Sergei is correct in assuming he will be "put out . . . to pasture. Soviet pasture" (59), perhaps forgotten, perhaps left to reminisce about glory days.

At this point in the story, conversation between Berman and his old friends breaks down. Gregory admits that he "should have left [the Soviet Union] when he had the chance" (60), while Roman expresses regrets or second thoughts about having left: "Don't be fooled, Grisha [Gregory]. I often think of going back" (60). Here the reunion between friends falters. Not believing Roman, Gregory assumes his friend is trying to console him: "I see your car. I see your apartment. I see how you struggle. Believe me, your worst day is better than my best" (60). In a perceptive and symbolic interpretation of this exchange, critic James Wood points out the story's "depictions of shifting hierarchies and the changed fortune that exile brings: the Soviet gold medallist is only a silver medallist in the West, and no longer the idol he once was; yet the struggling Russian immigrant, whose life seems to be day upon day of hard graft, is envied by the visiting Soviet" (2004). If Roman longs for his old life, where language would not be an enemy, where his skills and credentials would be acknowledged, he does not express envy.

* * *

When dealing with Bezmozgis's works, it is often tempting to point out parallels to his biography. This practice, however, devalues the crafted and created aspect of his fiction: to point out that details from Bezmozgis's life are close to many contained in stories such as "The Second Strongest Man" implies that the author is merely jotting down his life experience. While it is true that Bezmozgis emigrated to Canada from Riga, and while it is true that his father trained weightlifters and "on the side . . . ran a bodybuilding class, particularly popular with young Riga Jews" (Bezmozgis 2012b, 90), the fiction does not improve (or worsen) if we know the author's own story. Bezmozgis has often addressed this life-or-literature dichotomy in interviews. For example, in 2004 interview with *Quill and Quire* published after *Natasha and Other Stories*, he stated: "The stories may be called autobiographical fiction but the part that interests me is the fiction." He is clearly resourceful in mining his past for details that can meaningfully flourish in his fiction, much of which plays itself out in an in-between space.

Weightlifting proves the perfect sport for probing masculinity, in-betweenness, and how quickly athletic fame and prowess can fade. Like the immigrant whose life is split between a before and an after, the fading athlete moves into another realm of existence. Raising a bar above one's head in search of victory epitomizes individuality just as it epitomizes absolute, crystalline strength. Mark places Sergei on a pedestal, showing reverence but also taking him beyond the realm of the natural. "I had seen statues with such arms," says Mark. "I understood that the statues were meant to reflect the real arms of real men, but except for Sergei I had never met anyone with arms like that" (52). At moments like this, Sergei exists in an in-between space, on the margins of reality, between art and flesh.

WORKS CITED

Baer, Adam. 2004. "From Toronto With Love." *The Atlantic* 2004 (June). www.theatlantic.com/magazine/archive/2004/06/from-toronto-with-love/303128/.

Bezmozgis, David. 2004a. "Roman Berman, Massage Therapist." In *Natasha and Other Stories*, 19–36. New York: Farrar, Straus & Giroux.

Bezmozgis, David. 2004b. "The Second Strongest Man." In *Natasha and Other Stories*, 37–64. New York: Farrar, Straus & Giroux.

Bezmozgis, David. 2012a. "On Literary Love." *The Rumpus*, April 5, 2012. www.therumpus.net/2012/04/on-literary-love/.

Bezmozgis, David. 2012b. "Soviet Strongman: Grigory Novak (1919–1980)." In *Jewish Jocks: An Unorthodox Hall of Fame*, edited by Franklin Foer and Marc Tracy, 90–95. New York: Grand Central Publishing. Kindle.

Connor, Steven. 2011. *A Philosophy of Sport*. London: Reaktion Books. Kindle.

Dryden, Ken. (1983) 1999. *The Game*. Toronto: McClelland & Stewart.

Dunning, Eric. 1999. *Sport Matters: Sociological Studies of Sport, Violence and Civilization*. London: Routledge.

Exley, Frederick. (1968) 1988. *A Fan's Notes*. New York: Vintage.

Hemingway, Ernest. (1952) 2015. *The Old Man and the Sea*. Beirut, Lebanon: World Heritage Publishers.

Hemon, Aleksandar. 2015. "In Search of Lost Space." In *CEI Round Table at Vilenica "Reflections of Place,"* edited by Tanja Petrič and Nana Vogrin, 36–45. Ljubljana: The Slovene Writers' Association.

Hobsbawm, Eric J. 1990. *Nations and Nationalism Since 1780: Programme, Myth, Reality*. Cambridge: Cambridge University Press.

Kaloh Vid, Natalia. 2019. "The Challenge of (Not) Translating Russian-English Code-Switching in David Bezmozgis's *Natasha and Other Stories* (2004)." In *Translation and/und Migration*, edited by Ada Gruntar Jermol, Mojca Schlamberger Brezar, and Vlasta Kučiš, 168–78. Ljubljana: Ljubljana University Press. https://ebooks.uni-lj.si/zalozbaul/catalog/download/160/256/4123-1?inline=1.

MacDonald, Cheryl A. 2018. "Insert Name of Openly Gay Hockey Player Here: Attitudes towards Homosexuality among Canadian Male Major Midget AAA Ice Hockey Players." *Sociology of Sport Journal* 35: 347–57.

McGinn, Colin. 2008. *Sport.* Stocksfield, UK: Acumen.

Mercer, Rick. 2005. "Ken Dryden Song." First aired March 7, 2005. YouTube video, 0:51. www.youtube.com/watch?v=PmZUlEdp5so.

Oriard, Michael. 1982. *Dreaming of Heroes: American Sports Fiction, 1868–1980.* Chicago: Nelson-Hall.

Phillips, Laura. 2005. "The Long Shadow of the 'Old Country.'" Jewish Quarterly 197 (Spring): article 81. https://www.tandfonline.com/doi/abs/10.1080/0449010X.2005.10706913.

Q&Q Staff. 2004. "One Man Shock-And-Awe." *Quill and Quire*, March 15, 2004. https://quillandquire.com/authors/one-man-shock-and-awe/.

Stoffman, Judy. "'Escape to Purgatory': A review of *The Free World*, by David Bezmozgis." *Literary Review of Canada* 2011 (November). www.reviewcanada.ca/magazine/2011/11/escape-to-purgatory/.

Wood, James. 2004. "A Long Day at the Chocolate Bar Factory." *London Review of Books*, December 16, 2004. www.lrb.co.uk/the-paper/v26/n24/james-wood/a-long-day-at-the-chocolate-bar-factory.

Young, Darlene S. 1999. "Weightlifting." In *Encyclopedia of World Sport: From Ancient Times to the Present*, edited by David Levinson and Karen Christensen, 440–42. New York: Oxford University Press.

Weightlifting, Humour, and the Writer's Sensibility

An Interview with David Bezmozgis

This interview was conducted in February 2021 by email between David Bezmozgis's home in Toronto, Ontario, and Jason Blake's home in Ljubljana, Slovenia.

JASON BLAKE: Sports seem to have been a crucial part of your upbringing. Did sports have any sort of influence on your artistic path? Did they have any influence on your writing?

DAVID BEZMOZGIS: My father was in sports, both as a trainer and coach, and as an athlete. As a trainer and coach, he specialized in Olympic weightlifting and strength training. Before we left the Soviet Union, he achieved the level of international weightlifting judge, such that he could have officiated at the Olympics—though he never did. As an athlete, his sports were soccer and hockey. Growing up, I heard him talk about athletes and coaches he knew—some of them very famous—and we also watched a lot of sports together. It was the main area of commonality between us. I played a lot of sports growing up and was a passable athlete, though not as good as he was. The physical remains an important part of my life and my conception of myself. I think it's integral to who I am, but at some level, probably also a reaction against some effete stereotype of writers and artists. When I started to write, I was conscious of wanting to include the physical, including athletics, in the work. Also, I wanted to counter stereotypes of Jews as being mostly intellectual and neurotic, since the men I grew up with—my father's friends in particular—were very physical.

JB: Your writing has some deadpan humour and is also situationally funny. Do you actively think of humour or does it simply appear as your write?

DB: I think writers have sensibilities, the way they see the world. If you see the world as funny, somewhat absurd, it will find its way into the writing. What else? I think Jews are a funny people, and that humour and irony are part of the national character. Perhaps a function of being outsiders, often a minority within the larger majority—where humour is a useful tool and a defence mechanism. But it's a hard thing to talk about. You're only ever as funny as other people believe you to be.

JB: You've often mentioned the autobiographical background details behind your stories, though they are of course fiction. You've also mentioned that you are following in the footsteps of Richler and Roth by shining a fictional light on a community. How do you straddle the line between the public and the private?

DB: I think that's also a sensibility question. There must be something about me that enjoys blurring the line between the real and the fictional. It is a sort of game, one that writers like Roth and Richler played, often very well. There are others who have done it too—Leonard Michaels, a writer who was and remains very meaningful to me, is another. I think one reason for this is that I believed that family's immigration was compelling subject matter for fiction and so I just used what I had and elaborated from it. I kept much of the context—places, jobs, family dynamics—but invented most of the events. And I also like playing around with alternate versions of "myself," placing that self in situations that never happened to see what he would do. Not arbitrarily, but for some dramatic and thematic purpose.

JB: Was Grigory Novak in any way a model for the Sergei Federenko character?

DB: No, the model for Sergei Federenko was a different lifter, Gennady Ivanchenko. He was an extraordinary athlete, and the kind of natural phenom Federenko is described as being. My father knew him well and had some hand in training him, although his principal coach was a friend of my father's, an older Jewish coach named Misha Freifeld. These names are mostly lost to the fog of history.

JB: You manage to make a small, multilingual community understandable to any English-speaking reader. Is there an ideal reader you have in mind? (I am not suggesting that one has to be Latvian-Russian-Canadian/American-emigrated-in-the-1970s-Jewish to enjoy or appreciate your work!)

DB: I'm aware that I'm acting as kind of a tour guide and cultural interpreter for this quite marginal community. My goal when I write is to make it accessible to people outside the community but also authentic to those within it. Beyond that, my ideal reader is someone who likes the sort of books I read and the authors I like.

11

Adrian Markle

"It All Gets Beaten Out of You"

Poverty, Boxing, and Writing in Steven Heighton's *The Shadow Boxer*

Steven Heighton's modern CanLit classic *The Shadow Boxer* (2000) is about Sevigne Torrins, a boy who grew up in a working-class family in Sault Ste. Marie, "the Soo," a northern Ontario industrial city on the decline. Sevigne dreams of a different life than the one most people find there. He wants to be a writer, and on his journey toward that goal, he travels from the Soo to upper-class Cairo, then bohemian Toronto, and finally to harsh and spartan Rye Island in Lake Superior. In addition to being a writer, Sevigne is also a boxer, a pursuit he inherited from his father Sam Torrins.

Sport plays an important role in many authors' lives and sometimes their creative processes. Haruki Murakami, for instance, runs. As he puts it, "I run in a void . . . I run in order to *acquire* a void" (Murakami 2008, 17). He runs to distract his conscious thought with groaning muscles and to allow his "comprehension meter to shoot upward" so that he is "finally able to grasp something" (22). His athletic process here is complementary to his creative process: the one enhances the other. This complementary relationship is the case for many writers. However, the relationship between sport and the page is not as simple for Sevigne, not as singularly positive. Boxing—a term I use interchangeably with fighting and pugilism—is so closely tied to lower-class poverty that it is emblematic of it. In Heighton's novel, Sevigne's boxing, inextricably tied to his lower-class upbringing, actually impedes his progress toward success in writing—an activity associated with a higher social class.

It doesn't do this in an immediate way (he does not, for instance, skip a meeting with an agent in favour of a boxing tournament at the rec centre), but in an almost karmic way. Sevigne's boxing-as-relic-of-class-background *automatically* prevents him from truly succeeding within the writing class. This is not due to the machinations of any one individual, but to those of the universe itself, as if it were fated by the stars. His twin pursuits of writing and boxing occupy the shared space of his life but seem to repel one another, like oil sheening atop the rough waters of Lake Superior.

THE SOO AND BOXING AS LOWER-CLASS EMBLEM

"If you want to know who's at d'bottom of society, all you gotta do is look at who's boxin'," said DeeDee Armour, boxing coach at Woodlawn Boys Club in Chicago (in Wacquant 2006, 42). Indeed, "the overwhelming majority of boxers come from . . . the working class" (41). This makes sense, of course. Who else would do it? Boxers—at least the type who are serious enough about the sport to become competitive—must maintain a sometimes-monastic lifestyle and endure numerous injuries and ailments for an ever-diminishing chance to earn from an ever-diminishing prize pool. There aren't many who would view this as a reasonable investment of their time and health unless they had few other economic opportunities. Boxing as a pursuit is intrinsically tied to lower-class poverty.

While there are certainly boxers—both in literature and in life—who come from the upper class, they are the exceptions. Sevigne was born in and ultimately returned to Toronto, but between those periods of his life he grew up in the Soo, which is "squalid," and full of "dirt and dead leaves" and "thawing dogshit" in the spring (*Shadow Boxer*, 59). As an adult, he drives a "rotting Pontiac sedan" with a "prolapsed muffler" past "those slumped, wobbling derelicts who swilled Listermint or Sterno or Aqua Velva" to his low-paying job (17–18). With his father retired, Sevigne's "skimpy tips and paycheques made up the shortfall when the pension money wasn't enough for the booze" (17). However, Sevigne's low-class origins are not something he can simply leave behind when he moves to Cairo or Toronto. As Gavin Jones says, "poverty becomes a trait of identity, with class status coming to seem natural rather than contingent" (2008, 3). Poverty, Jones continues, results in "lasting behavioural patterns" (39). It is more than simply a backdrop: it is a fundamental part of who Sevigne is.

The same is true about boxing, both for Sevigne and, even more noticeably, for the older Torrins.

Sam Torrins (who I, like the novel, will simply call Torrins) was a dedicated amateur boxer in his youth, but his adult life was defined by his naval service and by working onboard freighters that sailed across Lake Superior. In his retirement, however, it is his time in the ring that most significantly informs his identity. We see this in Torrins's dedication to the routines of boxing. He begins his days "shadow-boxing" (11), "moving boxer-like foot to foot" (14) around the kitchen. He asks his son if he wants to go "a couple rounds after breakfast" (111), even after he can no longer actually fight those rounds. For much of his presence in the novel, Torrins is no longer in any real shape to box: "[H]e was lumbersome and wheezy and Sevigne could dance circles around him, landing jabs at will" (*Shadow Boxer*, 13). Despite his degenerating body and the fact that his boxing career ended years ago—and in disappointment—he and Sevigne both seem to demarcate his life according to the state of his body: he is either "still with a boxer's body" (10) or he is not, having instead "rheumy eyes and white stubble of a queen street drunk, nose cratered and veined, slack breasts. Gut soft, and the rotten old wineskin of his stomach scraped raw with a razor" (112). As Joyce Carol Oates explains, this focus on the body makes sense: "[A] boxer 'is' his body, and is totally identified with it" (1987, 5). Torrins is his body, and his body is boxing; he can't get away from boxing, nor, therefore, from the working-class anger and dispossession it has symbolized in his life. His last words in the book solidify this connection. Sevigne remembers the scene: helping Torrins to bed one night, the old man announces that he wants to tell him something—"Sum total of all I've gleaned. In one pithy summation." Smiling sardonically, Torrins pulls him close and then "says with casual finality, It all gets beaten out of you" (363). For Torrins, life was ultimately a series of losses in violent conflicts with the world. His identity as both a boxer and a lower-class worker centre on fighting—and eventually one must just quit fighting.

Late in life, Torrins's other sport, swimming, brings him a totally different state of mind. Even when Torrins was too old and drunk to box, "the old boy could still swim" (13), churning miles through the wild water outside their house in a way that awed Sevigne by the grace and purity of the movement, calling to mind Victor Turner's concept of flow: "the holistic sensation present when we act with total involvement" (1982, 55). The flow state is one in which we feel outside of time, becoming completely engaged with the singular task of the present. Flow state, in other words, is a state of "unified flowing from one moment to the next in which we feel in control of our actions, and in which there is little distinction between self and environment; between stimulus and response; or between past, present, and future" (56). Flow is the pure, timeless freedom of physicality. Torrins does not seem to feel it any longer when he tries to shadow box in the house or spar with Sevigne in the yard; he's too self-consciously limited by his decrepitude to lose himself mindlessly in the physicality of the sport. But he remembers how his boxing flow used to feel and can still access it while in the water—at least for a while. Torrins dies in the water, notably, on an occasion when he is unable to access the flow state because he is conscious to the point of distraction of "the burning of his gut" (112), the feeling that "his arms are dead weight" (112), the "whirling and vertigo" (113), and "his own heart, hugely amplified" (113). Here, Heighton reinforces the link between sport and identity: Torrins literally ceases to live when he ceases to feel like an athlete. Yet this athlete identity is not neutral for Torrins—it is not linked to just any sport. Although he swam successfully for longer than he boxed, made his living on the water for decades, and died by drowning, swimming is never the sport with which the old man most closely identified, nor the one with which others identified him. Long after Torrins's death, Sevigne recalls how "their father almost fought Ali" (128), invoking his father's unrealized boxing fantasy rather than the real accomplishments of his time on the water. In *The Shadow Boxer*, like in many novels about boxers, it is boxing that completely dominates the identity of the athlete.

Sevigne inherits his father's love for boxing. At the same time, ironically, boxing becomes for him a way to escape the negative things that the sport represented in his father's life: disappointment, trauma, and poverty. This is reminiscent of Stephen Lyng's concept of edgework: participation in dangerous activities as a means of escaping the kinds of "social conditions that produce stunted identities and offer few opportunities for personal transformation and character development" (2005, 6). Growing up in a social environment that left his father feeling that everything had been "beaten" out of him, Sevigne turns to an activity of physical danger to transform himself into someone who can endure that endless beating and won't be kept down by it. But this liberatory view of boxing is not shared by everyone. When Sevigne starts properly training and competing with his high school boxing club, the "aspiring artists and songwriters" who had become his friends deride his decision, claiming that boxing is "primitive" and "scum culture" (67–68). Sevigne immediately understands that this judgment is about class: "[B]oxing lived on the wrong side of the tracks" (68). Although his friends come from that same side of the tracks, they don't see boxing as a means of crossing them and aspire instead to more high-minded pursuits with which boxing appears incompatible. Heighton invites us to consider that while Sevigne may be able to use boxing to withstand his conditions, he may not be able to use it to overcome them. The identity of boxing is anchored in the body and in social class, and it appears to act as an anchor for Sevigne, who has internalized it and crafted it into a part of his identity. Boxing eventually gives him the confidence to leave the Soo, but it also prevents him from ever truly leaving his class-background behind.

CAIRO, TORONTO, AND WRITING AS UPPER-CLASS DOMAIN

As we've seen, Torrins's identity is tied to his body. Jamie Dopp, drawing a distinction between the body and the mind, might call him a "body-person" (2018, 95). Leger Grindon notes that the boxer specifically "personifies a division between the body and the spirit," where spirit refers to anything "beyond the body" (2019, 258). Grindon also refers to this division as a "mind-body split" (259). There is a separation or even conflict between the boxer's life of the body and the writer's or intellectual's life of the mind. Sevigne experiences this separation but, like many things in the novel, we first see it in Torrins.

Torrins is an avid reader, a devout lover of the classics, who plays a game with Sevigne in which the elder Torrins chooses a quotation from classic literature and Sevigne names the writer and the work. When referring to these famous authors, Torrins casualizes their names: "Ginny Woolf, Joe Conrad, Gus Herodotus—Torrins was on a nickname basis with them all, like a man who'd never expected to be let in to some elite coterie and now must constantly remind you of how fully, and by his own bootstraps, he has arrived" (*Shadow Boxer*, 15). But Torrins has not, in fact, been let into this coterie. He has not arrived. Torrins lives in a social class below the "elite." He lives in squalor, alone except for the intermittent company of Sevigne. No one consults him. No one includes him. Even his identification game—the primary way he discusses these works—simply indexes their contents and does not meaningfully interact with them. There is always a distance between him and them; they remain always inaccessible, even if ever present in his life. This tension plays out in different ways in Torrins's life, for example in Sevigne's brother's name. Their mother, Martine, had wished to name him Byron, after the poet. Torrins, despite his love of classic literature, refused that name, as if his inability to truly feel kindship with that elite coterie was so profound that he could not overcome it, even by blood relation. Torrins settles on a compromise, naming his son not Byron but Bryon (*Shadow Boxer*, 36).

Torrins has internalized the idea that writing and literature are innately upper-class concerns, and in that he is correct. Just as boxing is primarily the purview of the lower classes, literature and media in general are the dominion of the upper classes. As John Carlos Rowe says, "the traditionally defined proletariat is defined less by the theft of its *physical* power—labor power per se—than by exclusion from the diverse media through which the economy produces its effects" (1993, 62). Media, which includes literature, has long been a vehicle for "the production of social consensus" and as such has also long been primarily limited to those from the appropriate social stratum (74). So, while Sevigne may share the traditionally "bourgeois fetishization of the novel" (74), there are significant cultural barriers to his involving himself in (let alone seizing) the production of such a text. As Rowe says, "the exploitation of the postmodern working class begins with our exclusion from these media" (72). Gavin Jones makes a similar observation about the way in which poverty might exclude the lower class from engaging in activities with high cultural capital, though his explanation is more internal. He says that hunger, by which he means "the desire that constitutes the human subject," is, in its extremes, able to "destroy the intellectual self-consciousness of the poor, thus cutting them off the entirely from the realm of literate culture" (2008, 144–45). So Sevigne, like Torrins before him, may never truly become a part of that writing class; his background of poverty (embodied by his pugilism) is a fundamental element of his identity and as such will always remain a barrier.

When he was a teenager, Sevigne's parents divorced, and his mother and brother relocated to upper-class Cairo with their mother's new diplomat husband. Sevigne went with them briefly, but soon returned to live with his father in the Soo. As a boy in this town, Sevigne had grown up scrapping wildly with his brother, but as a high school student Sevigne commits himself to properly learning to box. He also commits himself to literature. In fact, Heighton reveals that the origins of literature and fighting in Sevigne's life are intertwined, perhaps giving truth to Sevigne's claims of a poem and a fight being "made from the same energy" (68). Sevigne begins "tearing through books at a rate of one or two a day," which is cause enough for other students in the school to beat him up, thus literally putting violence in opposition to literature from the outset (*Shadow Boxer*, 53). After physically defending his reading habits, Sevigne also begins "to fill dime-store notebooks with poems and stories of his own" (53). The intertwined origins of boxing and literature in Sevigne's life might give the impression that they are complementary, but they do not function that way in the novel. Though they are both central to Sevigne's life, his engagement with boxing regularly corresponds with diminished engagement or success in writing.

Sevigne boxes and writes throughout high school, but writing clearly takes a back seat. He rarely manages to do more than dash "urgent stanzas on the endpapers of his books" (72–73), demonstrating that his writing is the result of occasional inspiration rather than dedicated time or effort. This dynamic continues past his graduation. Heighton pays significant attention to Sevigne's amateur boxing career, in some cases even giving a blow-by-blow account of his exploits. By comparison, except for one summer when Sevigne is "focused on his books and his poems and his boxing" (82), he says comparatively little about Sevigne's writing. Then, all of a sudden, after a brutal bout in the North Ontario finals, Sevigne pitches "his bloody handwraps and shoes and mouthpiece into the trash" (89). This moment is not the end of his training, sparring, or even fighting, but it is the end of his participation in organized competition. With competition behind him, Sevigne finally begins to see success with his writing, and has a piece accepted by the *Toronto Poetry Review* approximately a year after his last competition.

Shortly after that acceptance, Torrins dies. Torrins is the only other character in the novel who understood the flow state of boxing and the allure of that experience. As the only other person in the novel who spoke that particular language of the body—the poetic energy of pugilism—Torrins's death leaves Sevigne without anyone who can fully understand him. Restless and lonely, Sevigne returns to his mother and brother in Cairo.

In Cairo, Sevigne remains unhappy much of the time. His relationship with his brother is strained, and although he does not physically fight with

Bryon in Cairo like he did in the Soo, there is conflict, and even violence. During a game of golf (a sport associated with the upper class), they argue and criticize each other, and Sevigne ends up "hacking away" at a dwarf palm with his five iron and seemingly purposefully driving the cart, with his brother screaming in the passenger seat, into the Nile (124). But they do not throw fists; they do not *fight*. Heighton suggests that actual fighting simply is not an option in this upper-class existence, even for those like Sevigne who identify with violence. But writing is another story. In Cairo, in a large house with servants and far away from the rough, hand-to-mouth life he lived with his father, Sevigne starts to write *Islands of the Nile*, the novel that comes to represent his literary success in the same way that boxing represents his class. Notably, this real literary progress is not made until he has removed himself from the place of his lower-class upbringing.

When Sevigne finishes the first draft of his novel, he also finishes with Cairo and moves back to Canada, landing in Toronto to meet up with some of the artists who had been his friends in high school. He lives a bohemian lifestyle of drinking, sex, and music while trying to make it as a writer. This new lifestyle does not make him happy. Heighton depicts Sevigne as being in a steady state of conflict with his environment, though this conflict rarely manifests as anything more than dissatisfaction. Sevigne does achieve moderate writing success, placing some poems and signing a deal for a poetry collection, but his great ambition still rests on *Islands of the Nile*, the completion and publication of which elude him to his increasing frustration and distress.

Sevigne is poor in Toronto, living in a cheap bachelor apartment he refers to as a "cell" (185) for "six fifty a month inclusive" (170), but he does not—for the majority of his time, at least—fight. This living situation seems to buck the trend of pugilism being an expression of poverty, but on closer examination that trend is still upheld. Sevigne's poverty in Toronto is voluntary, and perhaps even a facade. He has ample opportunity to make money; he simply chooses not to. He regularly argues with his magazine editor friend about the length of the book reviews he turns in, and therefore does fewer of them than he could. He takes, then quits, a one-dollar-per-word job writing book summaries for the type of CD-ROM encyclopedia popular at the time, and then he takes a job writing lyrics for advertising jingles that would pay him between "eight and fifteen grand per year" (204). This would be more than enough to cover his small bachelor apartment for "very little effort" or time, but he eventually quits this job too (290). So, while he does not have much money in Toronto, he is no poorer than he would like to be at any given moment. He is not truly poor, nor is the community he is a part of—which, being populated with artists, is also one of high cultural capital and high potential monetary capital. His boxing-free experience of poverty in Toronto underlines the ongoing incoherence of fighting in his existence in and pursuit of a higher social and monetary class, a conclusion supported by the events surrounding Sevigne's departure from Toronto.

After having been away from the working class for long enough, Sevigne finally gets some good news regarding *Islands of the Nile*. One of Toronto's major publishers announces their plan to partner with a major New York publisher and release his book, which is what he's been yearning for since moving to Toronto. He rides the high of that success until one night, when out for dinner with his more successful artist girlfriend Ike and her success-ful friends, he gets into a fight. Defending himself against a thin-skinned former friend, Ray, who has become jealous of Sevigne's new-found success, Sevigne leaves Ray "sprawled out on the icy flags" while "the guests look on" in "wary fascination" (268). After Sevigne fights Ray, he does not rejoin his upper-class girlfriend and colleagues, opting to save them the "embar-rassment" that his presence might now cause (269). His fighting thus causes a literal departure from this group of upper-class creatives.

Sevigne's re-engagement with fighting and the lower-class origin it sig-nifies causes a total break between him and all his upper-class pursuits. Soon after Sevigne's return to fighting, he receives notice that his big-deal publisher "may have been somewhat . . . prematurely optimistic" in con-tacting him about publishing his novel, and now has no such plans (282). He has fought again, and now he has "lost the book" (287). He also loses his girlfriend, whom he cheated on. Suddenly, he has lost all sense of belonging in this upper-class environment—what Heighton has called Sevigne's "false life" (2020, 22). But what is false about it? Sevigne shares the same artistic calling and sensibilities as his Toronto cohort, many of whom come from the same socioeconomic background as him without feeling their lives to be "false." Sevigne's feeling of falsity rests on the fact that boxing—and through boxing, an interiorized working-class poverty—remains a core element of his identity. Any life he built within extravagant, upper-class Toronto would be incompatible with his essential sense of self.

The Shadow Boxer is a novel of movement. The class and identity conflict the novel contains is there because the characters, especially Sevigne, move frequently through different environments. The family starts out in Toronto, then moves to the Soo, where ultimately Sevigne's parents divorce. Sevigne's mother Martine remarries and takes the boys to upper-class Cairo. Sevigne returns to live with his father; Bryon returns once to visit. After Torrins's death, Sevigne goes back to Cairo, then moves to Toronto, then to Rye Island. After this, he returns briefly to Cairo before going travelling. The presence or absence of fighting in Sevigne's (and, to a certain extent, Bryon's) behaviour is connected to his current class context and extends to the edges of his time in each place: the moments after he has decided to move from an upper-class to a lower-class setting but before he actually does so. The violence he anticipates in his future bleeds into his present.

The Torrins family spent the first years of Sevigne's life on the outskirts of Toronto, but financial considerations forced them to pack up and relocate, like "a shameful retreat after a bad beating" (43), to the Soo where Sam Torrins grew up. By comparing moving to a lower-class area to fleeing after a physical assault, Heighton creates the beginning of a key pattern for understanding the relationship between class and boxing in *The Shadow Boxer*: not only does violence in the form of fighting or boxing stem from lower-class areas, but such violence is, in fact, *solely* the province of those areas and the liminal spaces between classes. When the characters enter a lower-class context, they fight; when they enter a higher-class context, they do not, even though most other elements remain consistent. So, it is when the Torrinses move from the more cultured and affluent Toronto to the less cultured and affluent Sault Ste. Marie that Sevigne and his older brother Bryon "began to fist fight, the larger Bryon always winning, but Sevigne, even pinned and bloodied, unwilling to submit" (30). This fraternal violence continues throughout their time in the Soo; Heighton even introduces readers to new locations in the town as places where Sevigne and his brother "had once pounded each other bloody" (8). In the Soo, this violence is a part of their everyday lives.

Heighton presents Cairo as a clear cultural departure from the Soo, not only in terms of ethnic culture but also in terms of class. Everson Milne, Martine's new husband, lives in an "antique house . . . in the old city" (38) from which Sevigne's bedroom view is a "poetic and surprisingly clear panorama of Cairo" (39). Milne's lifestyle, which Martine, Sevigne, and Bryon now share, is characterized by "the comforts of his home . . . his hired help . . . the bounty of his table" (40)—a constant source of anger and conflict for Sevigne. This household experience is Sevigne's family's first encounter with upper-class life, and remarkably, though the boys have even more conflict in their relationship now than they did in the Soo (having sided with opposing parents and feeling differently about Milne and their new life), they cease to fight physically. While in the lower-class realm of their father's life they decide their differences with their fists, in the upper-class realm of their mother's life they do so with their words. In the world of *The Shadow Boxer*, Heighton not only associates pugilism with the lower class, but also sophisticated communication with the upper class. But as Sevigne's departure from Cairo approaches, this contextually appropriate mindset begins to shift. He becomes more combative with his mother, "slap[ping] at her until she pinned him down . . . or stormed out . . . or they embraced" (42). In this liminal stage of having decided to leave but having not yet left, Sevigne has a fractional return to physical conflict—slaps and tears—before returning to the fists and blood of his fights in the Soo.

Bryon demonstrates this same class-contextual engagement with violence later when, having returned to the Soo for a visit and getting into an argument with Sevigne over the dinner table, he ends up "shaking" with rage before "smash[ing] the bake-dish of poutine against the mural" (63). Bryon's smashing of the dish is not the full-on violence of the brothers' previous fights, but a behaviour that he is settling into as he readjusts to this lower-class experience. Bryon, like Sevigne, stopped fighting once he moved to Cairo. Unlike Sevigne, except for this one blip when he returns briefly to the Soo, Bryon never returns to violence in any form, distancing himself from it so much that he comes to refer to boxing as "caveman culture" (128). Fighting becomes "other" to him.

Sevigne enters another of these liminal, transitional spaces after being drawn into the fight with Ray that precipitates the collapse of his upper-class life and encourages his departure from upper-class Toronto. After this fight, as if in preparation for his social decline, he *starts* a fight for the first time in the big city, attacking and then getting beaten by a group of youths harassing a homeless man (298). We see Sevigne move back and forth between lower- and higher-class environments several times in the novel, and while his violence is largely confined to lower-class environments, we frequently see it bleed through at the tail end of his attempts to fit into higher society, signalling his mental shift to a different cultural context.

RYE ISLAND AND TRAUMA AS THERAPY

After losing his girlfriend, book, and sense of belonging in the upper-class society as a result (in part) of the expression of his lower-class upbringing in that false upper-class context, Sevigne journeys to Rye Island. This move echoes his father's much earlier decision to move from Toronto to the Soo—"a shameful retreat after a bad beating" (43), which in Sevigne's case happens to be literally true. Rye Island is a rough and wild place in Lake Superior that has long been a cornerstone of the moonshining mythology of his father's family. The island, and its harsh, ascetic lifestyle, will remove Sevigne from the Toronto culture that he never felt a part of and give him time to do nothing but finish his novel. It will allow him to punish himself, and thus perhaps atone, for his infidelity to his ex, Ike. He arranges to have himself dropped there in the summer, to be retrieved in the spring, and to be occasionally resupplied in the meantime. He will be the lone occupant of the island, living in an old bootlegging shack with historical significance to his family. Being alone prevents him from actually fighting anyone, but his willingness to engage in violent acts nonetheless returns when he descends to the class of the bootleggers, a shift that is evident when, for instance, he fires his rifle at a nearby pleasure boat of rich partiers who kill a bird he had befriended (322). To fill his days, he swims if the weather will allow it. He listens to the battery powered radio. He drinks moonshine that he finds hidden in the shack from an earlier age. He edits and re-writes *Islands of the Nile*. But beyond his new daily routine, he has not yet meaningfully changed.

Before leaving Toronto, Sevigne quit his lyric writing job because he couldn't bear to write one more jingle, saying "I'd hate myself if I did it." He adds, "Hate myself more, I mean" (290), demonstrating the depressed self-loathing that he feels before he sets off to remote Rye Island. In *Class Representation in Modern Fiction and Film*, Keith Gandal discusses how "traumatic self-loathing and depression" often result in a character "degrading his body" in narratives about masculinity and poverty (2007, 161). Gandal says that "the desecrated body is a central image" of these narratives (164), in which tropes of bodily decay and degradation are associated with purification and transcendence (160). Ultimately, the protagonist is delivered "from the bohemian depths . . . with a death or symbolic death near the end" (166–67). All of these observations are relevant to the events that soon play out for Sevigne.

Eventually, Sevigne gets "frostbite on his trigger finger and the pinkie of his right hand" (351). After a week of increasing infection and pain, he takes Torrins's hunting knife and "sets the blade at the very base of the pinkie and begins to cut," leaving his pinkie lying on the log like "nothing remotely human" (353)—a degraded (former) body part. While recovering from his act of self-mutilation, Sevigne is degraded further, his bowels violently spasming on the floor of the stillhouse (which he had been occupying since he accidentally burned down the bootleggers' cabin). At this point, Sevigne feels like nothing more than a "dead man rising up and throwing off his grave-clothes to soil his own tomb" (363). Sevigne's literal destruction of his pinkie is also symbolic: he removes the pinkie on his right hand—that is, his *punching* hand. The right hand is emblematic of boxing, and thus of his lower-class identity. It is the dominant hand, the power hand, the knock-out hand—and Sevigne mutilates it, the symbolic death of the boxer within him. Though Sevigne does eventually return to training (seemingly with no competitive interest), this symbolic death is what ultimately opens the door to his end-of-novel growth.

Gandal refers to this type of narrative arc as "trauma as therapy," a common trope for the emotional development of characters that come from lower-class backgrounds (2007, 155). Sevigne destroys his identity as a fighter, and by extension as a lower-class person, along with all the anger that connotes. When the boat finally comes for him in spring, he is "strong and sane and grateful," and "he stands on the shore and beams, clenched fists uplifted" (369), much more emotionally prepared to function in the world to which he returns, which is somewhere in between the two worlds of his past. He spends time in meaningful locations around the Soo, but only as a visitor. He lives again in Toronto but is far less connected to or interested in his old upper-class social and cultural contexts than before. He is calmer and more at peace. Ike notices the change and considers getting back together with him. His family notices as well. In trying to explain his transformation to himself, Sevigne speculates that the isolated, natural environment of Rye Island perhaps "reconceived a hunger for blood connections"—though that alone does not seem to satisfactorily explain the seemingly total lack of conflict with his brother or his brother's and mother's romantic partners, the latter of whom are obviously not "blood connections." He also suggests that "the writing of his novel seems to have exorcised other demons" in him (377), though he continues to write his novel even after Rye Island: "[E]very day. Same novel. I can't seem to finish it" (381). Years after the publication of *The Shadow Boxer*, Heighton explicitly claimed that "failure" was "the making of" Sevigne (2020, 23), but this explanation also doesn't fully explain the change in him. Sevigne began writing his novel long before Rye Island and would continue long after, and he had failed many times before: in the boxing ring, in love, on the page. The unique event with the power to exorcise his demons was the symbolic destruction of his identity as a working-class fighter.

* * *

Sevigne Torrins is a kid with dreams of a sophisticated life of the mind in the big city, but he is also a working-class kid. He is emblematic of the working class: he fights, both in the ring and out of it. His fighting is not the cause of his failure to achieve his dreams over the course of the novel, but it is the symbol of the cause. His love of boxing is illustrative of his origins in lower-class poverty and its influence on his identity. Each time he retreats from an upper-class context to a lower-class context, he demarcates that movement by fighting. His life of the body will not easily become a life of the mind; his life on the one side of the tracks cannot easily be transplanted to the other. He cannot resolve this conflict until he retreats to the lowest class he can, out of society altogether, to Rye Island, where destroys the symbol of his lower-class upbringing: his punching hand. When he returns to civilization, he is more equipped to function in that higher-class context emotionally and intellectually, and perhaps creatively as well.

WORKS CITED

Dopp, Jamie. 2018. "Hockey, Zen, and the Art of Bill Gaston's *The Good Body*." In *Writing the Body in Motion*, edited by Angie Abdou and Jamie Dopp, 139–51. Edmonton: Athabasca University Press.

Gandal, Keith. 2007. *Class Representation in Modern Fiction and Film*. New York: Palgrave Macmillan.

Grindon, Lester. 2019. "Body and Soul of the Screen Boxer." In *The Cambridge Companion to Boxing*, edited by Gerald Early, 258–72. Cambridge: Cambridge University Press.

Heighton, Steven. 2000. *The Shadow Boxer*. Toronto: Knopf Canada.

Heighton, Steven. 2020. *The Virtues of Disillusionment*. Edmonton: Athabasca University Press.

Jones, Gavin. 2008. *American Hungers: The Problem of Poverty in U.S. Literature, 1840–1945*. Princeton: Princeton University Press.

Lyng, Stephen, ed. 2005. *Edgework: The Sociology of Risk Taking*. New York: Routledge.

Murakami, Haruki. 2008. *What I Talk About When I Talk About Running*. Translated by Philip Gabriel. London: Penguin Random House.

Oates, Joyce Carol. 1987. *On Boxing*. London: Bloomsbury.

Rowe, John Carlos. 1993. "The Writing Class." In *Politics, Theory, and Contemporary Culture*, edited by Mark Poster, 41–82. New York: Columbia University Press.

Turner, Victor. 1982. *From Ritual to Theatre: The Human Seriousness of Play*. New York: PAJ.

Wacquant, Loïc. 2006. *Body and Soul*. New York: Oxford University Press.

On Boxing

An Interview with Steven Heighton

This interview was conducted via email between Steven Heighton at his home in Kingston, Ontario and Adrian Markle at his home in Cornwall, UK from February 17 to March 2, 2021.

ADRIAN MARKLE: What kind of research on boxing did you do for the novel, and how did that impact the writing process? Did you feel a particular fidelity to the facts or experiences you gained in that research, or were they always only in service to the greater narrative?

STEVEN HEIGHTON: All my life I've been in too much of a rush—sometimes a matter of creative excitement, sometimes just standard-issue impatience—to follow the path of the apprentice and learn the skills I've needed. I've written eighteen books now using just a couple of fingers (well, mostly just one) because I couldn't be bothered to take a typing class in high school. At sixteen I taught myself to fingerpick guitar with just two fingers instead of learning properly. I taught myself to skate at eighteen and quickly internalized all sorts of wrong techniques.

Likewise, on starting *The Shadow Boxer*, I threw myself into the project and didn't worry that the only boxing I'd done was a bit of amateurish outdoor sparring in the pine woods at Jasper Park Lodge, in the Alberta Rockies, where I worked as a dishwasher and then waiter in the months after finishing high school. I and the other boys had no idea what we were doing. Various undignified minor injuries were sustained. That half-assed experimentation turned out to be useless when it came to drafting the novel's boxing scenes. Naturally I barged on anyway. I figured if I simply recalled the feeling of being in our pine forest ring, then extrapolated and imagined while deploying lots of muscular verbs, I could build scenes that felt real.

But when I reread the novel's first draft, those scenes felt dead on the page. The language seemed lively but some crucial spark was missing. So I learned the hard lesson every stylist has to metabolize: you can revise and polish your cadences forever, but if that X-factor is lacking, you end up with nothing more than an exercise in fluency and euphony.

In this case the X-factor was, I guessed, actual bodily knowledge and experience of the ring. So I joined the Kingston Youth Boxing Club and over the following year and a half redrafted and repeatedly revised my boxing scenes while working out and sparring at the club. I loved it there. The place had been in operation for some thirty years but it felt and smelled as if it had been around since the 1920s. The coaches were gruffly, avuncular, like the cornermen in old boxing films. In due course I got my rib cracked by the Canadian junior heavyweight champion, a 200-pound 16-year-old named Alex White, to whom the coaches injudiciously fed me one night after he'd tired out or maimed all his other, usual victims.

The scenes I drafted while training at the club wrote themselves, as they say. I could feel a live current flowing through me as I drafted them, my palms sweating, heart speeding, body fully engaged. To some extent I still felt it even as I rewrote them—and when passages continue to feel alive to you, so that the repeated revision doesn't seem like mere chore-doing, you know they have a pulse and legs.

As for feeling a fidelity to facts/experiences—no, never. I'll unapologetically change facts, dates, quotes, etcetera, to suit the stylistic or thematic exigencies of the work.

AM: At one point Sevigne talks about the thematic and experiential similarities between boxing and writing. Could you talk a little more about that comparison—where it holds up and where it falls apart? And, just for fun, if your experience of writing this novel was a boxing match, how would you describe it as having played out?

SH: Fun answer first. Novels are impossible. All novels fail at some point or on some level, first novels especially. In this case I'd say the author lost the fight in a split decision, having taken a beating in the middle rounds, but he went the distance and scored a couple of knockdowns, especially in the early and late rounds.

As for parallels between boxing and writing, I think really we're talking here about the similarities between boxing and life; the sport is not just like writing, it's like any activity that involves strife and struggle, conflict with others/oneself (especially, always, oneself), self-doubt, self-destructiveness, fear of failure, failure, tests of stamina, and brief moments of triumph (a lousy word here but I'm going to stet it). Consider this: How many key adages or turns of phrase has soccer, the biggest sport in the world for a century, lent to our language? Few if any, because soccer (like hockey, or basketball, or baseball) is nothing like life. It's artificial, its rules arbitrary. And there's nothing wrong with artifice; to play tennis, you need lines and a net.

But boxing, like running, is less a sport than an adapted form of a primordial activity. Fight or flight: box or run. And since boxing and running embody basic human survival mechanisms, their terminologies are widely applicable—and also now so well embedded they're all but invisible, which is to say clichéd. To go toe to toe with someone. To stay on your toes. Roll with the punches. Be on the ropes. Keep your chin down. Be in someone's corner. Throw in the towel. Take it on the chin, then take a low blow. Hit below the belt. Down for the count. Beat the count. Saved by the bell . . . I'll embrace the clichés here and spell it out: life too often feels like a combat sport, the kind where you're trapped and fighting to beat the odds while dimly aware of faces watching from the periphery, a few cheering you on, most leering or at least indifferent, none able to save you. And of course we all get knocked down and need to get up again (cue dramatic music) and keep trying. The hackneyed nature of this paradigm is what makes it seem so puerile, but on some level it's all perfectly valid and true.

And where does the analogy fail? I would say that it falls apart—in the sense of becoming superfluous, irrelevant—only if, after years of disciplined spiritual work, you achieve the wisdom to stop fighting yourself or needing to fight with the world. But even at that stage—which must be so nice—a fight might be forced on you, or you might need to take one on, on behalf of others. Though I guess by that point an enlightened being would know how to respond with aikido instead of throwing punches.

AM: There is a pretty substantial tradition in western literature of "the boxing novel." Do you consider yours a boxing novel, or a novel with boxing in it, and did that distinction, if you even agree there is one, affect your decision making when writing the novel (re: genre convention, entering canonical dialogue, etc.).

SH: I can't imagine writing a book that could be called a boxing novel. What would that even look like? A bit like those fluent, entertaining hockey stories for boys that Scott Young—Neil Young's father—used to write and that I read as a pre-teen? *Scrubs on Skates* is one title I recall. Now those were true sports novels; they were built around practice, games, scoring goals, getting benched, all that. The characters, as I recall, were flat—mere delivery systems for the exciting sports scenes that many kids of that age like reading. To write an adult version of that sort of book now, focused on any sport . . . I just wouldn't be interested, let alone obsessed, and obsession is the pathological basis on which a writer has to found an edifice as large as a novel. Without obsession how would you ever finish building something of 100,000 words? (I'm not sure exactly what it is that does obsess me enough to finish my books; I am sure it isn't my job to describe it.)

Anyway, whether my characters box, serve as sailors and get shipwrecked in the Arctic, work as doctors, mechanics, or bakers, that's not exactly who they are. Their various jobs or vocations matter, in terms of public identity, but are not primary to their inner lives. Often they're accidental. (Our lives are often largely accidental.) And what a novel for grownups does is investigate inner lives as opposed to outer identities. In Leonard Gardner's small masterpiece *Fat City*—now there's an almost perfect novel—boxing is simply the medium, the ring, in which the main character learns some of life's necessary lessons. So while boxing is central to the book, I wouldn't call *Fat City* a boxing novel.

In my book, the sport's role is partly to furnish a useful metaphor for my protagonist's quarrel with the world and, above all, himself. "To shadow box" literally means to train by practicing your moves against a phantom opponent—and, sometimes, using a mirror, your own reflection—but to me the term also implies the kind of civil war our divided self constantly wages. Our public and private selves arguing; our ego, threatened by change, battling the deeper self that tries to enact same; complexes we inherited from one parent duking it out with obsessions bequeathed by the other. We're always throwing wild punches at shadowy projections, ghosts, memories, all of which are really aspects of ourselves.

The fact that boxing in my novel serves partly or largely as a metaphor might have been the most important reason I had to enter the ring and experience the sport first-hand. Metaphors in fiction have to be fully embodied and embedded, lest they seem merely conceptual, schematic, superimposed. Once my body and senses had internalized the sport, blow by blow, bruise by bruise, I was able to re-enact Sevigne's trials and to root his metaphor in the living physical world my novel was trying to incarnate.

12

Jael Richardson in conversation with Angie Abdou

Turn It Upside Down
Race and Representation in Sport, Sport Literature, and Sport Lit Scholarship

This conversation took place via Zoom in September 2022, with Angie Abdou at her home in Fernie, British Columbia, and Jael Richardson at her home in Brampton, Ontario.

ANGIE ABDOU: Since some of our readers are American or European, for people who might not know tell us—who is your dad?

JAEL RICHARDSON: My dad is Chuck Ealey. In 1968, he was recruited to play football for the University of Toledo. He grew up in Southern Ohio, so it wasn't a huge distance but a change from a little town to a big city. Also, 1968 is a critical time in history: the Vietnam war and the shooting of Martin Luther King. JFK had already been shot. It was a very turbulent culture time. The University of Toledo recruited my dad to play quarterback, a revolutionary move in an era of very few Black quarterbacks.

My dad had gone undefeated as a quarterback in high school, but University of Toledo had never seen him play a football game. They heard his record and saw him play basketball then recruited him for football. My dad competed as the team's starting quarterback and they remained undefeated from 1968 to 1971, winning thirty-five straight games, never losing.

My dad ended up going to Canada to play in the CFL afterwards. The NFL wanted him but not in a quarterback role. They gave him offers as the "back-up to the back-up" quarterback or as a running back. He wanted to be quarterback. So, he came to Canada and played for the Hamilton Tiger-Cats and became the first Black quarterback to win a Grey Cup.

AA: In 2012, you published *The Stone Thrower: A Daughter's Lessons, a Father's Life*, which explores the impact of racism on your father's sporting career. *The Stone Thrower* starts when you're thirty and you travel to Ohio with your dad for his fortieth high school reunion. You learn the reasons your father left Ohio. Can we sum up that reason as racism?

JR: Racism was an underlying reason he couldn't make choices other people might have been able to make. For example, other universities gave him offers in his grade twelve year based on his undefeated streak, but they all wanted him to play positions other than quarterback. At the time, he finished his high school football career with three years undefeated and had no offers because he refused to play other positions, even as a scholarship athlete. He was going to go and join the military potentially, the only option left available to him. His principal intervened and invited someone from University of Toledo to come watch him play basketball, which changed his trajectory.

AA: Why do you think he didn't tell you that information about his background? A protective impulse?

JR: My dad didn't talk about his past, even the NFL not taking him. He sent a letter to teams saying he would only play quarterback, and that's when the offers stopped, but he never talked about those inner workings. Researching for my book, I realized how racism shaped his opportunities. He didn't share those details for two main reasons. First, he didn't think they were important. He didn't see the relevance or meaning at the time or even now in some ways. Second, silence was his way of coping, managing the stress and disappointment of that experience.

He's about to get inducted into the College Football Hall of Fame, an incredible moment of him achieving recognition previously denied him because of racism. Now is the first time I've heard him admit that these achievements were things he deserved and wanted. He didn't talk about them being withheld from him because what was he going to do? How are you going to cope with the fact that you live in an unfair system? You can fight it and wrestle with it, but that's an exhausting way to live. Instead, my father chose to say: *This life isn't fair, and it's never been fair, but I'll do the best with what it's offering me.*

AA: Do you think you writing the book and the way you framed his life and the issues led to him seeing the influence of racism in sport culture differently?

JR: I think writing *The Stone Thrower* and spending time together, during the research and more so during the touring, did change his perspective. When the book first came out and we would travel together, I would share stories about my dad. For example, someone would ask him, "Did you experience racism growing up?" and my dad would answer, "No, not really." I would say "Excuse me?!!" and share stories of inequality that he himself had told me, about interactions I *knew* were racist. He would say "Oh yeah, but that's just the way things were."

He couldn't quite recognize how unfair things were. He'd just trained himself to ignore and move on and leave those negative instances behind.

Now when I hear him answering those questions about racism, he does answer them differently. He answers the questions about inequality and injustice more openly and honestly because he knows his answers help other people.

In our travels, when he shared the stories of injustice on and off the field, like sharing what people called him at games, audience members connected, saying "I've been there!" or "That must've been rough!" He finally admitted the hardship, and you could see the exchange of honesty and thoughtfulness. Knowing he's on that far side of those experiences has allowed him to share more honestly and see how being honest about racism he experienced can help other people, not just himself.

AA: Is that part of why you wrote *The Stone Thrower*, why you shared his story, to help other people?

JR: I wrote *The Stone Thrower* because I wanted people to know the story and the whole story. I also wrote about my dad's football career because I needed to know the whole story. I wove in my own story because I wanted people to understand not just that my dad had an incredible career, but that he had a very fractured way of sharing it. He didn't know quite how to talk about his experience with his family. Him not being able to be open about his struggles affected our relationship. I needed to see where my dad had been to understand why he raised us the way he did, why he talked to us the way he did.

I had all these White friends and felt confused about whether I wanted to be Black or not. Recognizing that my dad grew up around a lot of White people at a time of extreme racism helped me clarify things he'd said to me and ways we related to one another.

AA: I like the story behind the book's title. Can you explain why the book is called *The Stone Thrower*?

JR: When my dad was around ten years old, he lived in the projects in Portsmouth, Ohio. It was an all-Black neighborhood segregated from the rest of town. He would have to cross over train tracks. In most American cities, there's some sort of dividing line that historically marks the division between Black and White neighborhoods. In his town, it was these train tracks. He went to a White school, so he had to go over these train tracks every day. When the long coal trains passed, he got in the habit of throwing stones, aiming at certain letters to practice his precision. He said another skill the stone-throwing taught him was timing—how early to throw the rock, how quick to release it. Later, a university study showed that this practice contributed to his success because his timing was impeccable.

The title also alludes to a couple other important moments in my book—like when Martin Luther King Jr. talks about the 1960s as a moment like a stone thrown in the water, where the stone will drop and have an immediate effect, but it will also have a ripple that continues to affect people through history. The idea of stone throwing in my memoir, then, is also about the long-term effect of my dad's time as quarterback and civil rights movements happening during that time.

AA: How do the themes of racism and sport and the goals you set out to accomplish with telling your dad's story transfer over into the children's version of this book you more recently published?

JR: The picture book was tricky because the memoir has the long story of my dad's life and all his accomplishments, and it's too big for a children's book. I had to figure out a core focus for the children's book different than the adult book. My dad is passionate about ideas featured in his organization, The Undefeated Spirit. The main idea is that we all have to navigate hard moments with focused repetition and effort. *The Stone Thrower* children's book zooms in on the moment when my dad goes to the train tracks and throws stones for the first time—and how that focused throwing repetition led to his success.

The children's book also talks about transitioning that repetition and effort and success into the classroom. Importance resides not simply in being a good athlete, but my dad also had to repeat that hard work in school and be a good, successful student. He must repeat hard work at football practice, repeat hard work as a student, and repeat hard work as a leader.

Those skills learned through "stone throwing" translate well beyond the football field.

I think my dad actually likes the children's book more than the memoir because the kid version has that concentrated message that it wasn't just him throwing a football that made him really impressive. Rather what he learned through throwing a football helped him in other areas of life and continues to help him in business and as a dad and in all things.

AA: *The Stone Thrower* is about so many things—race, father-daughter relationships, communication, civil rights issues, the insidiousness of racism—but I'm approaching *The Stone Thrower* here mostly as a sports book, a story about football. Many sports books focus on father and son relationships. You've made a switch in writing a father-daughter sports book. Do you think coming at his career as a daughter instead of a son influences the story significantly?

JR: Yes, I think it's really interesting to come at the football story as a daughter instead of a son. My brother actually went to University of Toledo and played football there, like my dad. That's a story in and of itself, but the interesting thing about being a daughter is I don't even have the opportunity to play the same sport, so what is the father-daughter bond? What is the thing that connects us? What has my dad passed to me from his athletic career?

That is really exciting and special because I realized writing this book that my dad and I are very similar. I never thought of myself as someone who is focused and who repeats things over and over until I get them right, but I see now, in my professional life, the same diligence and same borderline obsession on getting things right and making sure everything is done well and making sure I'm leading responsibly. Like my dad. Also, like my dad, I learned some of those lessons in sport and carried them into my professional life.

AA: A lot of your work, both your writing and your work as founder and Executive Director of the FOLD, addresses racism and raises awareness about importance of diversity and equality. Are these issues the same inside of sport and outside of sport? Is sport a mirror of what goes on in larger society or is it completely different? What's your assessment of racism in sport?

JR: It's really tricky. Looking at books, the issues are much clearer: we need more stories by these groups or by this community. In sport, racism can be a lot more covert. People can say decisions just come down to talent or it's just about who's the best without recognizing how we disadvantage kids. Sports that are really expensive, for example—how does that cost disadvantage kids who might be good athletes, but their parents don't want to prioritize sports? There can be class-based inequities that are very prominent in sport. Class maybe weighs in more than overt forms of racism in sport, but when classism weighs in, race follows close behind.

I'm working on a project now about raising issues of diversity in sport, and it's been exciting to navigate those questions and to mix sport with what I do with the FOLD. Sport, for example, brings up questions about accessibility with disability. I realized recently that hockey helmets aren't created to make room for a cochlear implant, so at this point a child who has a cochlear implement simply cannot play hockey. These issues don't get discussed and addressed often, but I hope they do soon.

AA: If racism in sport is a little more invisible and harder to pinpoint, what can writers of literature do to help?

JR: What writers do that is so very important is we draw attention to things. Think of all the stories of sport that don't feature women or people of color, yet they're heralded as "amazing books." Readers love and celebrate classic sport stories without realizing how many faces are missing and how many people could've seen themselves in the book if attention would've been drawn differently, if thought had just been a little deeper.

Writers need to be doing this kind of thinking and evaluating about representation. Publishers need to make room for writers of different races, colors, and communities to make different kinds of stories, with a different focus of attention, available. Seeing yourself in a book is so important. The people who that kind of seeing seems insignificant to are the people who have seen themselves in books their whole lives.

If you're a girl and you've only ever seen boys in a hockey book or a basketball book, how do you think of yourself as that kind of athlete? Once writers put that female character on the rink, the story reflects a new possibility. That's the beginning of reshaping what a reader views as acceptable or possible.

A book doesn't have to directly tackle racism within the story, but the narrative can represent different types of people and represent events accurately; sometimes that kind of accuracy will expose ideology or behavior that readers recognize as wrong in a way they didn't before.

AA: My next question speaks to your role as the founder and director of the Festival of Literary Diversity. My co-editor and I both belong to the Sport Literature Association, as do most of the essay contributors. We have recognized within our association a concerning lack of diversity. When I started thirteen years ago, there were maybe three regular women. The society was made up mostly of White men. Now we're up to close to half women. But we're still very White. In a book like this one, the conversation has shifted, and we have diversity in terms of the sports, authors, athletes, and ways of understanding, but the list of scholars still lacks diversity. We've made efforts to include more diversity within our association and within our publications, but we've had very little success. How do you go about saying, "Okay, we want more diverse voices in this conversation," and then making that happen?

JR: Great question. That's the core of where many organizations must begin, recognizing that the lack of diversity as a problem and then recognizing they don't have an immediate solution. If there were an immediate successful solution, we'd implement it right away. The reality is that the work of diversity is a long work. I often say, "It's a long journey in a singular direction." You must commit to the stance that diversity is an important issue that you will continue to bring up over and over again as it continues to shift and change. In a lot of cases, that commitment requires honesty about what it might be like for someone from a marginalized group to join the community. Would the group be open and accepting or do they just create the appearance of being open and accepting? Then you must hand-recruit people to join the association. Ask yourselves: How can you actively recruit new members from these communities? It's like any kind of recruitment. You might ask twenty people and two say yes. So, if you want twenty people, you might have to ask two hundred people to join. Build a team with this specific goal of creating a space that's welcoming for different communities, and then actively recruiting folks to join and being willing to do that on repeat.

So you start with, "Can we continue to grow a group of people who feel that the organization is a welcoming place?" and then the next goal becomes, "Can you change the structure of the leadership?" Ideally, that's the end goal, but you can't change the structure of leadership if you don't have the body of people in the organization. Changing to a more diverse, inclusive, and open community is a long and intentional act.

AA: A group of younger scholars in our organization have started a committee with the specific goal of increasing diversity and welcoming scholars from a wide variety of communities. The other challenge is that BIPOC (Black, Indigenous, and people of colour) scholars are so in demand because everyone wants to hear from them, and they're overloaded and overburdened and overworked. So, when we say, "Will you write an essay for my collection?" they say, "No!" They're far too busy. We realize their time is valuable, and they have too much on their plate. What do you suggest as a strategy to include those voices without overburdening certain scholars?

JR: Yes! That's the challenge. It's like the pilot crisis right now. The industry let go of pilots, and now everyone wants pilots, but it takes a long time to become a pilot.

You have to look at "What are the qualifications?" and "How do those qualifications prevent us from making room?" Can you make space for those at a different stage or different entry point just to have those voices contributing?

That inclusion might involve a lot of cracking and breaking and reassembling what you've traditionally done. It might require turning everything on its head. Instead of looking for "qualified" scholars, look for the voices and stories you need and give them the opportunity to be part of the conversation on the path to getting qualified. If the end goal is to have more diversity in your association and in your publications, you start with that very specific target and ask how you can channel people to be more ready to contribute.

These scholars are in demand right now because they're "hot." But I remind people: this work is not trendy. It's just what we should be doing and should've been doing all along. It might require patience and rethinking how you've always done things. Maybe you approach a younger audience—undergraduates or masters students—and then they get a breakthrough moment with your publication, and you accomplish your end goal of diversity while elevating scholars who would normally have had to wait five more years to get a similar chance. Remember: Traditional qualifications might not always be the best indicator of talent or engaging content.

Contributors

Angie Abdou has published seven books and co-edited *Writing the Body in Motion: A Critical Anthology on Canadian Sport Literature* with Jamie Dopp. Her novel *The Bone Cage*, about Olympic athletes, was a Canada Reads finalist. Her two memoirs on youth sport hit the Canadian bestseller list. *Booklist* declared *Home Ice: Reflections of a Reluctant Hockey Mom* a "first-rate memoir" and a "must-read for parents with youngsters who play organized sports." Abdou is a professor of creative writing at Athabasca University and a nationally certified swim coach.

Jason Blake is a professor in the University of Ljubljana's English Department. He is the editor-in-chief of *The Central European Journal of Canadian Studies / Revue d'études canadiennes en Europe centrale* as well as the author of *Canadian Hockey Literature* (University of Toronto Press, 2010) and the co-editor (with Andrew C. Holman) of *The Same but Different: Hockey in Quebec* (McGill-Queen's University Press, 2017). He translates frequently from Slovenian, and less frequently from German, and he has published a trio of guides aimed at Slovenian students writing in English. In 2022 he received the International Council of Canadian Studies' Certificate of Merit.

Misao Dean is a professor at the University of Victoria, specializing in early Canadian writing. Her most recent book is *Inheriting a Canoe Paddle* (University of Toronto Press, 2013).

Jamie Dopp is an associate professor of Canadian literature at the University of Victoria. He is the author of two novels, three collections of poems, and many essays and reviews. In recent years his academic work has focused on sport literature in Canada. He has co-edited two earlier collections of essays, *Now Is the Winter: Thinking about Hockey*, with Richard Harrison, and *Writing the Body in Motion: A Critical Anthology on Canadian Sport Literature*, with Angie Abdou. He is currently nearing completion of a major critical work called *Hockey on the Moon: Imagination and Canada's Game*.

Adrian Markle is the author of the forthcoming novel *Bruise* (Brindle & Glass) as well as short stories in magazines and anthologies around the world, including *EVENT* and *Release Any Words Stuck Inside of You*. His critical work also appears in *Aethlon: The Journal of Sport Literature* and *The Power of Storytelling in Hong Kong Education* (Routledge, forthcoming). Adrian has a PhD from the University of Exeter and currently teaches English and creative writing at Falmouth University in Cornwall, UK, where he lives with his partner, the writer Eleanor Walsh. He likes old dogs.

Fred Mason teaches sport sociology and sport history in kinesiology at the University of New Brunswick. Fred's wide-ranging published academic research includes work on media coverage of parasports and women's sports, the history of sports medicine, fieldwork at the Women's World Cup and the Olympics, fictional hockey enforcers, and science fiction and fantasy writing with sport connections. He has published short fiction in chapbook collections and the *Canadian Writer's Journal*, poetry in the anthology *The Warbler's Song*, and photography in the magazine *incunabula* and on the cover of the *Canadian Bulletin of Medical History*. As of writing, he has completed twenty-nine ultramarathons, including three hundred-milers in Vermont, at Cape Chignecto, Nova Scotia, and on a treadmill.

Eva-Maria Müller studied at Gieß en University and the University of Alberta and is a postdoctoral researcher in the Department of American Studies at the University of Innsbruck. Her chapter in this volume developed out of her PhD thesis, "Rewriting Alpine Orientalism: Lessons from the Canadian Rockies and Austrian Alps." Her most recent mountain-themed publications include an article in *The New Review of Film and Television Studies*, "Cinematic Cultures of Descent: The Other Sides of the Mountaineering Story" (2023), and, with Christian Quendler, a co-edited special issue of the *Journal of the Austrian Association for American Studies*, "Mediating Mountains" (2022). She also serves as academic advisor for two cultural festivals in the Tyrolean Alps.

Gyllian Phillips is a professor in the Department of English Studies at Nipissing University. She co-edited (with Allan Pero) *The Many Facades of Edith Sitwell* (University Press of Florida, 2017) and has published articles on other modernist writers, 1930s film, travel writing, and postcolonial literature. Her most recent work, in research and teaching, focuses on decolonizing approaches to ecocriticism in outdoor adventure narratives.

Jael Richardson is the founder and executive director of FOLD—the Festival of Literary Diversity (https://thefoldcanada.org/). She is the author of *The Stone Thrower, Gutter Child, Because You Are*, and *The Hockey Jersey*. Richardson holds an MFA in creative writing from the University of Guelph and lives in Brampton, Ontario.

Veronika Schuchter teaches at Oxford University. She situates her research broadly at the intersection of contemporary literature, postcolonial studies, gender studies, and the medical humanities. Her current research project offers the first study of menopause as a literary trope in fiction, auto-fiction, and poetry by selected writers in the twenty-first century. Her PhD dissertation, "Imagining a Feminist Supermodernity: Non-Places in Contemporary British and Canadian Women's Writing," is the first major reconsideration of Marc Augé's theorization of supermodernity and its non-places through an intersectional feminist lens.

Heidi Tiedemann Darroch currently teaches Canadian studies at the University of Victoria and writing and literature at Camosun College. She has published on Atwood, Munro, Canadian drama, and mystery fiction, and she has a chapter forthcoming in the MLA's volume *Teaching Margaret Atwood*. She is working on a book-length study of Louise Penny and the landscape of Canadian crime fiction. Her PhD is from the University of Toronto.

Cory Willard holds a PhD in English literary and cultural studies from the University of Nebraska–Lincoln. He splits his time between teaching in the Department of English, Languages, and Cultures and working as a writing and learning strategist at Mount Royal University. His writing and research focus primarily on North American fly fishing literature with emphases on ecocriticism, place studies, and environmental ethics. When he's not trapped at a desk, you can find him streamside.